birth to a son, and he will be called Immanuel.

◈

PRESENTED TO:

_____

BY:

_____

DATE:

_____

CHRISTMAS BY THE HEARTH

Christmas

TYNDALE HOUSE PUBLISHERS

BY THE HEARTH

INC., WHEATON, ILLINOIS

Editor: Rick Blanchette
Designer: Raelee Edgar
Typesetter: Gwen Elliott

Cover photo: family scene copyright © 1996 by Jim and Mary Whitmer

Interior photographs copyright © 1996 by Dan Stultz

Published in association with the literary agency of Alive Communications, 1465 Kelly Johnson Blvd., Suite 320, Colorado Springs, CO 80920

New Living, NLT, and the New Living Translation logo are trademarks of Tyndale House Publishers, Inc.

Library of Congress Cataloging-in-Publication Data

Christmas by the hearth
    p.   cm.
    A collection of short stories both contemporary and historical by various authors about the Christmas season.
    ISBN 0-8423-0239-5
    1. Christmas—Juvenile fiction.   1. Children's stories.
    [1. Christmas—Fiction.   2. Short stories.]
    PZ5.C4674   1996
    [Fic]—dc20   96-11717

Printed in the United States of America

04 03 02 01 00 99 98 97 96
9   8   7   6   5   4   3   2

TABLE OF CONTENTS

INTRODUCTION

There is truly no other season like Christmas. It can mean so many things to many different people. To some it may mean trees, ornaments, family, and presents. To others it may be a very spiritual day to reflect on Christ's coming into our world to begin his work for our salvation. To others it can be a time of loneliness and depression. And to still others it may be a Christian holiday that they don't observe, yet they are happy to have the day off work.

It is also a time when people open their hearts to God—some of them may do so only in December. It is a time when people are willing to accept—even anticipate—miracles and evidence of God among us in the world. Contributions to charities increase; helping others less fortunate than ourselves seems more natural when we can say "Merry Christmas" at the conclusion of our deeds. It can be a wonderful, magical season, one that is all too short while here but that leaves us with the promise of returning next year.

Just as Christmas can be experienced in many diverse ways, so there are many ways to express the meanings and mysteries of Christmas. This collection presents a wide spectrum of short stories about Christmases past and present from some of the best-known authors in the Christian publishing industry, such as Calvin Miller and Francine Rivers, and from classic authors like Hans Christian Andersen and O. Henry. You and your family will travel back in time to the Holy Land to witness the Nativity, will venture to Europe to witness the writing of the Christmas hymn "Silent Night," will be transported to Virginia during the Civil War and to a German concentration camp. You will experience modern Christmases as well, witnessing angelic appearances and Christmas pageants, as well as learning the lessons God shows us in the ordinary events of any family's Christmas celebration.

It is our hope that you and your family will enjoy these stories together throughout Christmastime year after year, either while around the dinner table, cozied up near a fire, or while tucking the children in at bedtime. While all of the works in this collection draw us to focus on how God works—or can work—in our lives, parents may wish to read the stories first to make sure that each story is appropriate for the age of the children in the home, as younger children may not yet be able to appreciate all of the messages or plots.

We at Tyndale House wish your family a blessed and merry Christmas. It is our prayer that you experience God's grace and blessings in your lives. May the magic and mystery of Christmas be with you throughout the year.

PROLOGUE: THE CHRISTMAS STORY

❖

Now this is how Jesus the Messiah was born. God sent the angel Gabriel to Nazareth, a village in Galilee, to a virgin named Mary. She was engaged to be married to a man named Joseph, a descendant of King David. Gabriel appeared to her and said, "Greetings, favored woman! The Lord is with you!"

Confused and disturbed, Mary tried to think what the angel could mean. "Don't be frightened, Mary," the angel told her, "for God has decided to bless you! You will become pregnant and have a son, and you are to name him Jesus. He will be very great and will be called the Son of the Most High. And the Lord God will give him the throne of his ancestor David. And he will reign over Israel forever; his Kingdom will never end!"

Mary asked the angel, "But how can I have a baby? I am a virgin."

The angel replied, "The Holy Spirit will come upon you, and the power of the Most High will overshadow you. So the baby born to you will be holy, and he will be called the Son of God. What's more, your relative Elizabeth has become pregnant in her old age! People used to say she was barren, but she's already in her sixth month. For nothing is impossible with God."

Mary responded, "I am the Lord's servant, and I am willing to accept whatever he wants. May everything you have said come true." And then the angel left.

While she was still a virgin, she became pregnant by the Holy Spirit. Joseph, her fiancé, being a just man, decided to break the engagement quietly, so as not to disgrace her publicly.

As he considered this, he fell asleep, and an angel of the Lord appeared to him in a dream. "Joseph, son of David," the angel said, "do not be afraid to go ahead with your marriage to Mary. For the child within her has been conceived by the Holy Spirit. And she will have a son, and you are to name him Jesus, for he will save his people from their sins." All of this happened to fulfill the Lord's message through his prophet:

"Look! The virgin will conceive a child!
She will give birth to a son,
and he will be called Immanuel
(meaning, God is with us)."

When Joseph woke up, he did what the angel of the Lord commanded.

A few days later Mary hurried to the hill country of Judea, to the town where Zechariah lived. She entered the house and greeted Elizabeth. At the sound of Mary's greeting, Elizabeth's child leaped within her, and Elizabeth was filled with the Holy Spirit.

Elizabeth gave a glad cry and exclaimed to Mary, "You are blessed by God above all other women, and your child is blessed. What an honor this is, that the mother of my Lord should visit me! When you came in and greeted me, my baby jumped for joy the instant I heard your voice! You are blessed, because you believed that the Lord would do what he said."

Mary responded,

"Oh, how I praise the Lord.
How I rejoice in God my Savior!
For he took notice of his lowly servant girl,
and now generation after generation
will call me blessed.
For he, the Mighty One, is holy,
and he has done great things for me."

Mary stayed with Elizabeth about three months and then went back to her own home.

At that time the Roman emperor, Augustus, decreed that a census should be taken throughout the Roman Empire. All returned to their own towns to register for this census. And because Joseph was a descendant of King David, he had to go to Bethlehem in Judea, David's ancient home. He traveled there from the village of Nazareth in Galilee. He took with him Mary, his fiancée, who was obviously pregnant by this time.

And while they were there, the time came for her baby to be born. She gave birth to her first child, a son. She wrapped him snugly in strips of cloth and laid him in a manger, because there was no room for them in the village inn.

That night some shepherds were in the fields outside the village, guarding their flocks of sheep. Suddenly, an angel of the Lord appeared among them, and the radiance of the Lord's glory surrounded them. They were terribly frightened, but the angel reassured them. "Don't be afraid!" he said. "I bring you good news of great joy for everyone! The Savior—yes, the Messiah, the Lord—has been born tonight in Bethlehem, the city of David! And this is how you will recognize him: You will find a baby lying in a manger, wrapped snugly in strips of cloth!"

Suddenly, the angel was joined by a vast host of others—the armies of heaven—praising God:

"Glory to God in the highest heaven,
and peace on earth to all whom God favors."

When the angels had returned to heaven, the shepherds said to each other, "Come on, let's go to Bethlehem! Let's see this wonderful thing that has happened, which the Lord has told us about."

They ran to the village and found Mary and Joseph. And there was the baby, lying in the manger. Then the shepherds told everyone what had happened and what the angel had said to them about this child. All who heard the shepherds' story were astonished, but Mary quietly treasured these things in her heart and thought about them often. The shepherds went back to their fields and flocks, glorifying and praising God for what the angels had told them, and because they had seen the child, just as the angel had said.

About that time some wise men from eastern lands arrived in Jerusalem, asking, "Where is the newborn king of the Jews? We have seen his star as it arose, and we have come to worship him."

Herod was deeply disturbed by their question, as was all of Jerusalem. He called a meeting of the leading priests and teachers of religious law. "Where did the prophets say the Messiah would be born?" he asked them.

"In Bethlehem," they said, "for this is what the prophet wrote:

`O Bethlehem of Judah,
you are not just a lowly village in Judah,
for a ruler will come from you
who will be the shepherd for my people Israel.'"

Then Herod sent a private message to the wise men, asking them to come see him. At this meeting he learned the exact time when they first saw the star. Then he told them, "Go to Bethlehem and search carefully for the child. And when you find him, come back and tell me so that I can go and worship him, too!"

After this interview the wise men went their way. Once again the star appeared to them, guiding them to Bethlehem. It went ahead of them and stopped over the place where the child was. When they saw the star, they were filled with joy! They entered the house where the child and his mother, Mary, were, and they fell down before him and worshiped him. Then they opened their treasure chests and gave him gifts of gold, frankincense, and myrrh. But when it was time to leave, they went home another way, because God had warned them in a dream not to return to Herod.

"Let the little children come to me, and do not hinder them,
for the kingdom of heaven belongs to such as these."
MATTHEW 19:14, NIV

Francine Rivers

THE SHOE BOX

◆

Timmy O'Neil came to live with Mary and David Holmes on a cloudy day in the middle of September, two weeks after school started. He was a quiet little six-year-old boy with sorrowful eyes. Not very long afterward, they wondered about the box he carried with him all the time. It was an ordinary shoe box with a red lid and the words Running Shoes printed on one side.

Timmy carried it everywhere he went. When he put it down, it was always where he could see it.

"Should we ask him about it?" Mary said to her husband.

"No. He'll talk to us about it when he's ready," David said, but he was as curious as she was.

Even Mrs. Iverson, the social worker, was curious about the shoe box. She told Mary and David that Timmy had the box when the policeman brought him to the Youth Authority offices. Timmy's dad was put in prison. His mom had a job, but she didn't make enough to take proper care of Timmy. A lady in the apartment house where he lived found out he was by himself all day and reported it to the police.

"They brought him to me with one small suitcase of clothes and that shoe box," Mrs. Iverson said. "I asked him what was inside it, and he said, `Things.' But what things he wouldn't tell me."

Even the children at Timmy's new school were curious about the box. He didn't put it in his cubbyhole like things the other children brought. He would put it on top of his desk while he did his work.

His first-grade teacher, Mrs. King, was curious, too. "What do you have there, Timmy?"

"My box," he said.

"What's in your box?"

"Things," he said and went on with his arithmetic.

Mrs. King didn't ask him about the box again. She liked Timmy, and she didn't want to pry. She told Mary and David that Timmy was a good student. He wasn't the brightest by far, but he always did his best work. Mrs. King admired that about Timmy. She wrote a note to him about it on one of his math papers. "Other students will learn by your example," the note said, and she drew a big smiling face on his paper and gave him a pretty, sparkly star sticker.

Mary Holmes learned that Timmy liked chocolate chip cookies, so she kept the cookie jar full. Timmy would come home from school on the yellow bus and sit at the kitchen table, the box under his chair. Mary always sat with him and asked him about his day while he had milk and cookies.

Timmy asked Mary one day why she and David didn't have any children of their own. Mary said she had asked God the same question over and over. She said while she waited for an answer, she was thankful to have him.

Every evening when he came home from work, David played catch with Timmy in the backyard. Timmy always brought the box outside with him and set it on the lawn chair where he could see it.

Timmy even took the shoe box with him to Sunday school. He sat between Mary and David, the box in his lap.

When he went to bed at night, the shoe box sat on the nightstand beside his bed.

Timmy got letters from his mother twice a week. Once she sent him ten dollars and a short note from his father. Timmy cried when Mary read it to him, because his father said how much he missed Timmy and how sorry he was that he had made such a big mistake. Mary held Timmy on her lap in the rocking chair for a long time.

When David came home, they took Timmy out for a pizza dinner and then to the theater to see an animated movie about a lion. Mary and David both noticed Timmy's expression of wonder and delight.

When Timmy got off the school bus the next day, he was surprised to find David waiting for him. "Hi, Champ," David said. "I thought I'd come home early and share your special day." He ruffled Timmy's hair and walked with him to the house.

When they came in the kitchen door, Mary leaned down and kissed Timmy on the cheek. "Happy birthday, Timmy."

His eyes widened in surprise as he saw a big box wrapped with pretty paper and tied up with bright-colored ribbons on the kitchen table.

"It's for you, Timmy," David said. "You can open it."

Timmy put his old shoe box carefully on the table and then opened the bigger box with the pretty paper. In it he found a lion just like the one in the movie. Hugging it, he laughed.

Mary turned away quickly and fussed with the candles on the birthday cake so Timmy wouldn't see the tears in her eyes. David noticed and smiled at her. It was the first time she and David had seen Timmy smile or laugh about anything. And it made them very happy.

When Mary put the birthday cake on the table and lit the candles, David took her hand and then Timmy's and said a prayer of blessing and thanksgiving. "Go ahead, Timmy. Make a wish and blow out the candles."

Timmy didn't have to think very long about what he wished, and when he blew, not a candle was left burning.

Timmy's mother came to visit every other week. She and Timmy sat together in the living room. She asked him questions about school and the Holmeses and if he was happy with them. He said he was, but he still missed her. She held him and stroked his hair back from his face and kissed

4

him. She told him she missed him, too, but it was more important that he have a safe place to grow up. "These are nice people, Timmy. You won't grow up like I did."

Each time before she left, she always told him to be good and remember what she'd taught him. She picked him up and held him tightly for a long time before she kissed him and put him down again. Timmy was always sad and quiet when she left.

Fall came, and the leaves on the maple tree in the backyard turned brilliant gold. Sometimes Timmy would go outside and sit with his back against the trunk of the tree, his shoe box in his lap, and just watch the leaves flutter in the cool breeze.

Mary's mother and father came for Thanksgiving. Mary had gotten up very early in the morning and started preparing pumpkin pies while David stuffed the turkey. Timmy liked Mary's mother and father. Mary's mother played Monopoly with him, and her father told him funny and exciting fishing stories.

Friends came to join them for Thanksgiving dinner, and the house was full of happy people. Timmy had never seen so much food on one table before. He tried everything. When dinner was over, David gave him the wishbone. He told Timmy to let it dry and then they'd pull on it to see who would get their wish.

December came and brought with it colder weather. Mary and David bought him a heavy snow parka and gloves. His mother gave him a new backpack, and he put his shoe box in it. He carried it to school each day, and in the afternoon he'd hang the backpack on the closet door, where he could see it while he was doing his homework or when he went to bed at night.

It seemed everybody in the small town where Mary and David Holmes and Timmy lived knew about the shoe box. But nobody but Timmy knew what was inside it.

A few boys tried to take it from him one day, but Mrs. King saw them and made them pick up trash on the school grounds during lunch hour.

Sometimes children on the bus would ask him what he had in the box, but he'd say, "Just things."

"What kind of things?"

He would shrug, but he would never say.

The church where Mary and David Holmes took Timmy had a Christmas program each year. The choir practiced for two months to present the community with a cantata. Everyone dressed in costumes. This year part of the program was to include acting out the Nativity while the choir sang.

"We need lots of children to volunteer for the parts," Chuck, the program director, said. "The choir will sing about the angels who came to speak to the shepherds in the fields. And there's a song about the wise men who came from faraway lands to see Jesus. And, of course, we need a girl to play Mary and a boy to play Joseph."

"What about Jesus?" Timmy said.

"Latasha has a baby brother," one of the girls said. "Why don't you let her be Mary, and her baby brother can be Jesus?"

"That's a great idea," Chuck said.

Most of the children were eager to be part of the play. Even Timmy, but he was too shy to raise his hand. Chuck noticed the look on his face when all the parts were filled. He asked his helper to get the children started in a game and took Timmy aside. "We could use another shepherd in the play," he said carefully. "Would you like to be a shepherd?"

"I'd like to be a wise man."

There were already three wise men, but Chuck thought about it and nodded his head. "You know, the Bible doesn't say how many wise men came to see Jesus. There might have been four. There might have been more than that. I'll talk to the lady making costumes and ask her if she can make one more for you."

The lady was very pleased to make a costume for Timmy. She spent extra time on it because she wanted it to be very special. She made a long blue tunic that went to his ankles. She made a wide multicolored sash and an outer garment like an open robe of a beautiful brocade with purple and gold. Then she made a turban and put a big rhinestone brooch on the front and some colored plumes on the top.

When the night came for the program, everyone was so excited that no one noticed that Timmy was still holding his old shoe box instead of the fancy wooden jewelry box he was supposed to carry onto the stage. Everyone did notice when he followed the other three wise men out of the wings and into the lights.

One by one the wise men approached the manger and left their gifts, but everyone sitting in the audience in the big church social hall was looking at Timmy. Timmy's mother had come to see him in the cantata. Mrs. Iverson, the social worker, had come as well. So had Mrs. King and two other teachers from Timmy's school.

They were all holding their breath when it came Timmy's turn to put his kingly offering before the manger, where the baby Jesus was sleeping. He looked like a small regal king in his royal garb, the turban and jewel on his head. The lights were on him, and the sparkles in the pretty clothes made him shine. He carried the old worn shoe box with the red lid and the words *Running Shoes* in both hands and presented it with solemn respect to the child in the manger.

Then Timmy straightened and turned and smiled broadly at his mother, Mary and David, Mrs. Iverson, and Mrs. King and her two friends before he took his place among the other wise men at the far side of the stage.

They all let out their breath in relief, but they also sat wondering and watching Timmy. He was singing with the choir, not the least bit concerned about the precious shoe box he had left on the far side of the stage. In fact, he didn't look at it once. And they'd never seen him look so happy.

When the cantata was over, his mother took his hand and went with him for Christmas punch and cookies. Mary and David went with them. So did Mrs. Iverson and Mrs. King and the two teachers who had come with her. They all said how proud they were of him and what a good job he had done.

When it came time to go, Timmy's mother asked him if he wanted to go and get his shoe box.

"Oh no," Timmy said. "I gave it to Jesus."

They all were curious about what was inside the shoe box, but when they passed by the stage, they saw it was gone. Timmy noticed, too, but he didn't seem the least bit upset about it. In fact, he smiled.

"Here it is, my Lord," the angel said, kneeling before the throne of God. He held the old worn shoe box with the words *Running Shoes* printed on it and set it at God's feet.

Jesus took it and set it upon his lap. He put his hand over it and looked out at the gathering of thousands of angels and seraphim and saints. Even they were curious about what was inside. Only he and Timmy knew.

Peter the apostle was there and, bold as always, was the only one who dared ask, "What's in that box, Lord? What has the child given you?"

"Just things," Jesus said, smiling. He had watched Timmy from the time he was conceived. He had counted every hair upon his head and knew all that was in his heart. And he had waited for the day when the child would come to him with what he had to offer.

Jesus took the top off the shoe box, and all the angels and seraphim and saints leaned forward as he took out one item at a time and laid it tenderly upon his lap.

And what they saw were *just things*—very simple, very ordinary things:

The worn and faded silk edge of his baby blanket
A wedding picture of his mother and father

His mother's letters with a rubber band around them

Ten dollars

His father's note of love and apology

A math paper with a smiley face and a note from his teacher

A pretty star sticker

A movie ticket stub

Used birthday candles with dried icing on them wrapped in pretty wrapping paper and tied with a bright curled ribbon

A big side of a broken turkey wishbone

A pretty red maple leaf

An old baseball

And six chocolate chip cookies

There were unseen things, too. Hopes, dreams, prayers, and many worries and fears. All of them were in the box Timmy gave to the Lord.

Jesus put everything back in the shoe box with tender care. He put the red lid back on the box and then rested his hands upon it as he looked at the multitude before him. "Timmy has given the most precious gift of all: the faith of a child."

More angels were sent to guard Timmy from that day forth. They never left his side.

They were with Timmy when Mary and David invited his mother to come and live with them. She had a room right across the hall from Timmy. The angels were with him when Mary and David had a baby of their own. They were with him when his father got out of prison in time for his high school graduation. They surrounded Timmy as he grew up, married, and had children of his own.

In fact, angels surrounded him and protected him all the days of his life up until the very moment he was ushered into heaven, straight into the waiting arms of the Lord who loved him.

"Hail, Thou long-expected Jesus, born to set Thy people free; from our sins
and fears release us; let us find our rest in Thee."
"Hail, Thou Long-Expected Jesus," CHARLES WESLEY

John Leax

REMEMBERING CHRISTMAS

Looking back, I think my father ruined most Christmases for my mother.

He never meant to. If anything, he meant them to be occasions of joy—

high moments of family togetherness. The problem, however, was that he

seemed to think that when my mother changed her name from Smith to Baker,

all of her natural affections for her parents were transformed and reduced

to mere duty. Duty, he understood, was important. He recognized the command-

ment to honor parents. But it seemed he felt the obligations duty and of honor were met in the routine visits of ordinary life. These visits were always pleasant. Grandpa and Grandma Smith liked my dad, and he liked them. But on holidays he thought only of the Bakers. It was a blind spot he had.

For many years that was fine with me. My Grandpa Smith was a Methodist pastor with a spirit of St. Francis. He walked meekly in the world. He spoke softly, and as far as I could tell, he had no anger in him. As wonderful as this sounds—and he *was* a wonderful man—it made him rather vague to me. I guess I loved him, but nothing about him ever fixed in my mind.

My Grandpa Baker, on the other hand, was a rough, direct man. "Not that way," he growled. "Watch." I was six years old on my first fishing trip with him, and I was stabbing at a worm writhing on the bottom of the boat. "You have to pick it up," he said, taking it in his hand. "Hold it between your thumb and finger, then thread the hook through the collar." He made a quick little motion, and the worm was impaled. I cringed.

"Do mine," I begged.

"The first thing about fishing," he answered, "is baiting your own hook." When he handed me a worm that day, only my love and desire to earn his approval made me grasp it in my hand and dig the hook into its wiggling body.

A few minutes later I caught my first fish. A perch. Grandpa held it in one big hand and carefully worked the hook out with the other. Then he opened his hand and pointed out the dark bars down the fish's side. "Beautiful," he said. I looked at it, open-mouthed. Without speaking again, he lowered his hand into the water, and with a sudden thrust of its tail my fish swam free. I wanted to cry. I was that happy.

I sometimes wonder if my indifference to Grandpa Smith hurt my mother. I can't imagine it didn't, but I was a child, and I showed my affections as randomly and unconsciously as a dandelion scatters its seeds. My father, though, was an adult and should have been more aware. Normally he was.

He and my mother had a regular little dialogue they'd repeat a couple times a week. My mother would be at the sink doing dishes. He'd pick up a dishtowel, and she'd start, "What do you think you're doing? That's my job."

He'd answer, "I'm just being with my honey."

"Well," she'd say, "there are better places for that." Then they'd laugh.

Even I could see they loved each other. Yet strangely, in our relationships with parents, we often remain children and act blindly, our gropings toward love no better understood than our unintentional cruelties. I think that's the way it was with my father and his parents. He hadn't put away all childish things. But my mother needn't have suffered as long as she did. I see that now.

After dinner on each Christmas Eve, all of my father's family gathered at Grandpa Baker's. My aunts, uncles, and cousins. No one ever missed. Grandma always baked pies—apple, pumpkin, cherry, and mince—the same pies she baked for Thanksgiving. I always had cherry. Then we'd open gifts—not all of our gifts, just one.

That was maddening, but it was also the point. The adults made a game of it. They'd wrap the most mundane gifts, usually socks or underwear, in irresistible packages to tease us. They'd enclose bricks in boxes to make them deceptively heavy. They'd wrap overlarge boxes and not let us touch them until we agreed to open them. Or they'd wrap something in box after box to drag out the opening. Every Christmas we'd fall for their tricks, and they'd hoot at the disappointment on our faces when we realized we'd been fooled again.

Late in the evening we'd go to church. That was the hard part for my mother, for we'd always go to the Presbyterian church Grandpa Baker belonged to. What I remember most about Christmas Eve services was looking up into my mother's eyes while we were singing carols and seeing tears. Once I asked her why she was crying, and she whispered, "Because God is born a baby." Her answer made no sense to me then, and what sense it makes now, I think, is contrived. The Incarnation can be felt that way, but my mother was no theologian. Her answer was a cover. What brought those tears to her eyes was the desire she could not bring herself to speak: the desire to be in her father's church, to hear his voice announcing the birth of Christ.

Sometime around my tenth or eleventh year I began to sense a tension between my mother and father. I didn't understand; I simply became aware of nuances of feelings I couldn't grasp. Understanding of a sort came early in junior high school. I started wanting to do things with friends: go to movies or ball games and hang out at a drugstore that had a soda fountain. My father was dead set against me doing that. He said he wanted to know where I was and what I was doing at all times; I was too young for independence. Though it always resulted in nasty arguments, I disobeyed him and did as I pleased with some frequency.

I began to see him as a bully. What's curious to me, as I remember, is how little it mattered. What was happening to me was happening to all my friends, and rebellion was natural. In fact, the more my father pushed, the better I felt about ignoring him. But I couldn't stand it when he bullied my mother. He didn't bully her the same way he bullied me. There was nothing overt about his actions. He just seemed to discount her opinions and expect her to fall in with his. It bothered me, and I could tell by her slight stiffening and flattened tone of voice when it was bothering my mother.

It all came to a head about a week before Christmas the year I turned thirteen. I was in the kitchen making a sandwich, and I overheard Mom and Dad in the living room.

"Tom," my mother began, "I've been thinking."

It was easy to tell by her tone that something was up. I think my dad could tell too. His answer was guarded. "Yes?" he questioned.

"Christmas is coming. . . ."

"True."

"Listen to me," my mother snapped, her voice more filled with emotion than the words warranted.

"I'm listening," my father protested.

This conversation's over, I thought and prepared to beat it out of the house, but my mother got control of her voice.

"I want to go to my father's church this Christmas Eve, and I want you to come with me."

"No," my father said.

My mother was stunned. "No?" she said. "Nothing more? No reason? Just no?"

"We have a tradition. Mom and Dad count on it. We just can't change."

"We could take them with us. It would be different. Something fresh to make Christmas special."

"Christmas is special the way it is," my father answered.

"Maybe for you," my mother burst out, "but not for me. Not anymore."

I knew tears were coming and probably more words—words I didn't want to hear, so I left.

The next morning I sat quietly at the breakfast table until my dad settled down with his coffee. I waited for him to get real comfortable, then I said, "You know, some Christmas Eve I'd like to hear Grandpa Smith preach."

If my father had been a cat, the hair on his back would have been standing straight up. As it was, I saw his body tense before he turned to stare hard at my mother. Her face showed distressed bewilderment.

"It was just a thought," I said quickly. "If you think it's a bad idea, we can forget it."

"Let's," my father said. His body relaxed, and my mother turned away to the sink. I went back to my cornflakes as if nothing important had happened, but I went back to them thinking I knew something about my mother and father I'd never known—and I didn't like knowing it.

On Christmas Eve we went, as usual, to Grandpa Baker's. I went brooding and in no mood to celebrate. Grandma's pies were probably as flaky as ever, but I didn't notice. As we ate, my mother and father kept exchanging glances that made no sense. They seemed excited, as if they anticipated something wonderful. I didn't anticipate anything. The thought *What hypocrites!* fed me, and I was angry. I couldn't believe my mother's act. I wanted to stand up and shout that we didn't want to be there, that Christmas was bunk, that the gospel of jingle bells was a lie, that the Christ child was still-born. But I didn't. The thoughts hurt too much. As they pushed themselves on me, I realized I needed the Christmas story to be true. I wanted more than anything for the birth to be real, for the child to live, to grow up *God with us* and change our lives.

My thoughts that Christmas hadn't any of the clarity or shape I've given them here. I was just thirteen. Nearly inarticulate with the anger growing in me, I sat, nursed my discontent, and watched the celebration around me as if from a great distance. One cousin after another opened the single allowed gift. Socks. Underwear. Fruit. Mittens. Socks. It was all predictable. Except my father. An aliveness I'd never seen before possessed him. He didn't sit still. He darted from his chair to the tree, snatching gifts and handing them out, all the time grinning at my mother and laughing.

We were nearly through the gifts when my mother spoke to me. "Mark, come out of your corner and open something."

"I'll wait," I protested. But my father already had a package about the size of a shoe box in his hand and was pressing it on me. "OK," I grumbled and began to tear at the paper. Inside was a shoe box, and inside of it was another box—wrapped. I forced a grin as everyone laughed. "I hope no one's in a hurry," I said, and very deliberately, pretending to want to reuse the paper like Grandma, started to loosen the tape. Five packages later, I held a small heavy weight in my hand. I knew it was the end of my unwrapping, and I knew that when I opened it the night would somehow be different. I trembled, reluctant to go on, for I didn't know if the night would open to wonder or devastation.

"Come on," Grandpa Baker urged. "Other people have presents, too."

"I'm trying to guess," I said. "It's too heavy for underwear."

"Don't get excited," Dad said. "Some people in this family have been known to get a lump of coal."

"No." I shook my head. "This isn't coal."

He smiled and touched my mother's hand. I tore the last layer of paper free and opened the box. In it lay the bright red Swiss Army knife I'd been wanting for years. I have no idea how I must have looked. Nor do I know how long I sat without speaking. I was that surprised. Finally my mother spoke. "Cat got your tongue?"

Still I didn't say anything. *Why?* was running through my head. *Why have you done this tonight?* Then one of my smaller cousins, a recipient of socks, blurted out, "How come he gets something good?"

Laughter filled the room, and under its cover I risked looking directly at my mother and father. They were smiling at each other and holding hands.

About twenty minutes later we bundled into our coats to leave for church. I was confused. Christmas Eve seemed the same, but it had changed. Then, as we pulled out of the driveway, following Grandpa Baker, I understood, for he did not turn left to the Presbyterian church. He turned right to Grandpa Smith's. All of us—Grandpa and Grandma,

my aunts, my uncles, and my cousins—were going to my mother's
church.

In the darkness of the backseat, I sat with my collar up and the windows
down. I was thinking how little I knew about my mother and father. And that
made me wonder how much I knew about either the gospel of jingle bells or
the gospel of the Christ child.

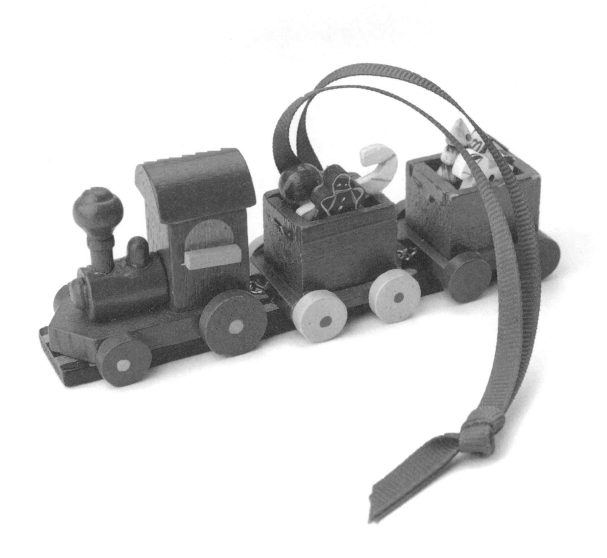

"It is more blessed to give than to receive."
ACTS 20:35, NLT

Danae Dobson

A CHRISTMAS LOST AND FOUND

❖

A lonely college freshman walked along the streets of Philadelphia on the day before Christmas 1975. Three weeks earlier his mother had written to break the news. The family could not afford to bring him home for the holidays. His father's business was in trouble, and there was no extra money for travel. That meant William Lambert would be forced to remain at the University of Pennsylvania during the entire Christmas season.

The winter break had been the most depressing period of William's life. With the exception of a foreign student who spoke little English, all the guys in his dormitory had left two weeks earlier in a flurry of activity. They talked excitedly about their moms' cooking and the families that awaited them back home. William had watched them pack and leave, feeling like the most wretched person on earth. His pain had become almost unbearable by that cold morning before Christmas.

Not even God knows that I'm alive, he thought to himself. *If he cares, why didn't he help me get home for the holidays?*

The question went unanswered.

In desperation, William boarded a bus for downtown Philly, hoping to find relief from his terrible loneliness. He pulled his collar around his neck to protect against the bitter wind and walked along the decorated streets. The laughing, happy people reminded him of his friends at home in Idaho. He thought of his mother's traditional turkey dinner and the family sitting around the Christmas tree. How his heart longed to be with them at that moment.

In his wallet he carried a crisp fifty-dollar bill, a present from his parents. He knew they had sacrificed to send it to him. The card had said, "Buy something special for yourself," but nothing sounded appealing.

William spent most of the day wandering aimlessly in and out of stores. It somehow helped to be surrounded by crowds. Then, late in the afternoon, his vision suddenly focused. There in a shop window was an electric train chugging through a tiny frontier town. In front of the window was a young boy, about nine years old, standing transfixed in front of the glass. It was as though he were hypnotized by the train.

William was reminded of his own childhood in Boise. There was a toy store near his house, where he had stood and longed for a beautiful Lionel train. He knew his father could not afford such an expensive gift, but he secretly hoped for a miracle that never came. Now he recognized that same disappointment in the face of the boy before him. The lad walked away, casting one last glance over his shoulder.

Why not? William thought to himself.

He strolled over to the boy and tapped him on the shoulder. "Hi! My name is William," he said.

"I'm David," said the boy.

"That's a beautiful train, isn't it?"

"Yeah," said David. "It's the best train I've ever seen."

"How would you like to have that train?" he said to his young friend.

The boy's eyes widened. "Oh, I could never own it," he said. "We couldn't—I mean, my mom doesn't have very much money."

"Come on," said William, leading David into the store.

William knew that his motives might be misunderstood by someone older than David, but he meant no harm to the boy. Indeed, this might have been the most unselfish moment of his life. Since he couldn't be a child again, he could at least enjoy making a boy's dream come true.

The salesclerk approached them and asked if he could be of help.

"That train in the window," William inquired. "How much is it—the whole set?"

"I believe it's about fifty dollars," he answered. "Let me check." In a few moments he returned to the counter. "It's $46.95. And worth every penny."

"That sounds terrific," said William. "We'll take it."

The salesclerk made his way to the storage room.

"Wow!" said David. "Do you really mean it? The train's for me? It's really mine?"

William gave the boy a pat on the shoulder and smiled.

"Hey," said David. "I live just around the corner. Wanna meet my mom? She's a really neat lady. I want her to meet you."

The salesclerk returned carrying a large box. "Here she be," he announced.

After William paid for the train, David said excitedly, "Come on! I wanna show Mom."

William struggled to carry the box and keep track of the boy who ran ahead. A block away they came to an old brick building. David ran up a dark staircase and pounded on a door marked 201. An apron-clad woman in her thirties soon appeared.

"Mom," said David. "This man is my friend. He bought me a new train. Can he come in, Mom? Huh? Please?"

William tried to maneuver the box so he could see the woman. "Hi," he said. "I'm William Lambert. I hope you don't mind what I've done. I saw David looking at this train, and I could see how much he wanted it. I would really be pleased if you would let him accept it."

"Well, sure," said David's mother. "Bring it on in. My name is Pauline Sanders. You'll have to pardon me. I'm not used to having my son bring people home with him."

"I'll be leaving in a minute," said William. "I just wanted to help David carry the box home."

"No, no," said Pauline, seeing the kindness in the young man's eyes. "Come on in."

Her warm reaction reminded William of his own mother, who would have responded the same way if he had shown up at the door with a stranger.

"Won't you have a seat?" Pauline asked.

As William removed his hat and coat, he noticed the humble surroundings. The living room was clean and neat, although simple in appearance. A fire crackled in the hearth, and a small Bible lay on top of the coffee table. In the corner stood a frail Christmas tree, covered with popcorn strings and red ribbon. He noticed there were hardly any presents underneath.

David grabbed William's hand. "Don't sit down," he said. "First come see my room."

As they made their way down the hall, Pauline called from the kitchen. "Son, did you remember to pick up those apples for me?"

"They're on the counter, Mom," David replied. He then opened the door to a tiny bedroom. "This is *my* room," he said proudly.

"Very impressive," William remarked, looking around.

Two posters hung on the walls, and a few model trains were displayed on the dresser.

"Did you make those models?" asked William.

"Yes," answered David. "All by myself!"

William picked up one of the trains and looked at it closely. "You did a good job," he said. "Better than I could have done."

David beamed with pride as they walked back to the kitchen.

"As long as you're here," Pauline said, "why don't you join us for

Christmas dinner? It's just David and me. It'll be good to have a guest with us."

She had prepared a bountiful meal of turkey, mashed potatoes, and green beans. It was clearly a sacrificial tribute that had been extracted from a small budget. William smelled the food and said he would be delighted to stay.

"Do you mind if we say grace before we eat?" asked Pauline. "David and I are Christians."

"Really?" said William. "I'm a new Christian, too. I became a believer last month at an InterVarsity meeting, but there's still a lot I don't understand."

They bowed their heads while Pauline thanked God for his blessings and for the birth of his Son, Jesus.

During the meal, Pauline talked about her late husband, Richard. He had died in Vietnam five years before. She had wanted to leave Philadelphia ever since his death, preferring to live on the West Coast with her family.

"Someday," she said, "we'll be able to move. That's my dream."

"Why didn't you visit your family this Christmas?" asked William. Immediately he regretted asking.

Pauline sighed. "I really wanted to," she said, "but I just didn't have the money this year."

William explained that he, too, had wanted to go home for Christmas, but financial woes had kept him in Philly.

"Then it must be God's will that you're here tonight," Pauline noted.

William smiled. "It must be," he agreed.

After dinner, William and David sat on the floor and began putting the train set together. Pauline served apple dumplings as they talked and laughed and told stories.

Finally, after three hours, the task was finished. William sat back in a worn easy chair. "All right, David, start 'er up," he instructed.

The young boy reached for the control and pressed the button. In a flash the train was on its way, winding around the tracks with an occasional whistle blow.

The joy-filled expression on David's face was worth every penny that William had spent. It was a feeling of immeasurable satisfaction knowing he had been able to make a boy happy at Christmas. After the train had made fifteen circuits, William announced he needed to get back to the university.

"I've had a wonderful evening," he said. "Thank you so much for making me feel at home. And the meal was delicious!"

"Wait just a minute," David pleaded. He ran from the room.

As William put on his coat and hat, he noticed that Pauline had tears in her eyes.

"I want you to know I've been praying the entire month for a way to buy David a nice Christmas present," she whispered. "Your kindness was not only a gift to David but also to me. It was an answer to prayer."

Before William could respond, David rushed back into the living room. He was holding a little white box in his arms. "Merry Christmas, William," he said joyfully.

As William lifted the lid, he was surprised to see the model train David had shown him earlier surrounded by crumpled tissue paper.

"It's not as good as the one you gave me," David apologized, "but at least we both got a new train for Christmas."

William reached out and gave his new friend a hug. "David, this is the nicest thing anyone ever gave me," he said.

A certain sadness came over William as he turned to leave. He knew he might never see the Sanderses again. Pauline and David thanked him for coming and for the gift, but William was the grateful one.

As he made his way to the bus stop, he reflected on all that had happened. He had found more satisfaction in his new friendships than in any Christmas celebration of the past. The words of Jesus, which he had learned as a child, rang in his ears. It really was more blessed to give than to receive!

As William rode the bus through the night, the meaning of the evening suddenly became clear—like a picture coming into focus. He and his new friends had each experienced a personal crisis before their chance encounter. Pauline had been on her knees, praying desperately for a gift to offer her fatherless son. Her little boy had longed for a prize that could never be his. And William had ached with unspeakable loneliness and despair. It was an impossible array of problems. There was no way, short of a miracle, that each set of needs could have been met simultaneously and in such a satisfying way. And yet it happened.

Could it be that a loving and compassionate Lord had been watching them on that day? Had he seen their distress and heard the longings of their hearts? Did he bring them together to provide kindness to one another on Christmas Eve?

"Yes," murmured William to himself. "He *does* care. He *is* there!"

"Happy Birthday, Jesus," he said as he entered the quiet dorm. "And thank you." Then he added, "But next year—could I celebrate in Boise?"

"He took up our infirmities and carried our diseases."
MATTHEW 8:17, NIV

Calvin Miller

EL NIÑO

The headlights nibbled at the white stripes on the dark asphalt. José nervously fingered the hand controls of his '78 Dodge pickup. On most trips he usually worried about the thin tread of his bald tires. But now he was more worried about an invisible film of ice that sheathed I-25 south of Belén. He hated driving on ice. He also disliked driving on Christmas Eve. Both he and María had known the baby would come in December. They had even prayed, for income tax reasons, it would. But now that their child was about to be born both the ice and the severity of María's pain had replaced their security with doubt.

Here and there along the glazed highway he could see shallow, dark adobe houses framed in glowing luminarias. The early evening fog that gave birth to the ice had cleared and left the road a gleaming sea of black ice. The great highway that bisected New Mexico through the Rio Grande valley was quiet and lonely.

"María," said José, "the stars are so beautiful that if I could give you any gift this *Navidad*, I would give you five minutes of sight." He tried to sound cheerful. He did not want María to feel the gnawing fear he felt at driving the dark, slick highway on treadless tires.

María was not taken in by his empty bravado. Only her eyes were blind. She saw clearly that José was troubled. But she played his game, his way, with mock cheer. "And if I could give *you* any gift this *Navidad*, I would give you legs. And once you had legs, I would give you an important job in Albuquerque."

He reached and took her hand. Their Christmas fantasies were absurd. Neither of them could give the other any gift. What meager money they made they saved and dared to hope that with Medicare and the state of New Mexico, their baby could be born in the "Indian hospital" in Belén. It was there they were headed, dreaming fragile dreams on an icy highway that forbade them any dreams at all.

José released María's hand and adjusted the steel shanks of his leg braces, pushing them back against the car seat. He didn't really know why he pushed his legs back. They were never really in his way. They were just there to be methodically pushed about; he had never given them much attention. He had been born with useless legs. Still, with his braces and crutches, he had excellent balance and could walk at a very brisk pace.

He took his eyes from the road ahead to look at her beautiful brown eyes. They always looked alive, but José was blind to her blindness. He never saw it at all. He saw only her beautiful eyes and face. To him her whole life was beautiful. They had met through a social agency of the county. The unspeakable loneliness that each of them had known while they were single was swallowed up in a wonderful togetherness that was about to know the joy of childbirth. They both believed that there was only one real handicap: loneliness. In the wondrous joy of their togetherness, his useless legs were of no consequence, and her blindness had ceased to exist. They lived and rarely thought about it. As María had said so often, "Love is the great miracle; in its light all handicaps disappear."

They had lived through the delirious months of María's pregnancy with joy. But now that the long anticipated time had come, José was less sure. They lived a long way from the hospital in Belén. And now María's contractions were coming at incredibly close intervals.

"José," she said sharply, "it's starting again!" She grew quiet, then moaned. Her body stiffened. It shuddered and moved from trembling rigidity to fall silently limp in the threadbare seat of their old pickup.

José knew that she was now trying to gather enough strength to endure the next spasm whenever it came. His hand urged the accelerator mechanism. Belén was still seventeen miles away. He had to hurry. Yet the glistening highway forbade him. Against all hope he urged the accelerator again. The old truck at first lurched straight forward in obedience, then it rocketed insecurely across the gleaming ice. Suddenly it slid. José froze in fear. Now the truck was spinning out of control. Gripped by horror, he realized there was no connection between what the pickup was doing and what he was doing with the brakes and steering wheel. The spinning intensified. Round and round hurtled the old truck as María and José strained against the safety belts.

The pickup shot off the highway and plowed a crystalline furrow through the ice-sheathed grass. It slid down the shallow embankment into a very low drainage ditch. Once in the ditch, it skidded into a fence post, slicing through the barbed-wire interstate fence. At last it came to a stop. Mercifully it was over. They were both unharmed, but there was no way to get the pickup back on the road.

José crossed himself. "*¡Gracias á Dios!* María, are you all right?"

She nodded quietly and smiled, then she gave a little cry as once again her small body stiffened with the pain. José inwardly cursed their predicament.

"*Mi amor*, it is madness, but I must try to go and find help," he said. The very idea of leaving her alone seemed as desperate as their plight. He opened the door and swung his legs outside. He stiffened his braces at the knee joint, clicking the metal shafts into "lock-extend." He pulled himself erect into the icy weeds, reached behind the seat, and pulled out his aluminum crutches.

"*¡Cuidado, mi amor!*" whispered María, feeling her body beginning to relax again.

"How close are your contractions?" he asked.

"*¡Cinco minutos!*" she replied.

"I'm going to try and find help," he promised. "I'm sorry, *mi amor*, to have to leave you. I'll be back as soon as I can."

"*Vaya con Dios*," she said.

"*A ti también*," he responded.

Those would have been his last words if he had not turned and shouted back as he closed the car door, "Start the engine if you get cold." In the pale illumination of the old pickup's dome light he watched María nod and was touched by the courage of her smile.

He turned and left. *What kind of a man would leave a blind woman all alone in the cold?* he asked himself. *Especially one who is about to give birth.*

The crisp air stung his face. A slight breeze had begun to blow. He was glad, for he knew in time the wind would cut the ice from the highway. He pulled his jacket around his chest and began swinging his body through his crutches, his plodding walk leaving uneven marks in the icy grass. Up, up, up, he came out of the low depression, where the pickup was sitting silently with its abandoned and needy passenger. In a moment he had made his way up out of the shallow drainage ditch. He could hear music as he reached the top, and once in the field above the ditch he broke into elation.

"*¡Gracias á Dios!*" he said again, nearly shouting in the night. The music was coming from a large but low adobe house, no more than two hundred yards to the side of the interstate. When he had closed some of that distance, he could see through the frosted panes that those inside were dancing. José was ecstatic. He made his way across a flat field, through patches of yucca and prickly pears to a barbed-wire fence. He dropped the crutches and fell on his hands in a hurried manner. Lying flat on the ground, he slid under the low wire, and reaching back under the fence, found his crutches and pulled himself upward again. He had torn his jacket in several places on the steel barbs, but he considered the incident of no consequence as he moved steadily toward the large house. He shuddered, suddenly aware that it was very cold. Nevertheless, he was sweating in the strenuous attempt he was undertaking to end the terror of María's lonely ordeal.

Finally he crossed the large level meadow, made crystal by starlight on ice. Furiously he moved. If a man on crutches can be said to run, José ran. At last he was at the house. As he approached the level stoop, a huge dog ran out of the shadows. Its barking stopped both the guitars and the dancing going on inside, but not for long; it started up once more. The dog barked again, and the merriment stopped a second time. During the second silence, José crossed the stoop and banged on the door with his crutch.

A heavily mustachioed face appeared in the glass. José breathed a sigh of relief as the orange porch light burst into illumination. The door swung wide open. "¡Hola! ¿Qué pasa, amigo?"

José felt a blast of warm air in his face. He gasped out, "¡Buenas noches!" and tried to move across the threshold. His right crutch snagged on a chair leg, and he stumbled and fell face forward into the room. In the process of the fall he threw his crutches to the side and caught himself with his strong arms and hands. He had long ago become accustomed to throwing his crutches during a fall; it was the only way he could guarantee himself the full use of his strong arms in breaking the fall. His hands were so numbed by the cold that it seemed to him the saltillo tile floor was warm by comparison. The crowd made a place for him as he put his hands underneath his chest and pushed himself upward. A couple of men stepped forward and lifted him up. Another handed him the crutches he had dropped when he fell.

Suddenly he was aware of the strong aroma of tortillas and marvelous pastries and pralines.

Those in the room with him could see that his jacket was torn. They could also see a look of terror in his eyes.

"Mi esposa . . . ¡Por favor, mi esposa!"

"Where is your wife?" several of them blurted at one time.

"In the truck," he offered. His lower lip—indeed his whole chin—was trembling. It was clearly apparent that he was a man in turmoil. "We've had an accident . . . she's having a baby! *Por favor, señores."* He stopped, his shoulders heaving. *"¡Por favor, por favor!"*

"¿Dónde? Señor. ¿Dónde?"

Quickly José told them that the truck was just off the road only a few hundred yards from the hacienda. Instantly, several of them were pulling on their mackinaws. They even found one for José. "I'm Manuelo," cried a big man, suddenly taking José's crutches and setting them aside. He picked José up and saddled him across his broad body piggyback fashion.

José's steel-braced legs stuck out at odd, stiff angles that seemed to protest passing the narrow door through which José had entered. *"¡Un momento!"* cried José. Manuelo set him down long enough for him to unstrap his leg braces. His legs fell limp as Manuelo hoisted him up again.

"Grab hold and don't let go," commanded Manuelo.

A group of seven or eight men rushed out with Manuelo and his terrified "rider." They crunched through the icy foliage back to the barbed wire in only a few minutes. The cutting, steel strands of the fence that had snagged José's jacket were easier crossed now with some aid. They all rushed on toward the old ice-encrusted pickup glistening in the starlight.

María's face lit up when she heard José's voice outside the frosted glass. She smiled as she groped for the roller handle and lowered the pickup window. Manuelo moved his "rider" to his knee as José leaned in, took María's face, turned it toward his own, and kissed her. Those who were with him pulled the door of the vehicle open, and María, made weak by her ever closer contractions, managed to stand, though feebly, outside the truck. There was a large blanket in the truck that the men double-folded into a strong but sagging litter. They held it firmly as María sat down on one side of it. Then Manuelo set José across his back, and the odd entourage moved again toward the troublesome barbed-wire fence. They laid the Indian-blanket litter on the ground, and then two men, bracing their feet on the ground, pulled the low wire high enough to slide the woman under the fence before they picked up the litter and continued toward the house.

When they were nearly there, María experienced another contraction. Her muffled outcry seemed to settle in their souls. They stopped as they felt her body stiffen with the ordeal of childbirth. As soon as she relaxed, they moved on into the house. The warm air, made delicious with the spirit of *Navidad*, greeted María. They moved her on through the main room to a bedroom that had been made ready for her.

"Muchas gracias," she offered weakly.

By the time they had made her comfortable in the bedroom, José had rebuckled his braces, grabbed his crutches, and reentered the room. "Señor," Manuelo asked José, "your wife is blind?"

"*Si*," agreed José.

"Then the waiting in the truck must have seemed a long time!"

"Perhaps," was all that José could say.

"Shall we call the ambulance in Belén?" asked Manuelo.

"*No hay tiempo*," said a husky old woman.

She was right! There wasn't time.

"José, this is Consuela Vieja," said Manuelo. "She is the midwife to our pueblo. She was there when nearly everyone in this room entered into the world. If she says there isn't time for the ambulance, you may depend upon it."

"*¡Agua caliente!*" ordered Consuela Vieja.

The room gathered itself around her command. The Christmas revelers would not have obeyed any faster had she been the surgeon general. Men carried water. Women came and left the room at her command. During the furor, one of the men began playing the guitar in a corner of the main room. It was an old Navajo Christmas lullaby. Its strains brought to silence all but the most necessary whispering. Over and over came a subtle litany of strings precisely plucked to form a melody for a baby that was changing worlds. The simple tune never stopped. Here and there a strummed chord interrupted the rise and fall of individual strings. Most of them knew the words of the Christmas lullaby. It was not a commonly known lullaby but one that was often sung in the villages where they grew up.

EL NIÑO

How-a-loo infant. See how he lies.
Navidad Niño from Navajo skies.
When God shouts loudest from heaven's throne,
On earth, a Navajo baby cries.

On and on the simple melody filtered through the waiting. Then, as if by signal, the guitarist quit playing. A baby cried. José strained at his crutches and rose from his chair. He moved to the door. He expected to be called through the door in a moment, but it was not so. He waited . . . and waited . . . and then finally Consuela appeared in the doorway. She entered the main room, closing the door behind her. Her face was bright. She smiled at José but said nothing. It was as though the news was generally good, but not altogether. Her smiling but ominous silence brought José to the edge of collapse.

"*¿Mi María?*" He shouted the question.

"She is well," answered Consuela.

"*¿Y el niño?*" Again he forced volume into his anxious question.

"He is . . ."

"It is a boy, then?"

"Yes, . . . a boy, and in most ways healthy."

"In most ways? How in most ways? Is he crippled like myself?"

"His legs are fine, I think," answered Consuela Vieja.

"Is he blind like my María?"

"His eyes, I think, are fine, too."

"Then tell me, *por favor. ¡Por favor!*" José was now leaning far forward on his crutches, making his whole body a plea.

"You may go in now," she said, "and greet your wife and son."

He passed by Consuela and burst into the room. He swung himself through the doorway like one whom Jesus might have healed. He was so light with joy he felt, for the first time, that he was not crippled at all. In the joy of seeing María, he threw his crutches aside. Only then did he look down, noticing he had forgotten to lock his braces. Why was he not falling? There could only be one explanation, but his joy was too great to stop and consider it. "María," he said, walking to her bed. He gasped. He suddenly realized what was happening.

"José! You walk!" The insane force of María's words had all but stopped her breathing. "What joyous madness is this? I've never seen you walk before!"

"Stop, María! Realize what you are saying! You have never *seen* me walk? You have never *seen* anything. Can our joy make madness of the impossible?" They were both laughing and crying at the same time. Why or how—it mattered not.

María extended her hand toward him. "*¡Gloria á Dios!*" he exulted. She reached to take his hand. *She reached!* How could she see to reach? He had always reached for her, but now she reached for him. Now he saw what was unbelievable to his reluctant soul. María saw, and reached to take his hand.

"So this is what you look like, my love?" she asked. "Of all that I have ever wanted to see, your face has held first place. *¡Te amo, José!*" she said.

In but an instant the joy they felt fell from their new madness to the child lying across her stomach. Was this child the source of all the joy that fell upon them both? José moved the towel that old Consuelo had draped across the wide-eyed infant.

"*Feliz Navidad,* my darling!" said María as José reached for their newborn son.

He picked the baby up and stood on his own legs, suddenly made strong enough to support them both. He turned two happy circles on the floor. "Yes," he said, "God brought you here to us!"

Suddenly he was aware that the guitarist and the old Navajo lullaby had started again in the main room. He heard the haunting strings of the guitar and the wonderful Christmas lullaby that they knew by heart. Now everyone in the room was singing it.

> "*How-a-loo infant. See how he lies.*
> *Navidad Niño from Navajo skies.*
> *When God shouts loudest from heaven's throne,*
> *On earth, a Navajo baby cries.*"

"*Feliz Navidad,* my darling!" María repeated.

María's wide eyes tried to drink in the intoxicating glory of seeing her paralytic husband dancing a kind of odd Navajo waltz. He held the baby close now and moved gracefully as though he had forever practiced this odd nativity ritual. Beautifully, powerfully, like a Navajo spirit, he moved and swayed to the lullaby born in the outer room, yet coming from somewhere farther—much farther—away. When the lullaby was finished, the music in the big room was clearly giving way to the Christmas party that had been going on before José's anguish had interrupted their evening. Only then did José give his new son back to María.

It was then that they both noticed the baby's hands for the first time. "María, look at his hands." The tiny hands were malformed. José's Navajo grandmother had a word she used for birth defects. In her special understanding the word meant, not *malformed,* but *specially made.*

José's spirit seemed troubled as he reached out his strong, bronze hand and touched the tiny malformed fingers. "What can this mean, María? The first moment we are well, our son is born imperfect."

He wanted to cry, but there are moments when joy is so great it stops the sadness before it has a chance to be born as tears. María joined her hand to José's and explored that of her infant.

"What can it mean?" she said, softly repeating José's question.

Furiously she loved this son she had carried so long in her blindness. She could not bring herself to feel bad that he was less than she had hoped. God had given her a son, exactly as God had created him to be. He was as beautiful as the night. He was *specially made.*

José's mind was far away. He thought distractedly of his old pickup parked in the icy weeds. He smiled when he wondered if he would ever be able to learn to drive a car using his feet on the pedals. His reverie returned to his new lightness of being. He had a child. He smiled again—*no hospital bills— at all! Gracias á Jesús* and, of course, *á Consuela Vieja.* Only gradually did his high elation return to the small twisted hands of his new son. He bent down and kissed those hands and then the beautiful María.

María gathered her strength. She knew José would want to show off mother and child to those who had been so nice to them at the Christmas fiesta. She waited for a few more moments and then swung her legs out of bed. It was hard; they felt leaden and yet young. She carefully stood.

"Do you feel strong enough to carry our son?" asked José.

She said nothing in reply. She only reached her trembling hands toward the baby. José handed her the child. She suddenly realized she had not combed her hair since going through the long trauma of childbirth. "My hair!" she cried, wincing.

"It's beautiful. You're beautiful!" said José.

Nonetheless, she pulled her shawl forward over her forehead. She leaned against José as he placed his hand on the doorknob, opened the door, and they entered the room. The dancing ceased. Every head swiveled in their direction. All conversation stopped. The paralytic was well! The blind could see! An old man sitting in a corner of the room rubbed his eyes as though the vision defied them. Consuela Vieja advanced slowly toward the new family. "Tonight," she said, "*¡Dios vino a Belén!* Yes," she said, "God has come to Belén."

"Then there will be no more dancing, no more singing!" said Manuelo.

"No, no, Manuelo! That's how you meet God every time he comes. Dancing and singing are the only language by which we mortals *can* greet him."

Consuela had said enough. Her words coaxed the first tentative chords from the quiet guitar.

Who knows all that stirs the deepest worship of old women? Perhaps it was the baby that drew the center of all esteem. After all, it was *Navidad!* Perhaps it was the grandmotherly memories of Consuela Vieja. But whatever it was, the old woman knelt. She offered no prayer. It was not as though she felt that the baby was worthy of worship, only respect.

46

"Consuela," said Manuelo, "do not kneel; this baby is not Jesus!"

"I know," said the old woman, "but every baby reminds us that once God willingly trusted himself to the keeping of mortals. Every baby born is a reminder of that!"

The tears in Consuela's eyes made her argument real.

Manuelo knelt beside her. *"Feliz Navidad!"* said Manuelo.

"It is good," said Consuela, "to have a baby at this fiesta."

The old woman stood slowly and with effort. The years had stolen all ease from the simple task of standing. She walked to María and spoke softly. "I have seen your son's hands. Do not grieve them. There is an ancient Navajo proverb known only to my father's clan.

> *"When a baby comes made special in the feet,*
> *Listen carefully to all the little one says;*
> *the child could be a prophet.*
> *When a child is born made special in his hands,*
> *Bow down; it could be God is back among us."*

There was light over Belén, New Mexico.

The dancing began again.

47

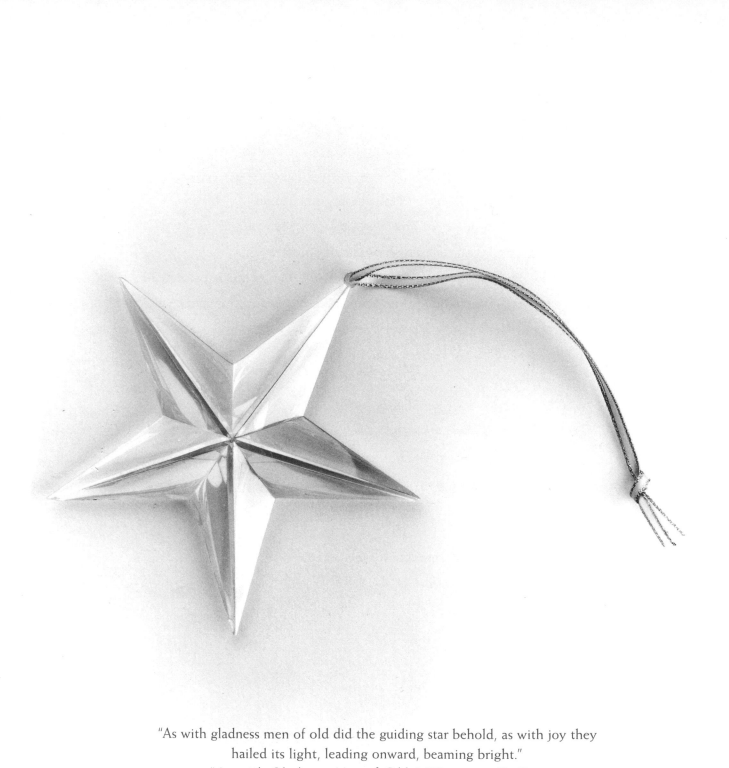

"As with gladness men of old did the guiding star behold, as with joy they
hailed its light, leading onward, beaming bright."
"As with Gladness Men of Old," WILLIAM C. DIX

Grace Livingston Hill

THE STORY OF THE LOST STAR

❖

About a week before Christmas in a small city of the East there appeared in the Lost and Found column this advertisement:

Lost. Sometime between the World War and the present morning, The Star of Bethlehem. The finder will confer everlasting favor and receive a reward of ten thousand dollars if returned to the owner between the hours of sundown and midnight on Christmas eve.

(Signed) George K. Hamilton,

Eleven, Harvard Place.

The type-setter blinked and paused in his busy work, read it again and wondered. Ten thousand dollars! Was it a joke? It must be a mistake! But no, it was paid for. It must go in. He punched away at his machine and the lines appeared in the type, but his thoughts were busy. Ten thousand dollars! With that he could, with self respect, marry Mary! He would not have been John if he had not thought of that first.

George K. Hamilton. That was the rich guy who lived in the big house, with one blind wall stuck on its side that everybody said was a picture gallery. He was rolling in wealth so it must be real. But what was this thing he had lost that was worth everlasting favor and ten thousand dollars? A jewel? A silver tablet? Something of intrinsic historic value perhaps? Something that must be well known, or the writer would not have spoken of it in that off-hand indefinite way as *the* Star of Bethlehem, as if there were but one. Bethlehem—Bethlehem—that was the place where they made steel! Steel! Why—steel of course. George K. Hamilton. Hamilton the steel king! Ah! Why hadn't he thought of it at once?

And why couldn't he go to Bethlehem and find out all about it? He was the first one, excepting the editor of the Lost and Found column, to see this ad. Why wouldn't he stand first chance of the reward if he worked it right?

To be sure there was a possibility that someone, who knew just what this star was, would be able to get on its track sooner, but if he caught the first train in the morning he would have a good start before anyone read the morning papers.

He would be through with his work by three a.m. at the latest, and there was a train at five. He would have time to get back to his boarding place and clean up a bit, perhaps scribble a note to Mary telling her to be ready for the wedding.

His fingers flew over the keys of his machine as he laid his plans, and his heart throbbed with excitement over the great opportunity that had flung its open door right in his humble path. Ten thousand dollars!

Early dawn saw him dressed in his best and hurrying on his way to Bethlehem amid a train load of laborers going out for the day's work. But he saw not pick nor shovel nor dinner pail, nor noted greasy overalls and sleepy-eyed companions. Before his shining eyes was a star, sometimes silver, sumptuously engraved, sometimes gold and set in sparkling jewels, leading him on into the day of adventure.

He essayed to question his fellow seatmate about that star:

"You live in Bethlehem? Did you ever see the Star of Bethlehem?"

But the man shook his head dumbly:

"Me no spak L'angla!"

Arrived in the City of Steel, he went straight to the news agent:

"Have you been here some time?"

"Born here."

"Then tell me, have you a Star of Bethlehem?"

The agent shook his head.

"Don't smoke that kind. Don't keep that kind. Try the little cigar store down the street." And he swung himself under the shelf and, shouldering a pile of morning papers, rushed off down the platform.

Out in the street John stopped a man whose foot was just mounting the running board of his car:

"Do you know anything about the Star of Bethlehem?"

"Never heard of it, Man. A Ford's good enough for me!" and he swung into his car and shot away from the curb hurriedly.

He asked a little girl who was hurrying away from the bakery with a basket of bread.

"Why, Star-of-Bethlehem is a flower," she said, "a little green and white starry flower with pointed petals. It grows in the meadow over there in the summer time, but it's all gone now. You can't find Stars-of-Bethlehem this time of year!" And she stared after him for a silly fool.

He asked a passer on the street:

"Can you tell me how to find out about the Star of Bethlehem?"

The man tapped him lightly on the shoulder with a wink and advised him knowingly, with a thumb pointing down a side alley:

52

"You better not mention that openly, brother. There's been several raids around here lately and the police are wise. It ain't safe."

And about this time the Bishop back at home was opening the morning paper at the breakfast table as he toyed with his grapefruit and coffee:

"Ha, ha!" he said as his eye traveled down the column idly and paused at the Lost and Found. "Listen to this, Bella. Poor old George has got 'em again. He probably thinks he is going to die this time. I'll just step in and have a little talk on theology with him this morning and set his mind at rest. No need for that ten thousand dollars to go out of the church. We might as well have it as some home for the Feeble Minded."

Bella left her coffee and came around to read the advertisement, her face lighting intelligently:

"Oh, Basil! Do you think you can work it?" she cried delightedly.

"Why, sure, he's just a little daffy on religion now because he's been sick. The last time I saw him he asked me how we could know any of the creeds were true when they were all so different. I'll smooth it all out for him, and make him give another ten thousand or so to the Social Service work of our church, and he'll come across handsomely, you'll see. I'd better go at once. It won't do to wait, there are too many kinds of crooks on the lookout for just such a soft ten thousand as this." And he took his hat and coat and hurried out.

The Professor at his meagre breakfast table, worrying about his sick wife, and how he could afford to keep his eldest son in college, happened on the item.

He set down his coffee cup untasted and stepped to his bookshelves, taking down several wise treatises on Astronomy.

A sweet faced saint in an invalid chair read and pondered and murmured thoughtfully: "Poor soul! What's happened to the man's Bible?"

Before night the one little shop in the city that made a specialty of astronomical instruments had been drained of everything in the shape of a searcher of the heavens, and a rush order had gone on to New York by telegraph for more telescopes of various sizes and prices, while a boy in the back office who was good at lettering was busy making a copy of the advertisement to fasten up in the plate-glass window, with special electric lights playing about it and a note below:

"Come in and order your telescope now before they are all gone, and get into line for the great sky prize! We have 'em! All prices!"

Far into the evening the crowd continued around that window, and many who had glasses at home hurried away to search for them, and build air castles of how they would spend the ten thousand dollars when they got it.

Even before the day was half over the office of the University was besieged by eager visitors come to question wise ones, a folded newspaper furtively held under each applicant's arm.

As evening drew on shadowy figures stole forth to high places and might have been seen scanning the heavens, and now and then consulting a book by means of a pocket flash light. More than one young student worked into the small hours of the night with reference books scattered about him, writing a many-paged treatise on the Star of Stars, some to prove that the star was a myth, and others that it was still in existence and would one day appear again as bright as of old. Even the police, coming suddenly upon lurking stargazers far toward morning, began to question what had taken hold of the town.

54

Coming home on the late train from a fruitless search for an unknown quantity which was not there, John Powers sat wearily back in the fusty seat of the common car and took out the worn advertisement from his pocket to read it once more.

The lost Star of Bethlehem! What could it be? He had searched the steel city from end to end without finding so much as a trace of tradition or story about a star in connection with that town. He had met with more rebuffs and strange suggestions than ever before in his life together, and he was dog-weary and utterly discouraged. If only he had not written that hopeful letter to Mary in the morning!

Now perhaps she would already be planning to have the wedding soon, and where was the money coming from to provide the little home?

Of course it just might happen that after all the star had been lost up in the city, else why should the advertisement have been put in the city paper and not in the Bethlehem local? But even so he had hoped great things from this trip to Bethlehem and now he had only wasted a day and the car fare, and had gotten nowhere at all.

At a local station a loud mouthed traveler got off, leaving his recent seat-mate without anyone to talk to, and presently he joined John Powers and entered into conversation, being one of those men who is never happy unless his tongue is wagging. In the course of their talk, John found himself asking the old question again:

"You say you are from Bethlehem? Did you ever hear of a star in connection with that town? Was there any memorial tablet or monument or emblem or anything in the shape of a star, that has been stolen away? Star of Bethlehem it was called, do you know anything about it?"

The stranger stared blankly and shook his head:

"Sounds to me as if it might be a song, or a book mebbe. If you knowed who wrote it you might find out at one o' the schools. My Johnny says you can find out almost anything if you know who wrote it. Ever been a Mason? Might be some kind of a Masonic badge, mightn't it?"

The man got out at the next station, and Powers leaned back wearily and thought how he had failed. His mind seemed too tired to think any longer on the subject.

An old lady in a queer bonnet with many bundles at her feet and a basket beside her out of which stuck a pair of turkey's feet, leaned over suddenly and touched him on the shoulder:

"Laddie, hae ye tried the auld Buik?" she asked timidly. "I'm thinkin' ye'll find it all there."

"I beg your pardon!" said Powers lifting his hat courteously and thinking how the blue of her eyes had a light like that in Mary's eyes.

He arose from his seat and went back to sit beside her. Then somehow the blue of her eyes made him unafraid, and he told her all about the ten thousand dollars and his fruitless trip to Bethlehem.

"Oh, but laddie, ye're on the wrong track entirely," said the old lady. "The Star o' Bethlehem's in the auld Buik. I ken it's no the fashion to read it these days, but the worruld lost sight of a lot besides the things it wanted to forget when it set out to put its Bibles awa! Hunt up yer Mither's Bible, lad, and study it out. The star arose in the East ye ken, and the folks who saw it first was those that was lookin' fer its arisin'. The star's *na* lost. It led to the little King ye ken, an' it'll always lead to the King if a body seeks with all the heirt, fer that is the promise: `An' ye shall find me, when ye shall seek fer me with all yer heirts.' May like the puir buddy who wrote the bit lines in the paper was longin' fer the King hisself an' wanted the star to guide him, but ye ken ye can't purchase the gifts of God wi' silver ner gold. The mon may lay his ten thousand baubles at the fut of the throne, but he'll find he must go his own self across the desert, and wait mayhap, before he'll ever see the shinin' of the Star. But you'll not turn back yerself now you've started, laddie! Go find the King fer yerself. Look in the Gospels an' read the story. It's passin' wonderful an' lovely. This is my station now, and I'll be leavin' ye, but it'll be a glad Christmas time fer you ef you find the little King, an *ye'll find Him* sure, if ye seek on with all yer heirt."

The doorway to the fine old Hamilton mansion on Harvard Place was
besieged from morning to night all that week by aspirants wishing to speak
with the Master, but to all the grave and dignified servitor who answered the
door replied:

"My master is away. He cannot speak with you until the time appointed.
If any then have found the lost treasure they may come and claim the reward.
But they must come bringing it with them. None others need present them-
selves."

Even the Bishop had not been able to gain admittance. He was much
annoyed about it. He was afraid others would get ahead of him. He had written a letter, but he knew it had not yet been opened, for the last time he
called he had seen it lying on the console in the hall with a lot of other
unopened letters. The Bishop was very certain that if he could have audience
first all would be well. He was sure he could explain the philosophy of life and
the mystery of the star quite satisfactorily and soothingly.

Before John Powers had gone back to work that night of his return from
Bethlehem, he had gone to the bottom of an old chest and hunted out his
mother's Bible. It was worn and dropping apart in places, but he put it tenderly
on his bed, and following an impulse, dropped to his knees beside it, laying his
lips against its dusty covers. Somehow the very look of the old worn covers
brought back his childhood days and a sense of sin in that he had wandered so
far from the path in which his mother had set his young feet.

All that week he gave all the extra time he had to studying about the
star. He did not even go to see Mary. He lost sight of the ten thousand
dollars in his interest in the star itself. He was now seeking to find that star

for himself, not for the reward that had been offered. He wanted to find the King who was also a Saviour.

The last night before it came time for him to go to his work, he dropped upon his knees once more beside the little tattered book, and prayed:

"Oh, Jesus Christ, Saviour of the world, I thank Thee that Thou hast sent Thy star to guide me to Thee. I worship Thee, and I give myself to Thee forever."

On Christmas eve when the door of the mansion was thrown open a large throng of people entered, **and** were speedily admitted, one by one, to audience with the master of the house, until, in an incredibly short space of time, the waiting room was emptied of philosophers and dreamers and ambitious ones. Even the Bishop had been courteously sent on his way. Only three were left. Three wise ones, and two of them were women!

One was an old woman with a burr upon her tongue and a Bible in her hand; one was a young girl with blue starry eyes and a bit of a Testament in the folds of her gown where she kept her fingers between the leaves to a place. The third was John Powers, standing within the shadow of a heavy curtain beside a deep-set window looking out at the great shining of a bright star, with peace upon his face. He turned about as the door closed after the Bishop and glanced at the two women. The girl looked up and their eyes met.

"Mary!"

"John!"

There was scarcely time to recognize the old woman before the door opened and George K. Hamilton, keen of eye, sharp of feature, eager of expression, walked in and looked from one to the other searching each face questioningly.

The young man stepped forward to meet him and Mary saw for the first time that a worn little Bible was in his hand.

But John was speaking in such a ringing voice of certainty:

"Sir, I want to tell you first that I have not come for your money. When I began this search it was in hope of the reward, but I've found the Star itself, and it led me to the King, and now I've brought it to you because I want you to have it too. You'll find it in this Book. It has to be searched for, but it's there. And when you have found it I've been thinking you'll maybe want to sell all that you have and give to the poor and go and follow *Him*. But *I* am not one of those poor any longer, for I *have found the King!* Come, Mary, shall we go?"

Then up rose the old Scotch woman from her place near the door:

"I've just one more word to say, an' ye'll find it in yon Buik: `Arise, shine; for thy light is come, and the Glory of the Lord is risen upon thee.' That star isn't lost, sir, an' never was! Never will be! It's up in the heavens waiting till the King has need of it again, and some day it will burst upon the world again and they will all know that it has been there all the time!"

The Master was left alone in his mansion with the book in his hand and a strange awed feeling of the Presence of God in his room.

He looked wonderingly, doubtfully, down at the book, and then wistfully out through his richly draped window to where a single star shone softly through the Christmas night.

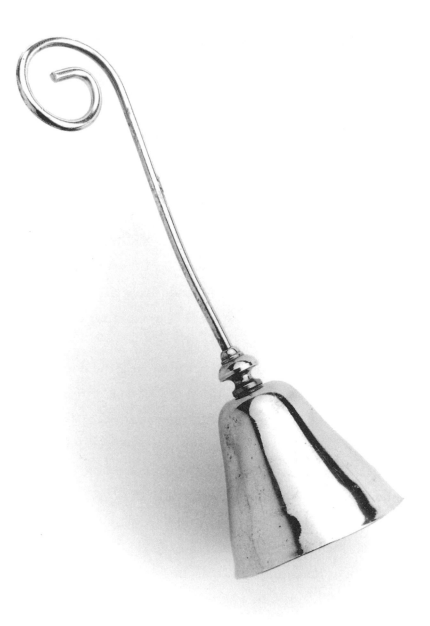

"I heard the bells on Christmas day, their old familiar carols play, and wild
and sweet the words repeat of peace on earth, good-will to men."
"I Heard the Bells on Christmas Day," HENRY W. LONGFELLOW

Joe L. Wheeler

THE BELLS OF CHRISTMAS EVE

"When will the bells ring?"

"Midnight, Miss Louisa . . . midnight."

"Thank you, Jacques. I'll . . . I'll be waiting. Don't forget the carriage."

"I won't, Miss Louisa."

She turned and walked to the hotel window, leaned against the sill, and waited. Waited, as was her custom, for the dying of the day. She sighed with a faint feeling of loss, for the sudden disappearance of the silver path to the sun that had so recently spanned the deep blue Mediterranean Sea and sky.

Losing all track of time, her soul's lens recorded on archival film every detail as the master scene painter of the universe splashed all the colors and hues on his palette across the gilding sky. At the peak of intensity, she felt like a child again, watching that last heart-stopping explosion of fireworks that transforms mundane evening darkness into a twilight of the gods.

Then, as suddenly as it had come, it was over—and the curtain of night was drawn down to the darkening sea.

And it was only then that the icy blade of loneliness slashed across her heart . . . and time ceased to be.

How much time passed before awareness returned, she never knew, for the breakers of awareness came in soft and slow, seemingly in unison with those breaking on the French Riviera shore outside the window.

Fully awakened at last, she slipped into her heavy coat, stepped outside, and walked across lawn and sand to her favorite rocky shelf. After snuggling down into a natural hollow out of the path of the winter wind, she spread her coat over her legs and wrapped a small blanket around her shoulders.

The tide was ebbing now, and with its departure she again realized how terribly lonely were the shores of her inner world. . . . If only *he* were here to hold her, to commune with her, to fill that void in her life that only he could fill, achieve that sense of completeness that only he could induce.

Scenes from the past summer flashed on the screen of her mind: his arrival in a huge carriage at the Pension Victoria; her almost instant recog-

nition of his weakened health; his stories detailing his involvement in the
ill-fated Polish revolt against Russian tyranny, his capture and incarceration
in a damp airless dungeon, and his eventual release.

Fresh from her service as a nurse in Washington during the recent
American Civil War, she noted the same battle symptoms that marked tens
of thousands of her own countrymen: the tell-tale signs of a weakened
constitution, and the lingering evidence of recent illness and almost
unendurable stress and pain. Instinctively, she steered the newcomer over
to a table near the largest porcelain stove. That simple act of kindness
supplied the spark that short-circuited the stuffy formalities of the day:
one moment they were complete strangers; a moment later they were
friends.

She was a thirty-three-year-old June to his twenty-one-year-old April.
But hers was a young-at-heart thirty-three, and his a maturity far beyond
his years, forged by the crucible of war and imprisonment. But it was his
seared, but cheerful still, spirit that won her heart. In spite of his recent
residence in hell, this bruised and tattered lark was a living embodiment of
the poetic portrayal of two men looking out through selfsame bars, one
seeing walls, the other stars. Ladislas Wisniewiski saw the stars.

Used to the cold formality and austerity of New England, she was totally
unprepared for warmhearted Ladislas, who smashed through conventions and
formalities as though they were so much kindling, a Mozart minuet stormed
by a Liszt rhapsody.

In truth, Louisa had been the object of many a lovesick swain through
the years, but none had been able to break through her self-imposed barriers

of reserve and indifference; prior to Ladislas, not one had been able to raise her temperature so much as one degree.

The days and evenings that followed were full of adventures, large and small. He taught her French, and she taught him English; he regaled her with the culture, history, and lore of the alpine country of Switzerland and France, and she introduced him to the New World of America; they rowed almost daily on beautiful Lake Geneva, framed by the snowcapped Alps; they explored the grounds of the chateau and area sights of interest such as the nearby Castle of Chillon, which Byron had immortalized; they took frequent tramps along the mountain sides, pausing often to drink in the stunning deep blue sheet of water spread out below them, the verdant hills around them, and the sawtooth mountains above them, cutting notches in the sky.

And woven into the fabric of that never-to-be-forgotten summer of '65 was talk—talk when talk added color, silence when talk was superfluous. Their talk recognized no barriers, no constraints. The subject was life, life with all its complexities, inequities, and unanswered questions. In the evenings, Ladislas would perform in the parlor (he was an accomplished professional musician), and Louisa would join the others and listen. Deep, deep within her, seas long dead would be stirred into tempests by Ladislas's fomenting fingers.

He was good for her—far better than she knew, for Louisa was (and always had been) a caregiver, a Martha, one who sublimated her own dreams and desires so others could fulfill theirs. All her life, others had always come first. She had grown up early, realizing while yet a child that it was her beloved mother who bore the full weight of the family's financial problems, for her father—bless him!—seemingly dwelt in another world. Like Dickens's immortal Micawber, he blithely assumed that something would always "turn up" to enable the family to muddle through. Certainly, God would provide. Somehow, some way, God always did, but in the process her mother, Abba, grew old before her time.

Louisa had early recognized that she, by nature and temperament, was born to be an extension of her mother. She had sometimes resisted and resented this burden, but not for long, for hers was a sunny disposition; duty was not an ugly Puritan word but something you shouldered with a song in your heart.

Rummaging around in her mind, Louisa took off a dusty cobwebby shelf a Christmas reel of her childhood: images of that bitterly cold New England winter flooded the walls of memory. They were down to their last few sticks of wood, and the winter wind howled around the snow-flocked house, icy fingers reaching in through every crack and crevice and chink. Besides the three sisters, a newborn was now at risk when the firewood was gone. "God will provide" was her father's rejoinder to his wife's worried importuning. "God will provide as he always has."

Just then, there was a knock on the door. A neighbor had braved the banshee winds to bring over a load of wood, unable to escape the conviction that the family needed firewood. "Needed firewood?" Abba's face resembled a rainbow on a golden morning.

Later that memorable evening, Father had disappeared for some time.

When he returned, stomping his half-frozen feet on the fireside hearth to restore circulation, he jubilantly announced that another neighbor, with a sick baby in a near-freezing house, had asked for help—how providential that the Lord had sent his family wood. Abba's face grew coldly pale: "You . . . you didn't . . . certainly, you *didn't!*" But she knew even before he answered that he had. How *could* he? *They* had a baby too! This was just more than flesh and blood could bear.

But before her pent-up wrath could erupt there was another knock on the door—and another load of wood waited outside. "I told you that we would not suffer," was her father's trusting response. Abba and her girls just looked at each other, absolutely mute.

66

Louisa stirred, aware of a change in the tide: it was beginning to return. A dream-like full moon had risen, and the breakers were now luminous with a ghostly beauty. The wind had died down at last.

Truant-like, before she knew they had slipped away, her thoughts returned to that golden summer in Vevey. How lonely she had been. At first, the mere idea of seeing Europe had entranced her; all she had to do was care for a family friend's invalid daughter: be a companion. But the girl was so insensitive to the beauty and history Louisa reveled in that her *joie de vivre* had begun to fade.

And then came Ladislas.

He filled a long-aching void in her life, for, growing up, she had been so tall, coltish, and tomboyish that romance could be found only in storybooks and in dreams. Her sisters were the soft, the feminine, the lovely ones.

Then, when she had grown up, this ugly-duckling self-image refused to go away, in spite of the refutation in her mirror and in the eyes of men. As a result, she remained shy and unsure of herself—and certainly, so far, success in her chosen career was mighty slow in coming.

Ladislas had unlocked an inner Louisa that even she had never seen before. Free for the first time in her life to be young without heavy responsibilities and worries, her day-by-day interactions with Ladislas brought new gentleness and vivacity to her face, and his open adoration, stars to her eyes. The older travelers staying at the pension watched the couple, subconsciously envying their youth and happiness. In the evening, in the flickering candlelight, Louisa's face was graced by that inner radiance that comes but once in a woman's life: from the full knowledge that she is loved and adored by the man she perceives to be her world.

She borrowed not from the future, but accepted each day, each hour, each minute, as a gift from God. The realities of life were swept aside to dissipate in the mists of the mountains as they lived each moment with the intensity of those who live on the slopes of a volcano or on an earthquake fault. Time enough for harsh realities later, when the cherubim of circumstance barred them from Eden with their flaming swords.

But like all Shan-gri-las, this one too had to end. As the cool autumn winds swept down from Mont Blanc, Louisa's invalid charge decided it was time to move to a warmer climate—southern France would be ideal.

Louisa tearfully packed her trunks. It was no longer possible to pretend that this idyllic island in time would be their home. The age differential, Ladislas's lack of livelihood prospects and his weakened health, their cultural differences, Louisa's commitments to her family as well as her own career uncertainties—and, of course, the slight tincture of the maternal in her love for him—all added up to a gradually growing conviction that it would never be. Even as they rowed together, it was her sister May whom she envisioned opposite Ladislas down through the years; her age equating with his, her love of music and art responding to his, her infectious love of life feeding upon his boyish blandishments, impulsiveness, and warm and tender heart.

But none of this took away from the bittersweet parting. Masking his intense feeling, he kissed her hand in the European manner. As she watched his waving scarf recede into a blur down the train tracks, her eyes filled with tears.

For what right had she to dream of marriage? She who had vowed to shore up her mother's failing strength, assisting her in every way possible; and then, when that beloved caregiver could no longer function very well, quietly and cheerfully taking her place.

Then, too, Louisa vaguely realized that she was out of step with most of the women of her age, in that marriage, children, and domesticity were really not her all in all. For she had career dreams of her own and had little inclination to turn over her life to a man, becoming old before her time by repeated pregnancies and brutally heavy housework.

But even that could not check the tears running down her cheeks . . . for love is not governed by the mind.

She pulled out her watch and, by the light of the climbing moon, discovered it was almost eleven. Just before midnight, she planned to take a carriage to the ancient cathedral and see the nativity scene everyone had been talking about. She hungered to hear the choir and pipe organ celebrate the birth of Jesus eighteen and a half centuries ago.

In her pocket was a letter from home (worn and tattered from many readings) that her fingers touched in the darkness. She had no need to reread it, for she knew it by heart: Father's lecture tours were not doing very well; Anna had just given birth to her second son (how good John was to her!); Mother continued to weaken, her gradual buckling to the resistless juggernaut of the years becoming ever more apparent to the writer of the letter, May; and as for May—how much she needed a chance to flower, to become a real artist: she must be given the opportunity to experience Europe, too.

And never far from mind was Beth—little Beth with her endearing ways, whose untimely death seven years before had left an aching void that time would never fill or completely heal. What a *dear* family she had! And how they loved each other! Wouldn't it be wonderful if she could use her writing talents to somehow recapture those magical childhood years, so permeated with sunlight and shadows, laughter and tears.

But every story, especially a story of four girls, has to have a hero, too. Perhaps—the image of a dark-haired Polish musician, forever teasing, laughing, and cajoling. . . . She could no more resist him than she could the incoming tide now lapping at her feet. Brother, sweetheart, and friend. But "Ladislas" would never do. Um-m . . . how about "Lawrence" . . . but she'd call him "Laurie."

She sank into a reverie outside the stream of time. She had no way of foreseeing the future: of knowing that four months later, "Laurie" would be waiting for her at the train station, and that for two wonderful weeks he, she, and Paris in the spring would coalesce in memories that would never die. Nor could she know that three years later, her book, the first half of the story, would be published, and a year after that, the second-half sequel would be snapped up by a constantly growing audience. The book would become the most beloved story ever written about an American girl. For, in spite of all her efforts to show off her sisters, offsetting their portraits with unvarnished depictions of her own frailties, mistakes, and weaknesses, she would fail in her purpose—for it would be Jo with whom generations of readers would fall in love.

And who among us could ever read that unforgettable passage, set in the eternally flowering gardens of Vevey, wherein Amy, still mourning the recent death of her sister Beth, looks up . . . and sees him standing there:

> "Dropping everything, she ran to him, exclaiming, in a tone of unmistakable love and longing, `Oh, Laurie, Laurie, I knew you'd come to me!'"

Yes, who among us can ever read that without sensing that the words were really Jo's, that the broken heart was really Jo's, and that the longing for a love that would forever remain imprisoned in the bud of might-have-been, never blossoming into the rose of marriage, was Jo's. Who among us can read that heart-broken call without tears?

"Miss Louisa?. . . Uh . . . Miss Alcott?"

"Uh . . . I'm sorry, Jacques, I guess I . . . I must have dozed off. What is it?"

"You asked me to have the carriage ready at fifteen minutes before midnight."

"Oh, yes! Thank you—Just give me a minute."

Soon Louisa was settled within the carriage. The horses snorted in the cold night air, and the wheels complained as they chattered and clattered over the cobblestone streets. She looked out her window and took in the festive crowd and air of expectancy that hovered over the city. She realized that she regretted nothing—even if she had the opportunity to live her life over again, she would change not one line. Joy and pain, hand-in-hand— without both she would have but a one-dimensional ditty or dirge; with both, a multifaceted symphony of life.

She could ask for no more.

Then she heard them, faint at first, soon gathering power as they were joined by other bells across the city. The crescendo continued until the ringing and the clanging swallowed up every other sound on earth.

It was Christmas. . . . Christ was born in a manger.

"This flower, whose fragrance tender with sweetness fills the air,
dispels with glorious splendor the darkness everywhere."
"Lo! How a Rose E'er Blooming," HARRIET KRAUTH SPAETH

Angela Elwell Hunt

THE PARABLE OF THE POINSETTIA

❖

Andelina Rodriguez was born on the twenty-sixth day of December, an almost-Christmas birthday. Though some people might think a birthday during the holidays is another wonderful reason to make merry, Andelina thought her after-Christmas birthday was about as much fun as watching trees grow. Many of her presents were wrapped in leftover red-and-green foil, and her friends never wanted to come to her birthday parties because they were too busy playing with their Christmas toys.

Andelina's parents did their best to make her birthday seem like everyone else's. They decorated the house with bright blue and pink balloons,
and her mother always baked an ordinary birthday cake. Her father made
certain that his gifts were never, ever wrapped in red or green foil.

Aunt Dominga seemed to understand, too. Though she lived far away
in Mexico, she always sent Andelina a beautiful birthstone for her birthday:
one year a ring, the next year a bracelet, the next a necklace. Andelina's
birthstone was icy blue, as delicate as a diamond, and Aunt Dominga's note
always said, "For my wonderful niece: the special December stone for a
special December child."

But when the doorbell rang on Andelina's tenth birthday, she opened the
door to discover a florist holding a large poinsettia plant. The attached card
said: "For my wonderful niece: the special December flower for a special
December child."

A poinsettia? That was a Christmas flower! Andelina carried the plant
inside and set it on the floor next to the drooping Christmas tree. She tried
to swallow the lump that rose in her throat. Aunt Dominga didn't understand at all.

December passed, and the Christmas decorations were put away.
Andelina took the poinsettia outside and left it on the back porch. The
bright red leaves curled and fell off, and soon nothing remained but a stalk.
"You should take care of your plant," her mother told her. "It's a living
thing, you know."

"It has sun and water," Andelina said, shrugging. "It's OK." And it was.

But that spring, as the little poinsettia grew full and bright with green,

Andelina's mother became very sick. She had to stay in bed all the time, so Aunt Dominga came from Mexico to help. *"Hola,* little one," she said, pressing her cheek to Andelina's after she had brought her suitcases into the house. "And how is my special niece?"

"OK, I guess," Andelina answered.

"You are so big!" Aunt Dominga knelt in front of Andelina. "I hope the plant I sent you is growing, too. The poinsettias in Mexico grow to be ten feet tall!"

"It's growing," Andelina said, not really caring how tall a poinsettia could get.

Spring warmed into summer. Andelina's mother did not get better, so Aunt Dominga took over the running of the house. She cooked the meals, cleaned the floors, and tended the garden. Often Andelina saw her aunt fussing over the poinsettia on the back porch. She kept the stalks trimmed and the soil moist, but Andelina didn't care.

As the autumn leaves began to toast golden brown and fall from the trees, Andelina's mother had to go to the hospital. She was very, very sick, Aunt Dominga explained, and no one knew when she would come home again.

Leaving her aunt in the house, Andelina went to the back porch and sat down on a bench. She felt like there were tiny hands wringing her heart, squeezing hard, until there was almost no feeling left. She lifted her eyes and saw the poinsettia she had ignored, now lush and green. How could it be so pretty, so *healthy,* when her mother was not?

"I hate you!" Andelina said, suddenly angry. "You're not alive, you're just a dumb weed!"

Gathering all her strength, Andelina lifted the plant. She carried it toward the woods behind her house, swaying from side to side as she struggled under the weight of the heavy pot. She found a dark spot under the evergreens, shaded from the life-giving sun. Andelina didn't care if the plant died. She didn't want Aunt Dominga in the house. And she didn't want that stupid poinsettia. She wanted her mother.

All through October, November, and early December, Aunt Dominga saw Andelina off to school in the mornings and then went to the hospital. Alone at home in the afternoons, Andelina did her homework and chores and then sat by the front window and prayed. Christmas was coming, but no one in their family had time for candy canes or parties or decorating. They were too busy praying for her mother.

On Christmas Eve Andelina's father called and said that she must pray very hard, for her mother was weaker than she had ever been. Andelina fell to her knees and cried, begging God for help.

A soft touch woke her the next morning. Aunt Dominga's hand was on Andelina's shoulder, shaking her gently. "Merry Christmas, child," she said simply, sinking to the floor where Andelina had fallen asleep. "God has answered our prayers. Your mother is better."

A flood of emotions poured through Andelina's heart: joy, relief, gladness . . . and guilt. "Oh, I'm so glad!" she cried, throwing her arms about her aunt's shoulders. "And I'm so sorry, Auntie. I was angry, I wanted you to leave, I even tried to kill the poinsettia you sent me."

Aunt Dominga's hand stopped stroking Andelina's hair. "What?" she asked, her voice a surprised whisper. "I wondered where it had gone."

"I hid it in the woods," Andelina confessed, palming tears from her eyes. "Deep under the trees, where it wouldn't get any sun."

Aunt Dominga was silent for a moment, and then her tired eyes brightened in a smile. "Come, child," she said, holding out her hand as she stood up. "Show me."

Andelina's heart was heavy as she led her aunt into the woods. She had done a wicked thing, for Aunt Dominga had done nothing but help. Now the poinsettia would certainly be ruined, for all plants need lots of sunlight.

When Andelina found the shady spot deep among the trees, she gasped. The poinsettia sat there still, but it looked nothing like it had when she left it. The leaves that had been spindly and green were now wide and red, as bright as a spill of crimson velvet over an emerald carpet.

"I thought it would die!" she whispered, staring at the lovely flowers.

Aunt Dominga's arms slipped around Andelina's shoulders. "You were upset, child, and you didn't understand the way God works. The poinsettia is a special plant. It needs long hours of dark to develop its pretty red leaves. If you had left it near the lights of the house, it would still be plain and green."

Carefully she turned Andelina to face her, then stooped to look into the girl's eyes. "You are as special as that poinsettia, child, and one day soon you will bloom just as beautifully. When you pass through long months of darkness and waiting, you can have peace, knowing you are in the hands of the Master Gardener."

"God?" Andelina asked, blinking back tears of wonder.

"Yes." Aunt Dominga's dark eyes softened as she looked at the exquisite plant. "It is fitting that we should find this today, at Christmas, for the world was dark and waiting when Jesus was born to bring us hope and light. That's why the poinsettia is the December flower."

"Aunt Dominga," Andelina said, moving toward the plant, "will you help me carry it back to the house?"

Aunt Dominga did. And when they reached the porch, they placed the poinsettia in a spot where everyone could see its splash of vivid color from inside the kitchen window.

As darkness drew down over the twinkling lights of the neighborhood, Andelina's father came home, a smile on his tired face. He hugged his daughter, wished her a merry Christmas, and said that her mother would soon be back home.

"And I," Aunt Dominga said, standing in the kitchen, "had better make plans for the birthday cake I will bake tomorrow. What sort of cake would you like, Andelina?"

"I think," Andelina said, smiling as she looked out the window at the bright blooms, "that I'd like a different kind of birthday cake this year. A white one, decorated with red poinsettias."

"Let no man despise thy youth; but be thou an example of the believers, in word, in conversation, in charity, in spirit, in faith, in purity."
1 TIMOTHY 4:12, KJV

Harriet Beecher Stowe

CHRISTMAS; OR, THE GOOD FAIRY

"Oh, Dear! Christmas is coming in a fortnight, and I have got to think up presents for everybody!" said young Eleanor Stuart, as she leaned languidly back in her chair. "Dear me, it's so tedious! Everybody has got everything that can be thought of."

"Oh, no," said her confidential adviser, Miss Lester, in a soothing tone. "You have means of buying everything you can fancy; and when every shop and store is glittering with all manner of splendors, you cannot surely be at a loss."

"Well, now, just listen. To begin with, there's mamma. What can I get for her? I have thought of ever so many things. She has three card cases, four gold thimbles, two or three gold chains, two writing desks of different patterns; and then as to rings, brooches, boxes, and all other things, I should think she might be sick of the sight of them. I am sure I am," said she, languidly gazing on her white and jeweled fingers.

This view of the case seemed rather puzzling to the adviser, and there was silence for a few minutes, when Eleanor, yawning, resumed:

"And then there's cousins Jane and Mary; I suppose they will be coming down on me with a whole load of presents; and Mrs. B. will send me something—she did last year; and then there's cousins William and Tom—I must get them something; and I would like to do it well enough, if I only knew what to get."

"Well," said Eleanor's aunt, who had been sitting quietly rattling her knitting needles during this speech, "it's a pity that you had not such a subject to practice on as I was when I was a girl. Presents did not fly about in those days as they do now. I remember, when I was ten years old, my father gave me a most marvelously ugly sugar dog for a Christmas gift, and I was perfectly delighted with it, the very idea of a present was so new to us."

"Dear aunt, how delighted I should be if I had any such fresh, unsophisticated body to get presents for! But to get and get for people that have more than they know what to do with now; to add pictures, books, and gilding when the center tables are loaded with them now, and rings and jewels when they are a perfect drug! I wish myself that I were not sick, and sated, and tired with having everything in the world given me."

"Well, Eleanor," said her aunt, "if you really do want unsophisticated subjects to practice on, I can put you in the way of it. I can show you more than one family to whom you might seem to be a very good fairy, and where such gifts as you could give with all ease would seem like a magic dream."

"Why, that would really be worth while, aunt."

"Look over in that back alley," said her aunt. "You see those buildings?"

"That miserable row of shanties? Yes."

"Well, I have several acquaintances there who have never been tired of Christmas gifts or gifts of any other kind. I assure you, you could make quite a sensation over there."

"Well, who is there? Let us know."

"Do you remember Owen, that used to make your shoes?"

"Yes, I remember something about him."

"Well, he has fallen into a consumption, and cannot work any more; and he, and his wife, and three little children live in one of the rooms."

"How do they get along?"

"His wife takes in sewing sometimes, and sometimes goes out washing. Poor Owen! I was over there yesterday; he looks thin and wasted, and his wife was saying that he was parched with constant fever, and had very little appetite. She had, with great self-denial, and by restricting herself almost of necessary food, got him two or three oranges; and the poor fellow seemed so eager after them."

"Poor fellow!" said Eleanor, involuntarily.

"Now," said her aunt, "suppose Owen's wife should get up on Christmas morning and find at the door a couple of dozen of oranges, and some of those nice white grapes, such as you had at your party last week; don't you think it would make a sensation?"

"Why, yes, I think very likely it might; but who else, aunt? You spoke of a great many."

"Well, on the lower floor there is a neat little room that is always kept perfectly trim and tidy; it belongs to a young couple who have nothing beyond the husband's day wages to live on. They are, nevertheless, as cheerful and chipper as a couple of wrens; and she is up and down half a dozen times a day, to help poor Mrs. Owen. She has a baby of her own about five months old, and of course does all the cooking, washing, and ironing for herself and husband; and yet, when Mrs. Owen goes out to wash, she takes her baby, and keeps it whole days for her."

"I'm sure she deserves that the good fairies should smile on her," said Eleanor; "one baby exhausts my stock of virtues very rapidly."

"But you ought to see her baby," said Aunt E.; "so plump, so rosy, and good-natured, and always clean as a lily. This baby is a sort of household shrine; nothing is too sacred or too good for it; and I believe the little thrifty woman feels only one temptation to be extravagant, and that is to get some ornaments to adorn this little divinity."

"Why, did she ever tell you so?"

"No; but one day, when I was coming down stairs, the door of their room was partly open, and I saw a peddler there with open box. John, the husband, was standing with a little purple cap on his hand, which he was regarding with mystified, admiring air, as if he didn't quite comprehend it, and trim little Mary gazing at it with longing eyes.

"'I think we might get it,' said John.

"'Oh, no,' said she, regretfully; 'yet I wish we could, it's so pretty!'"

"Say no more, aunt. I see the good fairy must pop a cap into the window on Christmas morning. Indeed, it shall be done. How they will wonder where it came from, and talk about it for months to come!"

"Well, then," continued her aunt, "in the next street to ours there is a miserable building that looks as if it were just going to topple over; and away up in the third story, in a little room just under the eaves, live two poor, lonely old women. They are both nearly on to ninety. I was in there day before yesterday. One of them is constantly confined to her bed with rheumatism; the other, weak and feeble, with failing sight and trembling hands, totters about, her only helper; and they are entirely dependent on charity."

"Can't they do anything? Can't they knit?" said Eleanor.

"You are young and strong, Eleanor, and have quick eyes and nimble fingers; how long would it take you to knit a pair of stockings?"

"I?" said Eleanor. "What an idea! I never tried, but I think I could get a pair done in a week, perhaps."

"And if somebody gave you twenty-five cents for them, and out of this you had to get food, and pay room rent, and buy coal for your fire, and oil for your lamp—"

"Stop, aunt, for pity's sake!"

"Well, I will stop; but they can't; they must pay so much every month for that miserable shell they live in, or be turned into the street. The meal and flour that some kind person sends goes off for them just as it does for others, and they must get more or starve; and coal is now scarce and high priced."

"O aunt, I'm quite convinced, I'm sure; don't run me down and annihilate me with all these terrible realities. What shall I do to play good fairy to these old women?"

"If you will give me full power, Eleanor, I will put up a basket to be sent to them that will give them something to remember all winter."

"Oh, certainly I will. Let me see if I can't think of something myself."

"Well, Eleanor, suppose, then, some fifty or sixty years hence, if you were old, and your father, and mother, and aunts, and uncles, now so thick around you, lay cold and silent in so many graves—you have somehow got away off to a strange city, where you were never known—you live in a miserable garret, where snow blows at night through the cracks, and the fire is very apt to go out in the old cracked stove—you sit crouching over the dying embers the evening before Christmas—nobody to speak to you, nobody to care for you, except another poor old soul who lies moaning in the bed. Now, what would you like to have sent you?"

"O aunt, what a dismal picture!"

"And yet, Ella, all poor, forsaken old women are made of young girls, who expected it in their youth as little as you do, perhaps."

"Say no more, aunt. I'll buy—let me see—a comfortable warm shawl for each of these poor women; and I'll send them—let me see—oh, some tea— nothing goes down with old women like tea; and I'll make John wheel some coal over to them; and, aunt, it would not be a very bad thought to send them a new stove. I remember, the other day, when mamma was pricing stoves, I saw some such nice ones for two or three dollars."

"For a new hand, Ella, you work up the idea very well," said her aunt.

"But how much ought I to give, for any one case, to these women, say?"

"How much did you give last year for any single Christmas present?"

"Why, six or seven dollars for some; those elegant souvenirs were seven dollars; that ring I gave Mrs. B. was twenty."

"And do you suppose Mrs. B. was any happier for it?"

"No, really, I don't think she cared much about it; but I had to give her something, because she had sent me something the year before, and I did not want to send a paltry present to one in her circumstances."

"Then, Ella, give the same to any poor, distressed, suffering creature who really needs it, and see in how many forms of good such a sum will appear. That one hard, cold, glittering ring, that now cheers nobody, and means nothing, that you give because you must, and she takes because she must, might, if broken up into smaller sums, send real warm and heartfelt gladness through many a cold and cheerless dwelling, through many an aching heart."

"You are getting to be an orator, aunt; but don't you approve of Christmas presents, among friends and equals?"

"Yes, indeed," said her aunt, fondly stroking her head. "I have had some Christmas presents that did me a world of good—a little book mark, for instance, that a certain niece of mine worked for me, with wonderful secrecy, three years ago, when she was not a young lady with a purse full of money—that book mark was a true Christmas present; and my young couple across the way are plotting a profound surprise to each other on Christmas morning. John has contrived, by an hour of extra work every night, to lay by enough to get Mary a new calico dress; and she, poor soul, has bargained away the only thing in the jewelry line she ever possessed, to be laid out on a new hat for him.

"I know, too, a washerwoman who has a poor lame boy—a patient, gentle little fellow—who has lain quietly for weeks and months in his little crib, and his mother is going to give him a splendid Christmas present."

"What is it, pray?"

"A whole orange! Don't laugh. She will pay ten whole cents for it; for it shall be none of your common oranges, but a picked one of the very best going! She has put by the money, a cent at a time, for a whole month; and nobody knows which will be happiest in it, Willie or his mother. These are such Christmas presents as I like to think of—gifts coming from love, and tending to produce love; these are the appropriate gifts of the day."

"But don't you think that it's right for those who *have* money to give expensive presents, supposing always, as you say, they are given from real affection?"

"Sometimes, undoubtedly. The Saviour did not condemn her who broke an alabaster box of ointment—very precious—simply as a proof of love, even although the suggestion was made, `This might have been sold for three hundred pence, and given to the poor.' I have thought he would regard with sympathy the fond efforts which human love sometimes makes to express itself by gifts, the rarest and most costly. How I rejoiced with all my heart, when Charles Elton gave his poor mother that splendid Chinese shawl and gold watch because I knew they came from the very fullness of his heart to a mother that he could not do too much for—a mother that has done and suffered everything for him. In some such cases, when resources are ample, a costly gift seems to have a graceful appropriateness; but I cannot approve of it if it exhausts all the means of doing for the poor;

it is better, then, to give a simple offering, and to do something for those who really need it."

Eleanor looked thoughtful; her aunt laid down her knitting, and said, in a tone of gentle seriousness, "Whose birth does Christmas commemorate, Ella?"

"Our Saviour's, certainly, aunt."

"Yes," said her aunt. "And when and how was he born? In a stable! laid in a manger; thus born, that in all ages he might be known as the brother and friend of the poor. And surely, it seems but appropriate to commemorate his birthday by an especial remembrance of the lowly, the poor, the outcast, and distressed; and if Christ should come back to our city on a Christmas day, where should we think it most appropriate to his character to find him? Would he be carrying splendid gifts to splendid dwellings, or would he be gliding about in the cheerless haunts of the desolate, the poor, the forsaken, and the sorrowful?"

And here the conversation ended.

"What sort of Christmas presents is Ella buying?" said Cousin Tom, as the servant handed in a portentous-looking package, which had been just rung in at the door.

"Let's open it," said saucy Will. "Upon my word, two great gray blanket shawls! These must be for you and me, Tom! And what's this? A great bolt of cotton flannel and gray yarn stockings!"

The door bell rang again, and the servant brought in another bulky parcel, and deposited it on the marble-topped center table.

"What's here?" said Will, cutting the cord. "Whew! a perfect nest of packages! Oolong tea! oranges! grapes! white sugar! Bless me, Ella must be going to housekeeping!"

"Or going crazy!" said Tom; "and on my word," said he, looking out of the window, "there's a drayman ringing at our door, with a stove, with a teakettle set in the top of it!"

"Ella's cook stove, of course," said Will; and just at this moment the young lady entered, with her purse hanging gracefully over her hand.

"Now, boys, you are too bad!" she exclaimed, as each of the mischievous youngsters was gravely marching up and down, attired in a gray shawl.

"Didn't you get them for us? We thought you did," said both.

"Ella, I want some of that cotton flannel, to make me a pair of pantaloons," said Tom.

"I say, Ella," said Will, "when are you going to housekeeping? Your cooking stove is standing down in the street; 'pon my word, John is loading some coal on the dray with it."

"Ella, isn't that going to be sent to my office?" said Tom; "do you know I do so languish for a new stove with a teakettle in the top, to heat a fellow's shaving-water!"

Just then, another ring at the door, and the grinning servant handed in a small brown paper parcel for Miss Ella. Tom made a dive at it, and tearing off the brown paper, discovered a jaunty little purple velvet cap, with silver tassels.

"My smoking cap, as I live!" said he; "only I shall have to wear it on my thumb, instead of my head—too small entirely," said he, shaking his head gravely.

"Come, you saucy boys," said Aunt E., entering briskly. "What are you teasing Ella for?"

"Why, do see this lot of things, aunt! What in the world is Ella going to do with them?"

"Oh, I know!"

"You know! Then I can guess, aunt, it is some of your charitable works. You are going to make a juvenile Lady Bountiful of El, eh?"

Ella, who had colored to the roots of her hair at the *exposé* of her very unfashionable Christmas preparations, now took heart, and bestowed a very gentle and salutary little cuff on the saucy head that still wore the purple cap, and then hastened to gather up her various purchases.

"Laugh away," said she, gaily; "and a good many others will laugh, too, over these things. I got them to make people laugh—people that are not in the habit of laughing!"

"Well, well, I see into it," said Will; "and I tell you I think right well of the idea, too. There are worlds of money wasted, at this time of the year, in getting things that nobody wants, and nobody cares for after they are got; and I am glad, for my part, that you are going to get up a variety in this line; in fact, I should like to give you one of these stray leaves to help on," said he, dropping a ten dollar note into her paper. "I like to encourage girls to think of something besides breastpins and sugar candy."

But our story spins on too long. If anybody wants to see the results of Ella's first attempts at *good fairyism*, they can call at the doors of two or three old buildings on Christmas morning, and they shall hear all about it.

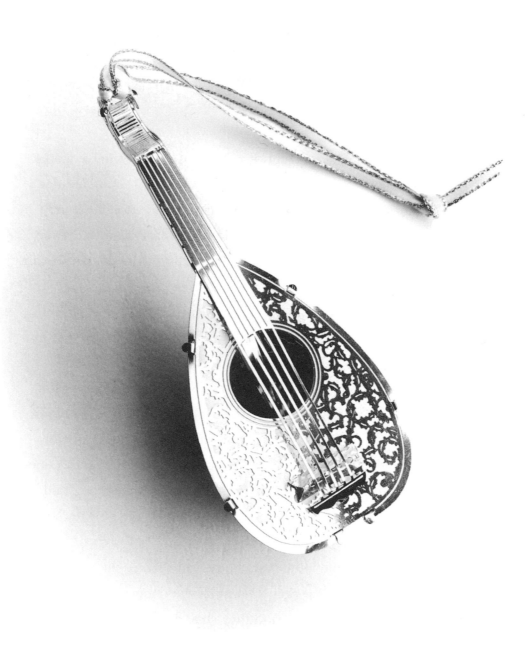

"Silent night! holy night! All is calm, all is bright."
"Silent Night! Holy Night!" JOSEPH MOHR

Grace Johnson

AUSTRIAN CAROL

❖

Long ago, in a poor cottage partway up the mountain lived a woodcutter, Karl, and his wife, Maria. Maria was with child, a child whose birth was expected close to Christmas. And on this particular day she sat propped up in the bed, watching her friend Hilda take a tall candle out of a box.

"There's a beautiful old legend," Hilda was saying, "that the Christ child walks about at Christmastime seeking to enter the hearts of men—and it's a candle in the window that invites him across the threshold."

Hilda placed the candle on the window ledge. She struck a match, and the candle glowed in the gathering darkness of the late afternoon.

"It's so beautiful," said Maria. Then she shivered and pulled a faded quilt more closely about her. "But it doesn't look right in here." She gazed about the barren little room. "Look at these bare walls! And the ceiling beams are about to fall down and—"

Hilda sat down on the bed. She looked into the dark, pretty eyes. "Ah, dear child, you are more than a little weary tonight?"

"I'm frightened, Hilda—"

"About the baby?"

Maria turned away. "I can't help it. Last year a baby was born dead. Why does life have to be so hard?"

"Oh, Maria," said Hilda gently, "there's not a heart without its hurt." She took Maria's hand in hers. "You must send Karl for me the moment the pains start." She smiled reassuringly. "And remember, I've helped many a baby into the world. And Jesus will be here. That's the heart of Christmas—that he *came* to give *light* to those who sit in darkness."

"To give light to those who sit in darkness," Maria murmured softly.

Hilda squeezed her hand. "Just like the candle, Maria. Just like the candle."

Franz, Oberndorf's church organist, surveyed the array of tools, pipes, and bellows strewn around him on the floor. The jumble of parts seemed to mock him. But being a man of steady resolve, he took a deep breath and lifted up his hammer along with his voice. "Joy to the world! the Lord is come; let earth receiver her King—"

He hit his finger and jumped up, yelling, *"Ach Himmel! Ach du lieber!"*

He sucked at his finger briefly. Then, hands on hips, he peered at the mess on the floor. "Sniggling little bunch! Bits and pieces of metal and wood are you? I suppose you think it's the better of Franz you'll be getting! Nein! Nein! I shall have you yet!"

He sat down on the bench and picked up a wrench and a small piece of piping. He grimaced. "I should drop all of you in the Danube River!"

Franz worked earnestly for another quarter of an hour. Finally he stood up, shaking his head. He grabbed a heavy cloth sack nearby and began to dump everything into it.

"Himmel! You miserable contraption, you! So, it's into the sack you go! Ah— trembling with fright are you? Well, you'd better. I shall take you to Haugan's shop, and if he has not the parts—*into the river you go!"*

Franz slung the sack over his back and started out the door, looking only a very little like the good St. Nicholas.

The wind swept down the street of the little village of Oberndorf. It blew whiffs of snow against its shops and cottages and swirled in little eddies over the cobblestones.

The pastor put his head down and thrust his hands deep into his pockets against the chill December wind. He was on his way back to his office in the church. His feet slowed on the cobblestone village street, for he was not overly anxious to reach his destination.

He sighed. The weight of his parish duties had taken its toll. So much sorrow; so many puzzlements. And Christmas so close! Not only should he be studying for his sermon, but there were calls he should make. He should go up the mountain to visit Maria and Karl. He sighed again. What could he say to them? No money, a cottage with almost nothing in it, a baby almost here, and Christmas in a week!

He stopped and threw back his head, staring with unseeing eyes at the sky. And what of the Christmas Eve service? *What*, that these villagers had not already had go in one ear and out the other? "Lord, maybe I have a dried-up heart," he murmured softly.

Someone cleared her throat loudly next to him. It was a woman wrapped in a bright red coat trimmed with fur. She was carrying a large purse along with what seemed to be numerous boxes, bags, and satchels. To top it all off, on the crown of her black bonnet a silly rosette waved gaily in the wind.

He bowed politely. "Frau Schneider."

She nodded, indicating the heavens. "I suppose you see what others don't and are getting *inspiration* from looking at the sky."

Now if there was anyone who could quickly divest him of any inspiration he *might* have found, it was Frau Wilhelmina Schneider. However, he managed to keep a pleasant expression.

She smiled knowingly. "Oh, it must be so *inspiring* to be a pastor at the Christmas season! You know, it's just *providential* that I ran into you! I've several things that I want to bring to your attention."

"Perhaps you could drop by my study at the church." With a brief bow, he turned to go.

"Nein, nein!" She began to set the greater part of her baggage down on the cobblestones. "It will only take a few moments."

"But—" he protested to no avail.

"To begin with, five of us ladies were to make marzipan candy—you know, to give to the children after the Christmas service. We had it all ready to shape, and would you believe Ulrica Zeissman *forgot* to bring the almonds! I tell you! Sigrid was so upset she burned the plum filling for the Linzer cake."

"I'm so sorry—"

"And we ladies don't have a *moment* to spare between now and then! And you know how disappointed the children would be not to have a marzipan and a piece of Linzer cake!"

"Perhaps you could stuff a candy cane in each little mouth as they go by."

Frau Schneider's eyes flew open wide. "You do jest!"

"You'd be surprised," he muttered under his breath. Then he quickly said, "Of course—of course, Frau Schneider. Surely someone will find the time to make it."

"Well—we can only hope. Next, I went to get the candles out for the service, and would you believe they were bent over in a quite ridiculous fashion from the heat of last summer? Whatever shall I do?"

"Couldn't you just set them up and call them `praying candles'?"

"Pastor!"

He took a deep breath. "Lay them out by the hearth and when they warm enough, you can straighten them out."

Frau Schneider looked impressed. "Ja! How very astute!"

"And now if you'll excuse me." He bowed and started off.

"Ja." She began to pick up bags and boxes. "Oh!" she cried. "I nearly forgot! Pastor!" She began to run after him.

He stopped and spoke without turning around. "Wilhelmina—Frau Schneider! I *do* have things to do!"

"Ja, of course. I'll take only another moment." She took a deep breath and plunged on. "Sigrid and I were readying the greens—pine and spruce—to decorate the church. And suddenly Sigrid says, `Wilhelmina,' she says, `did you know that in days gone by greens were used to banish *demons* lurking in the darkness?' Well, Pastor, I was just *appalled* at such superstition! So now my question is this: Do you feel we have sufficiently `Christianized' these customs to have greens in the sanctuary?"

The pastor nodded. "Ja, I do. Meanwhile, I am strongly thinking we have taken some *Christian* customs and paganized *them!*"

Again Frau Schneider's eyes flew wide. "Really?"

"What does the Incarnation mean to you?" he asked suddenly.

"The Incarnation? What is it?"

"Frau Schneider," he said in exasperation, "it's the birth of Christ! God coming to us as a human baby!"

"Oh—you mean the Christmas event."

"Exactly. What does it mean to you?"

"Oh—well—when you put it that way. . . ." She stood perfectly still for a few moments thinking. Then she said, "It means that I must be hurrying on to Haugan's shop. You know I have my handicraft and my bakery goods, and if I don't get them there to be sold, how will I have the money to buy the things that make Christmas Christmas?"

"So true," he responded, poker-faced.

"Well, I must leave you to your contemplations. As I say, it must be so *inspiring* to be a pastor at the Christmas season!"

The pastor watched her go. "An old German proverb says, `God gives the nuts, but one must crack them by one's self,'" he said to no one in particular. "How do I crack *that* one?"

Hilda reflected that it had been a very long afternoon in the woodcutter's hut up the mountain. She was physically weary. But thankful.

Now as darkness descended, she trimmed the wick and lit the candle in the window. She watched its flame leap high, sending dancing patterns over the room. Tonight its light touched rough beams and wooden planks and etched them in enchanting softness.

Only a few minutes ago, she had laid a small, warmly wrapped little bundle in the crook of Maria's arm. She smiled as a tiny fist waved in the air. Maria pulled the little one close as Karl, kneeling beside the bed, wept tears of joy.

There was a knock. Hilda, thinking it a poor time for *anyone* to come calling, opened the door.

There stood the pastor with his collar turned up against the cold. "Perhaps I should not have come so late, but it seemed tonight I should come up the mountain to see how Maria and Karl are—"

Karl was on his feet. "Come! Come in—and you shall see how we are!"

As the pastor entered, his eyes quickly took in the scene. "Oh! Maria, I'm afraid I've not come at the right time."

Karl clapped him on the back. "Oh, it's a *good* time! See him, Pastor! He's healthy!"

"And so beautiful," Maria murmured happily.

"God is good," the pastor said heartily. "Now, my child, how can I help you?" He looked about the room. "You need many things. I'll send some of the church ladies in."

Maria smiled a smile that seemed to light up the room. "Pastor, before the baby came, my list was long. It seemed I needed everything! Now I know that Karl and I are very rich." She pulled the small bundle closer. "I think we'll understand Christmas better this year."

The pastor nodded. "Perhaps I will, too."

The pastor, trying to be patient, tapped his pen restlessly. Light slanted in from the high window of his small study. The light illuminated the little rosette on the top of Wilhelmina Schneider's bonnet as, purse propped upon the desk, she leaned toward him. *Silly little rosette,* he thought, deciding that he would try to concentrate on *it* rather than the flow of words from the ever voluble lady before him.

"So I said to her, `Sigrid,' I said, `forget about demons! Pastor has assured me they're no problem.'"

"Excuse me," said Franz in the doorway. "I didn't know you were here, Wilhelmina."

"I'm just going." She nodded at Franz and turned back to the pastor. "As I say, I was most relieved about the demons."

"Demons?" inquired Franz.

"Getting mixed up with the greens in the sanctuary. Pastor says there's no problem."

"Oh?"

"We've `Christianized' them." Wilhelmina gathered up her purse. "Now I must be off. Sigrid is in a stew with the plum pudding!"

"And how about the candles, Frau Schneider?" the pastor called as she went out the door. "Are they still praying?"

"Some are. But they'll get straightened out eventually. *Guten Abend*, Pastor, Franz."

When she had gone the pastor went back to his papers.

Franz stood very near him, turning his hat thoughtfully in his hand. "Demons are no problem."

"I'm pleased they don't trouble you," said the pastor as he wrote.

"And some of the candles are still praying?"

"It would seem so."

Franz sat down. "Good friend, are you well? Has the season `affected' you?"

"I am well, and the season does affect one, one way or the other, Franz," he said, still writing.

Franz surveyed him for a few moments, then shrugged. He ran his hand through his hair. "Well, I can't fix it. I took the parts to Haugan's. It's no use!"

"I won't worry about it."

Franz stood up. "What do you mean you won't worry about it? You always worry about it! *We have no organ for the Christmas Eve service!*"

"We'll make do. Here." The pastor handed Franz a sheet of paper. "I need help with this."

"What is it?"

"Words! Words, Franz. I was coming down the mountain last night after visiting Maria and Karl. They've had a baby."

"That's ganz gut! But, my friend, your mind is somewhere else." Franz wrinkled his brow in puzzlement. "Or something inside you is different. What is it?"

"I'm trying to tell you! On my way down, I stopped on a crest overlooking the village. Stars were the clearest I've ever seen. And suddenly, *other* things became clear!" He rose from his chair, spreading his hands in excitement. "Into the hopelessly common, desperate dark of life came the pure *light* of the Son of God!" He sat down again. "I saw a room, Franz—dingy, falling to pieces, nothing lovely in it—but a candle that invited the Christ. *And then a baby was born!* And the room was filled with pure, holy *light!* Peace! Peace, Franz, beyond the dull gray of life." He stopped and pointed. "So read."

Franz scanned the paper he held. "This is very beautiful."

"So! I came home. I wrote. I finished at four o'clock this morning."

"You must be weary."

"Weary, that I am. Now you take it and make a song of it."

"You jest!"

"Nein."

"I'm no composer!"

"You can do it, Franz."

"We have no organ to play it on!"

"Your guitar will do. You have five days. Go now. I need to sleep. You need to compose. You pray—God will help you."

The little church was old but beautiful, framed by spruce and pine and with the stars of Christmas Eve above. Candlelight from within beckoned the worshipers. Maria entered, walking slowly, carrying a small bundle. Karl, strong and protective, strode beside her.

As the pastor rose to speak, a stillness pervaded the old church. He closed his eyes momentarily and shifted on his feet. Then he spoke, his voice gathering strength. "A week ago, I had nothing to say that I had not said many a time and was uninspired to repeat. Then, maybe a bit like Moses, I went up the mountain and saw the glory of God!

"It was a rough, barren little room—but lit by an *event*. A human baby, most helpless of all creatures, and a woodcutter's hut was filled with *peace and light!*"

Karl tightened his arm about Maria's shoulders.

The pastor's face was alight. "On the way down the mountain, God gave the words, and Franz has made a song of them." He leaned toward them over his pulpit. "No one will remember the *song*. But the message you must *not* forget! God is love! The Son of God—he is Love's pure light! Sent to reconcile—to redeem. His birth was the dawn of redeeming grace!"

The pastor sat down, and Franz moved to the front of the platform. Softly he began to strum on his guitar. And then he sang.

> *"Silent night! Holy night!*
> *All is calm, all is bright*
> *'Round yon virgin mother and Child.*
> *Holy Infant, so tender and mild,*
> *Sleep in heavenly peace,*
> *Sleep in heavenly peace."*

When the last note had died away, there was a deep, wonderful quietness among those who had heard. The baby stirred and made soft little sucking sounds in his sleep. Maria touched his cheek softly and blinked tears of joy.

"The wolf will live with the lamb, . . . and a little child will lead them."
ISAIAH 11:6, NIV

Rick Blanchette

THE BLUE AND GRAY CHRISTMAS

The snow was falling gently over the Virginia landscape. A soft, white blanket covered the fields and roads, moonlight making the trees sparkle as if they were wrapped in tinsel. It was a perfect night, a perfect Christmas Eve.

The snow covered the steeple of the tiny church outside of Culpeper. Wagons were parked out front, the horses pawing through the snow, searching for an evening snack. From inside, the strains of a piano and fiddle could be heard. At first only the instruments sounded; then voices joined in. "The first Noel, the angel did say was to certain poor shepherds in fields as they lay. . . ."

On this Christmas Eve, the soft wind could not make up its mind about which direction it wanted to go. First it would carry crystalline flakes eastward, then would, without any rhyme or reason, take them back to where they had begun and even farther west. This meandering wind also carried the voices of the villagers and farmers out to the fields on either side of the small sanctuary. "In fields where they lay . . ." would echo eastward then fade as "keeping their sheep, on a cold winter's night" would filter westward.

The first ears to hear this song, on the east side that is, belonged to a cold, dirty drummer boy. He was dressed in a blue uniform that was too large for his eleven-year-old frame. The cuffs of his trousers were rolled up three times so his heavy boots would not get caught up as he marched. His sleeves were six inches too long for his arms, but he didn't care because this way he could tuck his hands in to keep them from freezing stiff. For if his hands froze, he couldn't play his drum to entertain the Federal soldiers at the camp or lead them into battle.

He missed his family tonight—tonight more than most nights in the faraway land of the South. His mother and sisters were back in Illinois, and his father and older brothers had been taken prisoner after the battle of Fredericks-burg over a year before. He could have gone home, but he was the only man in their family left to fight for his country. So he stayed, and he played.

Tonight, even though he was lonely, he sat outside the small camp while the men in his company told stories and remembered Christmases past. Those were grown-up stories though, and he didn't understand why they didn't talk about sticks of candy and handmade wooden toys. So he sat at the edge of camp and tapped slowly on his drum. His taps soon took a pattern, and he began to sing with each tap: "Noel, Noel, Noel, Noel, born is the King of Israel."

He stopped and for the first time noticed why he was playing and singing that song. Somebody else was, too! There were voices, and instruments in the wilderness. He listened closely and decided the music was coming from someplace west of their camp. He leapt to his feet and ran back to camp.

"Lieutenant! Lieutenant!" he called. "There's people singin'! People's singin' Christmas songs!"

Lieutenant Barnes stood up from around the fire and tried to calm the boy down. "Are you sure you heard people? You weren't just remembering a Christmas back home?"

"No!" cried the drummer boy. "The voices are real. They're celebrating Christmas!"

The lieutenant looked around and tried to listen for the music. He didn't hear anything but the sounds from the campfire. Looking at the excited young boy, he said, "It might be a Confederate camp singing and celebrating. And if it is, we need to know about it." He motioned to a group of three soldiers standing nearby and called them over. "There's music out there somewhere, and I want you to find it. If there's Rebs around, I want to know where." Looking back to the boy, he ordered, "Since you heard it, you can lead these men to where you thought it was comin' from." With that, he headed back to the warmth of the fire.

The drummer boy couldn't believe he was commanding three full-grown privates! He smiled really wide and led them back to where he was playing. Once there, he strained his ears to locate the mystery music. "Joy to the world, the Lord is come." He heard it. And so did the others. They grabbed their rifles tightly, ready for the carolers to leap from the trees. But no one attacked. The song continued peacefully, unaware that it had caused a panic.

"Let's go find where they're singin'," ordered the drummer boy as he darted into the brush.

The soldiers shrugged and followed, anxious to have something to take their minds off their loved ones back home.

After a few minutes of walking, the group came upon a clearing. They saw a tiny church with a snow-covered steeple. Candles were glowing in the windows, and it was obvious the songs were coming from Christmas worshipers, not Rebel soldiers.

"Let's go in, huh?" the drummer boy urged. When the men frowned, he begged some more. "But we're supposed to go to church on Christmas! My mama would take me over her knee if I told her I didn't go in when I was so close. Please?"

The men were cautious, but the building did look warm. And they didn't have to stay long. Just long enough to thaw out. The oldest private nodded and tousled the drummer boy's hair as the soldiers headed for the church.

To the west of the church, another set of ears heard music coming from the trees. "Let every heart prepare him room, and heaven and nature sing. . . ." The gray-clad youth sat up quickly, dropping his drum in the new snow.

This drummer boy had been walking around the camp, unofficially keeping guard while the grown-ups told their favorite Christmas memories. They had bored him, so he picked up his drum and pretended to be a real soldier, using one of his drumsticks as a rifle. He stopped after only a minute. The game had been fun before he took part in his first battle. Now, after seeing the damage that muskets and rifles could do, pretend soldiering wasn't amusing, but tragic. So he sat down against a tree, wrapped his arms around himself, and thought himself back home to Richmond and into his family's church. He was sitting next to his mother and aunt as they attended the Christmas Eve services. They were singing "Joy to the World," and Mister Evans was singing off-key right into his ear.

But the music grew sweeter as he thought about it more. Soon it sounded as he had never heard it before. No one ever played a fiddle in their church!

He sat up, dropping his drum. *I gotta tell the sergeant*, he thought. Jumping to his feet, he picked up his drum and sticks and ran to the center of camp.

"Sarge! Sarge!" he called. "Come quick! Someone's out there!"

The old sergeant stood at his place near the campfire. "What you talkin' 'bout, boy? Who's out where?"

"People singin' out in the woods!" he gasped, out of breath from excitement. "I was sittin' outside camp, and I heered people singin' Christmas music!"

Chuckles erupted from those who could hear the conversation. "Maybe them Yankees are bringin' a goose for us to eat while they sing for us," someone joked.

The drummer boy didn't find it funny. "I ain't makin' it up. There's someone out there! I swear!"

"OK, I believe you heard somethin' out there," the sergeant said. He winked at a couple of soldiers and said, "You two, bring your weapons. If we're huntin' Yankees, I want to be ready for them!" Looking back at the boy, he ordered, "Now show us where you were when you heard these people. We'll capture them and make the camp safe." He almost couldn't keep the smile from his lips.

Unaware that the grown-ups were making fun of him, he led them to the tree where he had been sitting. He motioned for silence, then tilted his head to the east to catch the wondrous music.

Softly, chords from a piano drifted down from the treetops. Soon voices could be heard, too. "Away in a manger, no crib for a bed . . ."

The Confederate soldiers couldn't believe their ears. Somewhere in this wilderness people were having a party—a Christmas party.

"Anyone familiar with this part of the country?" the sergeant asked. The men all shook their heads. "Well, let's see who's makin' the music. Maybe they got a few extra pies to spare us poor soldiers protectin' their land."

"It's comin' from this way," the drummer boy said as he plunged into the forest. The men followed closely, the suggestion of a fresh pie making even the most tired of soldiers march double time.

Within minutes they approached a clearing. In the center of the clearing was a tiny church with a snow-covered steeple. The soldiers took a quick look around, then headed for the church and the warm, dry pews.

When the Union soldiers entered the church, several heads turned and cast disapproving looks in their direction. Whether it was because they were interrupting their service or because they were the enemy was hard to tell. But the drummer boy led the soldiers to a vacant pew on the left side, near the front of the room. They stood with the congregation and joined in the singing: "The stars in the sky looked down where he lay, the little Lord Jesus asleep on the hay." Satisfied that they were not going to cause trouble, the rest of the congregation resumed their worship.

The Confederate soldiers entered the church and removed their forage caps in respect. They stood near the back, looking for some open seats. Looking to the right, the drummer boy spotted an open pew, located toward the front. He started up the aisle, the soldiers following, surprised by the strange expressions of the worshipers as they sang. Their faces looked worried and frightened. *Don't they know we're on their side?* the drummer boy wondered. Once in place, they sang along: "O holy Child of Bethlehem, descend to us we pray. . . ."

111

The Rebel soldiers were relaxing, enjoying the warmth of the church and the simple act of worshiping in a church again. But during the second verse of "Hark! The Herald Angels Sing," the drummer boy saw why everyone was so nervous. *Yankees!* Three pews up and to the left were three soldiers and a young boy about his age. *Did they, too, hear the beautiful Christmas music and come in to worship?* The drummer boy continued to sing, not sure of what to do.

A moment after the Southern drummer boy noticed him, the Northern drummer boy glanced around the church as he sang. He hadn't been this close to Southern people before, except in battle. They sure didn't look like the monsters they were supposed to be. The boy thought they looked just like the people in his hometown. As his eyes passed along the right side of the church, he stopped. *Rebels! Four of them! Did they see us yet?* The boy wasn't sure of what to do next. Should he tell his companions and risk a battle inside of God's house? Or should he pray that the Rebels would leave without noticing their blue uniforms?

He didn't have to wonder long, for the man next to him turned his head to see what the boy was looking at. His hand quickly grabbed his rifle as he kicked his comrade to get his attention.

One of the Southern soldiers saw the commotion to his left and stood up quickly, snatching up his own rifle. Within moments, six armed men faced each other across the center aisle, guns raised and ready for battle. The singing and music stopped abruptly. Mothers hugged their children. Old men tried to move the people out of the line of fire but could not budge the terrified civilians.

The standoff continued, neither side sure of what to do. The soldiers were sweating and trembling. The drummer boys on each side stared at each other, armed only with their instruments. Their wide, children's eyes were confused, just like their companions'.

Softly, one voice trembled above the quiet: "Silent night, holy night! All is calm, all is bright." It was the blue drummer boy, doing the only thing he could do in the war—make music. Each Christmas his sisters and he sang "Silent Night," accompanied by their mother on the piano. He was not able to be with them this Christmas, but singing their song now seemed the right thing to do. And maybe his sisters and mother were singing at this moment, too.

The gray drummer boy joined in: " 'Round yon virgin mother and Child. Holy Infant so tender and mild, sleep in heavenly peace, sleep in heavenly peace."

The soldiers were even more confused now. The Union men looked to each other, unsure of the next action. The Rebels did the same.

Slowly the Union drummer boy walked toward the front of the church. "Silent night, holy night! Shepherds quake at the sight. . . ." When he reached the pulpit, he turned around, faced the people, and closed his eyes as he sang.

"Glories stream from heaven afar, heav'nly hosts sing Alleluia. . . ." The Southern drummer boy also began walking to the front and stood next to the young blue drummer boy.

The pastor, frozen in place until now, carefully motioned to the pianist to begin playing. The old woman at the piano took a big gulp and lightly played along with the duet. The fiddler also joined in and began to sing with the boys.

With confidence, the pastor sang along, looking straight at the soldiers on both sides of the battle lines. "Son of God, Love's pure light. Radiant beams from thy holy face, with the dawn of redeeming grace, Jesus, Lord, at thy birth, Jesus, Lord, at thy birth."

The soldiers knew they couldn't fire in the church, not on Christmas. A Union soldier lowered his weapon and sang, staring into the eyes of a Rebel. The Rebel sergeant lowered his rifle as well, and sang the hymn. A few moments later, all the guns were lying on the pews, forgotten, as the celebration of Christmas continued. "Silent night, holy night! Wondrous star, lend thy light. With the angels let us sing, Alleluia to our King; Christ the Savior is born, Christ the Savior is born."

As the congregation sang the final carol, "O Come, All Ye Faithful," the drummer boys played their drums. The snare drums added a victorious note to the music, which was appropriate, since a battle had been fought and won in that tiny church with a snow-covered steeple—and not one shot had to be fired.

After the service, the opposing soldiers gathered in the center aisle like neighbors might. They spoke of hometowns, families, wives, and children. And the drummer boys sat near the altar and became friends. The soldiers hated to leave, but they knew they had to return to their camps and to the war. The men exchanged simple gifts of whatever they were carrying. The Northern soldiers gave the Rebels a couple packets of coffee and some dried beef. The Southern soldiers gave the Yankees the only thing they had to give—three small bags of Virginia tobacco. The gifts weren't wrapped in pretty packages, but each soldier knew the others would go without what they gave until the next rations were issued.

The drummer boys were the last to leave the small church. They carried nothing of value to exchange, except their drums. Reverently, they unstrapped the instruments and swapped them, the Northern boy giving up his factory-made, expensive drum for the hand-crafted simple version his friend gave him. He sounded a drum roll and smiled at the sound. The Southern boy tapped a few notes of "Dixie" on his new drum with his old, hand-carved sticks and smiled.

As they stood outside the church, the snow still falling, they called out farewells.

"Keep your heads low, Rebs!" a Union man warned.

"You too, Yanks! I'd hate to know I shot one of y'all," a Confederate returned.

They tipped their hats and walked off toward their camps.

"Merry Christmas, Johnny Reb!" the blue drummer boy called.

"Merry Christmas, Billy Yank!" the gray drummer boy called. "Maybe we'll see each other next Christmas!"

"Maybe," the blue boy agreed, then headed back to the war.

"Some have entertained angels unawares."
HEBREWS 13:2, KJV

Penelope J. Stokes

ONE GIFT FOR THE JESUS CHILD

◆

Isabel Montgomery arrived early on Christmas Eve to find the main hall of the

Sunday school building dim and chilly. Carefully balancing the huge cake in

both hands, she stomped the snow off her boots and, without removing her coat,

made her way in the darkness toward a row of child-size tables. She had almost

lost the cake once this evening when she slipped on a patch of ice getting into the

car. The thermostat could wait for a minute or two until she made sure her great

surprise was safe.

It had been all Isabel's idea, putting on the "Birthday Party for the Baby Jesus" for the four- and five-year-olds. The older children were in the Christmas pageant, and the babies would be taken care of in the nursery. This way, with Isabel entertaining the "middle children" in the Sunday school hall, their parents could relax and enjoy the show without worrying about their little ones disrupting things. It was Isabel's gift to the mothers and fathers of the congregation.

It was also Isabel's gift to herself, if she was going to be perfectly honest. Single and childless—an old maid by most people's standards—she had no family, no nieces and nephews to dote on. And Christmas was a special time for children, after all.

Isabel turned on the lights, adjusted the thermostat, and looked around. All her hard work had paid off, that was certain. The Christmas tree in the corner glowed with lights and ornaments, and even a little toy train ran around and around the base. The red and green streamers held in place by clusters of balloons lent a festive air to the basement room. The place had been transformed into a wonderland that would make any tot's eyes shine with joy. And she had done it all herself.

As she poured apple cider into the huge coffeepot to heat, Isabel imagined the children sitting around the tables, listening intently as she made the Christmas story come to life on a flannel board. She would tell them about the Virgin Mary and Joseph traveling a great distance to Bethlehem, only to be turned away by the innkeeper. She would ask them, "Would you turn Jesus away if he came to your house?" And a chorus of intense voices would answer in unison, "No!"

Isabel had made the flannel donkey herself out of a scrap of furry tan material that was sure to delight the little ones. And she had fluffy white sheep and even a black-and-white cow with dark button eyes and whimsical long eyelashes. After the story, they would sing Christmas carols and make a Christmas tree hot pad out of Popsicle sticks to take home as a memento of the wonderful birthday party for the baby Jesus.

While the cider heated, Isabel laid out the paper plates and napkins, arranged the paper cups, and set her personal little gift at each place. It was only a bit of Christmas candy wrapped up in silver paper and tied with ribbon, but the effect was charming.

She walked around the room, surveying her handiwork with satisfaction. The cake, bought with her own meager funds, had a manger scene in the middle and the words *Happy Birthday, Jesus* scrolled across the top. The sheep peering over the manger looked a little like a thundercloud with feet, and one of the wise men came out so tall that his head stuck up over the top of the stable and made him look as if the Angel of Glory were nesting in his hair. But all in all it was a good job, and the children probably wouldn't notice.

It was going to be a wonderful evening, an evening the children would never forget. An evening Isabel herself had anticipated for a long, long time.

At 6:55 Isabel counted eleven four- and five-year-olds in the Sunday school hall, most of them familiar faces. She had planned for fifteen, and it wasn't likely that many more would show up, since the older children's Christmas pageant began at seven. They were obviously on their best behavior—the boys dressed in their tiny sports coats and clip-on ties, the girls primped in velvet dresses with lace petticoats. At the base of the tree knelt four of the lads, watching in wonder as the Christmas train made its way in and out of the branches. Several of the girls were *oohing* and *ahhing* over the cake, and others shook the small packages on the table, trying to guess what was inside.

Only one child sat apart from the group—a serious-looking girl, perhaps four years old, with lank, dishwater-colored hair, huge brown eyes, and a threadbare sweater over a dress two sizes too big. She had settled into one corner of the room and sat holding something in her arms, rocking back and forth and humming.

Isabel went over and knelt down beside her. "Hi there, honey," she said softly, putting a hand on the girl's shoulder. "I'm Miss Isabel. What's your name?"

The child's liquid eyes rose to meet Isabel's. "Sissy," she said, with a slight lisp. "Sissy Minot. My brother Mark's in the big show. He's a shepherd."

"Well, that's fine," Isabel said. "What do we have here?" She pulled back the edge of a tattered bath towel to reveal an obviously well-loved baby doll.

"It's the baby Jesus," Sissy whispered reverently, holding the doll at arm's length so Isabel could get a look, then clutching it to her heart. "He's mine." Her eyes filled up with tears, and her face contorted as she tried not to let them spill over. "I told them I could be in the show, too—I had the baby Jesus and everything. But they said—" She gulped and wiped her nose on a corner of the towel. "They said I was too little. That I wouldn't understand it, and that I'd mess up the pa—pag—what's that word?"

"Pageant." Isabel smiled and patted the girl on the head. From the looks of her, she hadn't been in church very often. She certainly stuck out among these other well-groomed Sunday school kids. Perhaps Isabel's well-planned agenda—the flannel-graph presentation of the Christmas story, the carols, the interaction with the other children—would be good for the child. Clearly, if she thought her doll was the baby Jesus, she didn't understand the true meaning of—

Isabel's thoughts were interrupted by a commotion at the door. She turned to find herself face-to-face with the most beautiful little boy she had ever seen—a blond, blue-eyed five-year-old with a dimple in his chin and a dazzling smile. *A charmer,* Isabel thought instantly. And someday, a real heartbreaker.

With a parting smile at Sissy, she got to her feet and went to the doorway.

"This is Brandon Colton," the Sunday school superintendent said, urging the boy forward.

"Bandy," the child corrected, bringing a blue security blanket to his cheek and gazing at Isabel with the expression of a love-struck cherub. "I came for the birthday party."

An absolute angel, Isabel decided. Her mind flashed for an instant to an image of adorable Bandy Colton sitting at her feet, drinking in the flannel-board gospel and being the first in the group to say no when she asked if they would turn Jesus away at the inn. This was the child of her dreams. With a face like that, he had to be the best little boy in the room.

Behind Isabel, the Sunday school hall had grown quiet as death. She glanced over her shoulder. The boys who had been playing with the train stood at attention like little soldiers, eyeing the newcomer. The girls huddled in a group next to the cake. Only Sissy Minot had not moved.

She still sat in her place, rocking the baby Jesus and humming softly.

As soon as the door had closed behind the superintendent's back, little Bandy Colton launched into motion. With his blanket trailing behind him, he blazed through the room, parting the cluster of little girls like Moses lifting his staff over the Red Sea. He slid to a stop in front of the cake and surveyed it with a sneer. "What's this dumb thing?" he said, prodding his finger into the thunder-cloud sheep and licking off the icing. "And what about this stupid bird?" With a mighty swipe he raked the Angel of Glory into his mouth, turned, and quick as a snake wiped his frosting-covered hand down the front of Susie Stinson's green velvet dress.

Susie burst into tears and began scrubbing at the mess. In three strides Isabel was across the room. She grabbed Bandy's hand before he could do any more damage and turned him around to face her. "This is the house of the Lord, young man, and this is Jesus' birthday party. You will behave yourself, or—"

Bandy narrowed his eyes at her. "You're not my boss," he said in a menacing tone. "And if you do anything to me, I'll tell my father, and he'll really make you pay!" He stuck his blanket to his cheek and glared at Isabel as if daring her to take action.

Isabel looked around the room. Except for Sissy Minot, still rocking and singing in the corner, every child in the room was looking on with expressions of abject terror. Isabel might never have met the angelic-looking Bandy Colton, but obviously everyone else had. And they seemed determined to keep their distance at any cost. Susie Stinson had gotten too close, and look what had happened to her!

Well, things weren't going to get out of control—not at Isabel Montgomery's birthday party for Jesus. She had waited all year for this evening, and one pint-sized terrorist wasn't going to spoil it. Not for her, and not for the other children.

Still gripping Bandy's hand, she met his steely gaze. "As I said," she resumed, calmer now, "you will behave yourself, or you will not be allowed to enjoy the party like the rest of the children." She let go of his hand and squatted down to his eye level. "We're going to have cake and cider, Bandy," she said in an entreating voice. "And we're going to tell the story of Jesus on the flannel board—"

That was when Isabel made her big mistake. She turned—just slightly—to look at the flannel figures on the board, her sweet-faced fluffy sheep and the tan fur donkey she had worked so painstakingly to make. Before she knew it, Bandy was at the board, jerking the donkey from the background. He tore its tail off and ripped out its eyes, then in a single motion smashed it into the cake.

"Bandy!" Isabel gasped. "Don't you want to hear the story of Jesus?"

He looked at her, gripping his blanket so hard that his little knuckles turned white. "I dunno who Jesus is," he said, "but I bet my father could beat him up."

Isabel grabbed for him, but before she could reach him, Bandy careened behind her and wrapped his blanket around her ankles. She went down, hard, and lay on the floor, gasping for breath. Bandy headed for the Christmas tree. With a swift kick he derailed the toy train, and the tree began to rock precariously. Children scattered everywhere, the girls whimpering and the boys making a beeline for the opposite end of the room.

Then, just as he was about to round the room for another pass at total destruction, Bandy Colton saw Sissy Minot, still in her corner, rocking the

123

baby Jesus doll. He slid to a halt in front of her and stood with his hands on his hips, defiant. Isabel saw it coming, but she couldn't get up. She couldn't stop it from happening.

"Who are you?" Bandy demanded.

"Sissy," she said simply, and kept on rocking.

"What's that?" He kicked a foot at the doll's head, and she drew back just in time.

"It's Baby Jesus."

"Give it to me."

Sissy looked at him with wide brown eyes and shook her head. "No."

"I said, give it to me!" He wrestled the bundle from her arms, and Sissy jumped to her feet. The towel unrolled, and the naked doll went flying. Bandy stood there holding his own blanket in one hand and the baby Jesus wrapping in the other.

Tears filled the little girl's eyes, but she said nothing.

Bandy threw the old towel on the floor and put one foot on top of it. "Aren't you afraid of me?"

She shook her head. "No."

"My father can beat up your father."

Sissy looked at him. "I don't have a father." This stopped Bandy for an instant. Then she whispered, "But I have Jesus."

Bandy's beautiful blond head snapped up, and his blue eyes went wide. "I just killed your baby Jesus," he said, pointing to where the doll lay in a heap on the floor.

"You can't kill Jesus," Sissy said. "Jesus lives here, in your heart—if you'll let him. He can make you . . ." She paused and took a deep breath. "He can make you not be mean."

Bandy reached out and slapped her, hard, across the face. "Take it back."

But Sissy stood her ground and leaned her head to the other side.

"What are you doing?" Bandy demanded.

"Turning the other cheek," she said. "It's what Jesus said we're s'posed to do."

He raised his hand as if to strike her again, but she didn't move. Didn't flinch. Didn't close her eyes. Instead, the hint of a smile crept onto her lips.

Bandy slowly lowered his hand. "What are you smiling at?"

She shrugged. "At you. I don't think you're really mean," she said. "I think you just need somebody to love you. Somebody like Jesus."

Bandy began to tremble. He dropped his security blanket and, without a word, dashed through the Sunday school room and out the door. Sissy Minot looked around for a minute, then gathered up his blanket and the baby Jesus doll and followed.

By the time Isabel Montgomery got to the fellowship hall, the after-pageant coffee hour was well under way. It was 8:15, and she never had the chance to give her flannel-graph gospel lesson. Never cut the cake. Never sang a single Christmas carol. She limped in on her sprained right ankle, with ten awestruck four- and five-year-olds in tow, and the Sunday school superintendent wasted no time in beginning his interrogation.

"Isabel, what on earth happened? You look like you've been through a war."

She arched an eyebrow at him. We had an . . . ah, incident."

His face went pale. "Brandon Colton?"

Isabel nodded. "Yes. And a little girl I've never seen. A Sissy Minot. They're both missing."

Missing? The superintendent mouthed the word, but no sound came out. He closed his eyes for a moment, then turned briskly and clapped his hands for attention.

"Mr. and Mrs. Colton?" he announced. "I need to see you for a moment. And . . . ah, Mr. and Mrs.—"

Isabel tugged at his sleeve. "There's no Mr. Minot," she whispered.

"Mrs. Minot," the superintendent corrected. "In the pastor's office, please."

Isabel limped into the office, followed by the superintendent and a handsome blond man and his snooty-looking wife, both impeccably dressed. She assumed them, rightly, to be the Coltons.

"What's the meaning of this?" Mr. Colton boomed.

"This is Miss Montgomery," the superintendent explained. "She was in charge of the little children's birthday party in the Sunday school hall."

Mr. Colton looked Isabel up and down, his lip turned up on one side as if he found her distinctly unappealing. She probably did look a sight, she admitted to herself, with her hair disheveled and her ankle swelling up like a basketball.

"Well, where is my boy?" he demanded. "Surely you didn't leave the children unchaperoned down in the basement?"

"No, sir, I—," Isabel began.

"We have a little problem," the superintendent interrupted. "Your boy— and a little girl—are missing."

"Missing?" Mrs. Colton put a diamond-adorned hand to her heart and gasped. "If this is your idea of a well-orchestrated church function, then I—"

"Never mind that," Mr. Colton snapped. "Let's just find him."

"Them," Isabel corrected. "The little girl—"

"Right, right," Mr. Colton muttered impatiently.

Just then the director of the Christmas pageant stuck her head in the door. "There's no Mrs. Minot here." She frowned. "Apparently no one has even heard of her."

"The child said she had a big brother playing a shepherd in the pageant," Isabel said. "Named Mark, I believe."

"Mark? Mark Minot?" The director scratched her head. "No, that name doesn't ring a bell. I'm certain we didn't have a Mark. We had a—"

"Let's just get moving, all right?" Mr. Colton snapped.

Enlisting the help of all the able-bodied parents and some of the older children and teens, they searched everywhere: the sanctuary, the choir room, the library, the kitchen, even the broom closet. Nothing. No sign of Brandon Colton or his diminutive victim, Sissy Minot.

At last the cry came from the parking lot: "We found him!"

Mr. and Mrs. Colton, along with the superintendent and a weak and limping Isabel Montgomery, grabbed their coats and headed outside.

Sure enough, there in front of the church, standing calf-deep in new-fallen snow, stood Bandy Colton, his blond head haloed by the lights from the outdoor manger scene. The child stood shivering next to a five-foot plywood wise man, while a two-dimensional Jersey cow gazed over his shoulder.

Mr. Colton dropped down in the snow and jerked off his overcoat, wrapping it around his son. "Bandy! Are you all right?"

The boy nodded, turning a face streaked with frozen tears toward the manger scene. "Jesus loves me," he whispered. Then he pointed to the manger.

The rough wood feeding trough had been empty earlier this evening—from the road, nobody could see anything but the hay anyway. But now there was something in the manger, something blue and soft.

Mrs. Colton reached past Isabel and snatched it up. "Your good blanket! Brandon Colton, you've gone and gotten your expensive handmade blanket all filthy. Look at this!" She began picking pieces of dirty hay out of the soft fibers, but suddenly Bandy grabbed it back.

"No, Mama! It's for Baby Jesus."

Tenderly, and with infinite patience, he lifted the naked Jesus doll out of the manger and wrapped it in his blanket, then laid it back in place and gazed at it.

"But that's your favorite blanket, Bandy," his mother protested. "You never go anywhere without it."

"No," he said firmly. "It's mine, and I'm giving it to Jesus."

Isabel extended a hand and put it on the boy's shoulder. "Bandy," she said softly, "where is Sissy?"

Bandy twisted around and looked up at her, a puzzled expression on his little cherub face. "She was here a minute ago. She brought me out here to put the baby Jesus to bed." He brightened. "I guess she went home."

Isabel looked around the snow-covered church lawn. From the parking lot, four sets of hurried footprints scuffed through the snow out to the manger scene. From the front sidewalk, one set of tiny prints made its wandering way across the yard, ending where Brandon Colton now stood. There was no sign of Sissy Minot. Isabel let out a shuddering sigh.

One set of footprints. One baby Jesus doll, saved from the frigid night by the gift of a treasured blanket. And one little boy who, God willing, would never be mean again.

Brandon Colton stood on tiptoe and leaned into the manger to plant a kiss on the faded plastic face wrapped in his cherished blue blanket.

"Happy birthday, Jesus," he whispered. "I'm sorry I ruined your cake."

Then, giving a wide angelic smile to Isabel Montgomery, Bandy took his father's hand and walked away.

129

"O come, O come, Emmanuel, and ransom captive Israel,
that mourns in lonely exile here, until the Son of God appear.
Rejoice! Rejoice! Emmanuel shall come to thee, O Israel!"
"O Come, O Come, Emmanuel," JOHN M. NEALE

Bodie Thoene

DACHAU NIGHT

◆

Cold, silent night had come without darkness or peace to Dachau. A huge stone wall topped by electric wires ringed the massive prison compound. From the towers, machine guns bristled and stern, black-shirted sentinels kept watch. Harsh floodlights glared down upon the stark white walls of the barracks, bleaching color and life from the scene.

From the door of Barracks 11, a thin skeleton of a man emerged dressed in a black-and-white striped uniform. He stood blinking up into the lights and turrets, then stumbled

131

from the step. His face colorless, he walked with a jerking motion as he moved toward the forbidden area where the lights beat down unrelentingly and signs declared that those who stepped across the low wire would be shot. The figure did not seem human. His thin clothes flapped in the chill wind like the rags on a scarecrow.

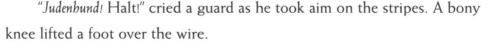

Scharf Geschossen! The black lettering warned.

The scarecrow trudged on toward the forbidden line. He did not look at the guards who shouted to him, or halt at their command. Like an image on a black-and-white celluloid film, he lurched across a bleak cold screen. The guard dogs barked, straining on their leashes. One guard, then another, then still another clicked rifle bolts into place; the sound echoed hollowly across the silent night, a grim counterpoint to the crunch of ragged shoes against the snow.

"*Judenhund!* Halt!" cried a guard as he took aim on the stripes. A bony knee lifted a foot over the wire.

The figure seemed not to hear the words, the threats, the shouts. His hollow eyes stared past the harsh lights as though searching for something— some color, perhaps a single star.

Then, in a rattle of machine-gun fire, the black-and-white stripes jumped forward in a strange jerking dance that tore and stained the fabric—red, perhaps, if there had been color. But there was no color—only the white glare of the lights, and a body tumbling forward as a spirit broke free and sailed over the walls of Dachau toward colors and stars.

The entire incident had taken only moments. Shouting sentries fell silent once again. They would let the body lie where it had fallen as a warning for other inmates.

Inside the long, unheated buildings, Jews and Social Democrats, Catholics and Protestants huddled in close-packed rows, trying to sleep, trying to keep warm, trying to forget the sound of the gunshots. Thousands of them were crammed into barracks that had been built for only a few hundred at best. In the morning there would be numbers missing from the roll call. They would die tonight and be cremated, along with the one who had committed suicide by crossing the forbidden line. Then they would be shipped home in little boxes like Christmas packages. A slip of paper would offer the explanation: Died of natural causes.

These were Hitler's gifts to the German people and the Greater German Reich. He had swept the cities clean of beggars. He had pulled dissenters from their pulpits and public offices. Day by day more Jews were defrauded of their property; their belongings were scooped into the coffers of the public building funds or the armament industry. The humans themselves had been swept into grim, black closets like Dachau. The Aryan cities of the Reich were becoming pure for German culture once again. Those who were missing were those who had somehow disturbed the conscience and peace of mind of the German people. What difference did it make if a few thousand, more or less, came back in ashes? A handful of dust to spread in the rose garden? What difference would it make if eventually a few million died, more or less—as long as there were no beggars, no gypsies, no Christian dissenters, no Bolsheviks, no Jews. The Aryan race of the great Thousand-Year Reich must be pure! Society must be pure! Sweep the dust into Dachau and forty other camps in Germany. Had not the Führer proclaimed his purpose in the Christmas broadcast? "I am doing the work of the Lord!"

After four months in solitary confinement, Theo Lindheim had come into Dachau. Like Pastor Niemöller and Pastor Jacobi, he had been given a false name and a new identity with the prison identification number. He was too well known among the people of Germany for the S.S. to risk some news of his fate being leaked. Those men who had been prominent or popular before Hitler came to power were all called by other names within the walls of the camps.

But somehow, it made no difference. Theo was listed on the records as Jacob Stern, but still prisoners quietly saluted this unnamed war hero when he passed by in the exercise yard. To speak his name and be heard would mean a beating with a rubber truncheon, or worse. And so, faceless men, cold and ragged, saluted Theo with their eyes when he passed. They spoke without speaking, and between them was a covenant to remember what Germany had been before all this—a covenant to remember that although they were imprisoned, those who lived outside the walls were also captives of Hitler's brutal rule.

No one was free in Germany now. *No one!* The streets were clean. Great buildings of white stone were being erected everywhere to the glory of the Reich. There was no disagreement and no freedom. Germany was a nation of prisoners, ruled by a government of jailers. Göring himself had said, *"I would like to see all of Germany in uniform, marching in column."*

Tonight, outside the walls of Dachau, neat rows of field-gray uniforms marched through the streets of Berlin and Munich and Hamburg in eerie torchlight procession. Perhaps they were warmer than those inside the walls of Dachau; perhaps they had more to eat; but they, too, had lost their names.

They had no faces. Their breath sucked color and life from the very air as they raised their arms as one mob to shout, *"Sieg Heil! Heil!"*

Like Faust, the mob had sold its soul to the devil for the sake of . . . what? Clean streets? New buildings? Jobs and possessions stolen from another human being in the name of "Aryan racial purity"? In the name of this purity, Hitler had robbed even the Christ Child in the manger of His identity, declaring: *Jesus was not Jewish; it could not be! His young mother was not Jewish! We must eliminate these slanders from the German Christian religion! We must expunge all traces of Judaism from our churches! The very thought that Christ was Jewish is unthinkable!*

Tonight the Nazi storm troopers and Hitler Youth marched row on row. *"Gott mit uns*—God with us" was inscribed on every belt buckle. The sound of their boots on the pavement was like the echo of the Roman legions on the stones of Jerusalem's streets when a young Jewish woman gave birth to a son in a cave above Bethlehem. That son had grown to manhood with the sound of marching legions in His ears. The crash of soldiers' boots had followed Him to his execution; the ring of their hammers had crashed again the spikes in His hands and feet, and a soldier in field gray with a swastika on his arm had driven the lance into His side. Soldiers had killed the Jewish child called by the Hebrew name *Emmanuel . . . God with us.* Like the S.S., they had come by torchlight to arrest Him in the night. They had thrown Him into prison, pulled out His beard by the roots, and beaten Him. *"Hail King of the Jews!"* they had jeered.

Yes, there were echoes of that time and place tonight in Dachau. In the endless rows of skeletons dressed in rags lived the poor and the homeless, the shepherds and wise men alike who looked for a Messiah to deliver them. In the arrogant cruelty of Hitler's army, once again the generals of Rome sought to crush even the barest ember of hope from men's lives. But even here there was forbidden light—even in the hell of Dachau.

In the corner of Barracks 8 men huddled together for warmth tonight. They jokingly called their corner the *"Herrgottseck"*—*"The Corner of the Lord."* As Theo Lindheim crouched on a wooden pallet between a Catholic priest and a Jewish cantor from the synagogue in Strassburg, he thought that perhaps the only free men left in Germany shivered within these thin walls. Here, with all else stripped from them, these men could be only what they were, for good or for evil. It was almost Christmas. It was just past Hanukkah. Tonight a priest without vestments, a cantor without tallith remembered the Festival of Lights and the One who was proclaimed to be The Light.

For the holiday, the prisoners had been given an extra ration besides their five ounces of bread to eat. Guards had distributed a raw potato for each man in the barracks. The eight in the Herrgottseck had carefully hoarded their treasures for the feast tonight. Now, eight potato halves were placed in a circle before each man. They had been hollowed out, and a wick made from an oil-soaked rag had been placed in each one to form a candle. At great risk, the priest had stolen a match from the kitchen.

A cold draft sifted up through the boards of the barracks' floor. Theo shivered and pulled his thin blanket around his chin. He prayed that the draft would not snuff out their match. Somehow the lighting of these candles tonight had become the focus of his existence, the reason he continued to breathe and think and hope when so many had given up.

Outside their circle of eight, someone mocked them in a hoarse, bitter whisper. "So, Priest. Here is Christmas. Peace on earth. Of course this is not earth, ja? But purgatory. Almost hell, only not warm enough. Hell would be better. Warmer."

"Shut up!" another voice hissed from the darkness. "Let them alone."

"You think your little candles will warm you?" mocked the voice again.

Yes! Theo wanted to shout. *Yes! This one defiant act of worship will warm me. Please, dear Lord, do not let the flame die. Please let our candles burn!*

"Come closer," said the cantor, and the eight pressed in shoulder to bony shoulder, ribs and spines and skulls forming a wall against the threat of a hostile wisp of air. The potato candles were moved forward into a tight circle, their wicks placed together at the center. The cantor held a small bundle of straw and the priest held the match. The only match.

137

"Tonight," the priest said quietly, "God has provided only one match. And so we who are both Jews and Christians worship as one in this place."

Theo could not see the priest's face. They all looked the same in the darkness, but there was a smile in the voice of the priest. So it had taken Dachau to bring priest and cantor together. Dachau, 1937. Christmas. Hanukkah. A moment of covenant among men who suffered together.

The cantor's voice was like a song as he spoke. "Tonight we remember the great miracle that happened in the temple. After the enemy had desecrated our place of worship and we drove him out from Jerusalem, there was oil enough to light the lamps for only one day. And God caused the flames to burn for eight days until more oil was sanctified. On this darkest night of our souls, when we find no light within ourselves, we ask God for a miracle—"

"What miracle can you expect here?" taunted the voice outside the circle.

"Only that the light will burn. That we will remember God is with us," replied the cantor.

"*Gott mit uns!* God is with the Nazis! Can't you read it on their buckles? I was beaten by one of those buckles," he scoffed.

The priest began to sing softly:

"O come, O come, Emmanuel,
And ransom captive Israel,
That mourns in lonely exile here
Until the Son of God appear—"

Other voices joined him softly in the song.

"O come, Thou Rod of Jesse, free
Thine own from Satan's tyranny;
From depths of hell Thy people save
And give them victory o'er the grave."

From the far corners of the barracks, weak voices added their strength to the song. Theo closed his eyes and sang loudly. Never mind that the *Kapos* would come and beat them—*never mind!* And if they were shot for singing, what did it matter?

"O come, Thou Dayspring, come and cheer
Our spirits by Thine advent here;
And drive away the shades of night,
And pierce the clouds and bring us light!"

Theo opened his eyes as the one match sputtered into flame. The tiny, fragile flame touched the bundle of straw, and the cantor, his voice clear and bell-like as he sang, touched the fire to the wicks of the eight Hanukkah candles.

"Rejoice! Rejoice! Emmanuel
Shall come to thee, O Israel!"

For an hour the candles burned as the cantor and the priest led the men in songs of hope and deliverance. And indeed, a great miracle happened there that night: no guards came near the barracks; no clubs smashed the heads of the thousand who joined the songs. For one hour that barracks in Dachau became synagogue and cathedral, where men lifted their hearts with one voice to the One God.

"Calm on the Listening Ear of Night," E. H. SEARS

Colin Pearce

NA-NA THE SINGING GOAT

◆

Na-Na was a beautiful little goat.

Her mother was a pedigreed Tannenburg-Angora cross of royal bloodlines, and her father was the son of the noted Morgan Thasbah III, the grandest goat champion of champion goats.

Na-Na lived in the backyard of the hotel. When she was big enough, she would be let out into the goat pasture with the other goats, but the children had asked Dad if they could keep her as a pet when she was a kid.

"All right," Dad had agreed, "but I don't want her treated like a baby. She has to go out to pasture one day and have kids of her own, you know! I don't want her to be a nuisance."

The children were delighted and called their new pet Na-Na.

She was so pretty. Her coat was a soft gray color. Her ears hung down like two warm oven gloves, and her eyes were a rich violet color—almost black and full of a goaty sort of love.

And everyone who saw her loved her.

Everyone except Dad.

You see, although Na-Na was beautiful, she was a bit silly.

She ate things. Not just goat food things, but other things—things in the garden, like bulbs and blossoms and bushes, plants and petals and pots; and things off the wash line, like socks and stockings and sheets, tea towels and trouser legs and tablecloths.

She nibbled on this, munched on that, took a bite here, took a gnaw there, ate up, fed on, gulped down, tucked into, picked at, champed, chomped, chewed, and swallowed—everything!

When they tied her up, she ate the rope and started all over again.

But that's not what made Dad mad. Although he didn't like Na-Na eating things, there was something else Dad was really mad about.

You see, Na-Na sang!

Now goat singing is not good singing at the best of times, but Na-Na's singing was awful. It wasn't so much *how* she sang or *what* she sang or *where* she sang—it was *when* she sang.

She sang in her sleep, and she only slept at nighttime because she was

too busy eating things in the daytime to sing then. And so she only sang at
night when everyone else was asleep.

And what did she sing? It's almost too strange to tell.

Every night she dreamed that the sky caught on fire. In her dream the
sky filled with fiery lights of reds, oranges, yellows, and greens.

And she dreamed that the sky sang! Yes, sang! And Na-Na loved the fires
and the singing so much that she joined in, too.

"Naa-naa-naa-naa," she would sing.

"Naa-naa-naa." She thought she made beautiful music, but it was tune-
less, toneless, terrible, and *very* loud. And she did it every night.

Nothing Dad or the children could do would make Na-Na stop once she
started. Dad kept a supply of stones and bones on his window ledge to throw
at her in the night, but even when the stones hit her she didn't notice, and
even when he shouted at her she wouldn't stop.

Guests in the hotel did not like being waked up by Na-Na's singing,
and they complained to Dad. Some of them left the hotel. There were lots
of visitors coming to town soon, and Dad was afraid that people would not
want to come to the hotel to stay.

At last, one night, in a very bad temper, Dad stomped through the house
and stamped out into the backyard. He grabbed Na-Na's collar and dragged her
roughly into the shed. He was very cross. He threw her into a corner full of
junk. He hooked a rusty chain to her collar and tied her to a post.

"There," he shouted. "You're off to the butcher tomorrow, you pest.
You're not good for anything but chops and sausages. And then a man
might get some peace at night and run his business properly."

He slammed the door shut and said bad words all the way back to bed. Poor Na-Na.

She stood there in the shed, in the dark, bruised and breathless, with big goaty tears spilling out of her violet eyes. A minute ago she had been singing with the sky music, and now she knew she would never sing again.

Poor Na-Na.

She stood there in the dark, shivering and shaking, dozing off now and then, but not really sleeping. The first sound to say it was morning was the shed door scraping open. There he stood: the butcher, with blood on his hands and knives in his belt.

Na-Na shut her eyes and waited. She knew about butchers. Some of her uncles had been taken to the butcher, and she had never seen them again.

Dad and the butcher began to poke Na-Na and feel her all over.

"There's not much meat on her," said the butcher. "I could only give you a few dollars. The only good thing about her is her wool. Why don't you keep her yourselves, just for the wool?"

"Because she's too noisy," Dad snapped. "I've got other goats for wool."

"All right! All right! But I won't need her until tomorrow. The town will be full of visitors tomorrow, and when they're hungry, they'll eat anything. I'll come for her in the morning."

"Pick her up anytime," said Dad.

Na-Na tried to think of other things all day. The thought of being eaten was sickening. She felt so sick that she couldn't eat anything herself. She wouldn't touch the grass or the water that the children brought her, and when they offered her a whole geranium plant to herself, she just hung her head, closed her eyes, and cried.

The only thing she hoped for was to fall asleep at night and dream her wonderful sky dream for the last time.

And that's what happened.

The children patted her good night.

Darkness fell.

The shed fell quiet.

And Na-Na fell asleep.

She didn't hear the shed door open early in the evening.

She didn't hear the donkey walk in.

She didn't hear the man and the lady talking quietly.

She didn't hear the man rustling straw and spreading out blankets to make a bed.

She didn't notice when they began to move about and talk later in the night.

But she did hear the sky music.

And she did see the sky catch on fire.

And what a sight it was! It was the best she had ever seen it. There were reds and yellows and oranges and greens as usual, but this time there were silvers and golds and purples and whites. There were flashes of light and sparkles of color. There were sparks like rainbows, and a brilliant burning bright star in the center of it all. It seemed so real, she wondered if it were really a dream at all.

And the sky music was so loud and so beautiful that Na-Na joined in straightaway and sang at the top of her voice.

"Naa-naa-naa-naa," she sang. "Naa-naa-naa."

She was so busy with singing and loving the sky music that she didn't notice the kind brown hands unhook her chain and lead her out of the corner. Half waking and half sleeping, she began to realize that her dream was not a dream at all. She could see through the cracks in the roof, and there was *real* sky music, and there were *real* fiery lights in the sky. And right in front of her was a gracious lady and, in her lap, a new human baby.

Na-Na was only a goat, but she knew something important had happened. Deep in her heart she knew that all the sky music that had ever been and would ever be was for this baby.

The gracious lady reached out and touched Na-Na's warm ears and spoke to her.

"Little goat, thank you for singing your lovely song for my baby boy. Your singing made him happy."

It seemed to Na-Na that all the kindness in the world was in the lady's voice and in the baby's face.

"I'm so glad you're here," she said, "because your people have given their lives for my people's sins for such a long time. Now my baby has come into the world to take my people's sins away forever. Your people will never again suffer for our sins, and my people need not be afraid to die."

Because Na-Na was only a goat, she didn't really understand, but just hearing the words made her feel better. Strangely, she no longer felt afraid of the butcher. She gave out a little song of happiness.

"Naa-naa-naa," she sang.

The lady smiled.

Na-Na lay down and rested her head in the lady's lap. She fell asleep to the suckling sounds of the baby taking milk from his mother.

The first sound to say it was morning was the shed door scraping open. And there he stood: the butcher, with blood on his hands and knives in his belt.

This time Na-Na wasn't afraid.

Na-Na waited by the lady's side while the man with the kind hands spoke to the butcher and to Dad. Suddenly the butcher marched away crossly, and the man with the kind hands gave Dad some money.

He had paid the money to save Na-Na's life.

"We couldn't let that pretty face go off to the butcher shop, now could we, little goat?" the man said to Na-Na.

"You're ours now. You can be the baby boy's pet. He likes you. And I think you know who he is, don't you?"

Na-Na was so happy she started to eat the man's shoe, and the lady laughed.

After a few days the little family moved away and took Na-Na with them.

She grew up as the baby boy grew up.

She still ate everything and sang every night.

She had kids of her own as the years went by, and they, too, became the boy's pets.

He learned to walk holding Na-Na's collar.

He learned to run chasing Na-Na.

He learned to play as Na-Na butted him gently with her head.

The man with the kind hands milked Na-Na, and the boy grew strong from drinking her milk.

The beautiful lady clipped the fine wool from Na-Na's coat every year and knitted warm boots and gloves and coats as the boy grew bigger.

Each year she would unravel the garments and knit or weave something for the next size, always adding fine new wool from Na-Na's coat.

When the boy was nearly a man and Na-Na had lived a very rich and contented life, she died. From her last clip of wool and from the fine wool of the past years, the gracious lady wove the young man a lovely long coat.

He wore it everywhere. And Na-Na would have been very proud of him. The boy turned into a man—a good man who pleased God and loved people. When he spoke, they listened. And if they were sick, he touched them and prayed over them—and they got better. He was easy to spot in a crowd. People saw him in the coat and ran up to him to listen to his wise words and loving sayings.

Later in his life, bad men came with blood on their hands and knives in their belts—and they killed him.

He died, just as the gracious lady had said, so that you and I need never be afraid to die and so that our sins would be forgiven.

And at the place where he died, the bad men gambled and squabbled about who should steal his lovely long coat, the coat made from Na-Na's fine wool.

"I knew you before I formed you in your mother's womb.
Before you were born I set you apart."
JEREMIAH 1:5, NLT

Frederic Loomis

THE TINY FOOT

◆

"Doctor, just a moment, please, before you go into the delivery room."

The man was about thirty-five, well-dressed and intelligent, an executive of a large oil company. His first baby was to arrive within the hour. He had spent the preceding hours by his wife's bedside, miserable with the feeling of helplessness and anxiety common to all prospective fathers at such a time, but nevertheless standing by to comfort her by his presence.

"I must tell you one thing before the baby gets here, Doctor," he said. "I want that baby and so does Irene, more than we ever wanted anything else, I think—but *not* if it isn't all right. I want you to promise me right now that if it is defective—and I know you can usually tell—you will not let it live. No one need ever know it, but *it must not live.* I am depending on you."

Few doctors have escaped that problem. I had not been in California long before I encountered it there, just as I had encountered it elsewhere. Fortunately, it is a problem that usually solves itself. Babies that are defective, either mentally or physically, after all are infrequent. Yet the possibility of having one hounds almost every waiting mother. Her first question on opening her eyes after a baby is born is always either "What is it?" or "Is it all right?" Whichever question comes first, the other invariably follows, and the one as to its condition is always the more important.

However they may feel about it in individual instances, doctors rightly resent and resist the rather persistent effort to make them the judges of life and death. Our load of responsibility is enough without that. "Judgment is difficult," Hippocrates said, "when the preservation of life is the only question." If the added burden of deciding whether or not life *should* be preserved were placed upon us, it would be entirely too much. Moreover, the entire morale of medicine would be immediately threatened or destroyed.

Two years after I came to California, there came to my office one day a fragile young woman, expecting her first baby. Her history was not good from an emotional standpoint, though she came from a fine family.

I built her up as well as I could and found her increasingly wholesome and interesting as time went on, partly because of the effort she was making to be calm and patient and to keep her emotional and nervous reactions under control.

One month before her baby was due, her routine examination showed that her baby was in a breech position. As a rule, the baby's head is in the lower part of the uterus for months before delivery, not because it is heavier and "sinks" in the surrounding fluid, but simply because it fits more comfortably in that position. There is no routine spontaneous "turning" of all babies at the seventh or eighth month, as is so generally supposed, but the occasional baby found in a breech position in the last month not infrequently changes to the normal vertex position with the head down by the time it is ready to be born, so that only about one baby in twenty-five is born in the breech position.

This is fortunate, as the death rate of breech babies is comparatively high because of the difficulty in delivering the after-coming head, and the imperative need of delivering it rather quickly after the body is born. At that moment the cord becomes compressed between the baby's hard little head and the mother's bony pelvis. When no oxygen reaches the baby's bloodstream, it inevitably dies in a few short minutes. Everyone in the delivery room is tense, except the mother herself, in a breech delivery, especially if it is a first baby, when the difficulty is greater. The mother is usually quietly asleep or almost so.

The case I was speaking of was a "complete" breech—the baby's legs and feet being folded under it, tailor-fashion—in contrast to the "frank" breech, in which the thighs and legs are folded back on a baby's body like a jackknife, the little rear end backing its way into the world first of all.

The hardest thing for the attending doctor to do with any breech delivery is to keep his hands away from it until the natural forces of expulsion have thoroughly dilated the firm maternal structures that delay its progress. I waited as patiently as I could, sending frequent messages to the excited family in the corridor outside.

At last the time had come, and I gently drew down one little foot. I grasped the other but, for some reason I could not understand, it would not come down beside the first one. I pulled again, gently enough but with a little force, with light pressure on the abdomen from above by my assisting nurse, and the baby's body moved down just enough for me to see that it was a little girl—and then, to my consternation, I saw that the other foot would *never* be beside the first one. The entire thigh from the hip to the knee was missing, and that one foot never could reach below the opposite knee. And a baby girl was to suffer this, a curious defect that I had never seen before, nor have I since!

There followed the hardest struggle I have ever had with myself. I knew what a dreadful effect it would have upon the unstable nervous system of the mother. I felt sure that the family would almost certainly impoverish itself in taking the child to every famous orthopedist in the world whose achievements might offer a ray of hope.

Most of all, I saw this little girl sitting sadly by herself while other girls laughed and danced and ran and played—and then I suddenly realized that there was something that would save every pang but one, and that one thing was in my power.

One breech baby in ten dies in delivery because it is not delivered rapidly enough, and now—if only I did not hurry! If I could slow my hand, if I could make myself delay those few short moments. It would not be an easy delivery, anyway. No one in all this world would ever know. The mother, after the first shock of grief, would probably be glad she had lost a child so sadly handicapped. In a year or two she would try again, and this tragic fate would never be repeated.

"Don't bring this suffering upon them," the small voice within me said. "This baby has never taken a breath—don't let her ever take one. You probably can't get it out in time, anyway. *Don't hurry.* Don't be a fool and bring this terrible thing upon them. Suppose your conscience does hurt a little; can't you stand it better than they can? Maybe your conscience will hurt worse if you *do* get it out in time."

I motioned to the nurse for the warm sterile towel that is always ready for me in a breech delivery to wrap around the baby's body so that the stimulation of the cold air of the outside world may not induce a sudden expansion of the baby's chest, causing the aspiration of fluid or mucus that might bring death.

But this time the towel was only to conceal from the attending nurses that which my eyes alone had seen. With the touch of that pitiful little foot in my hand, a pang of sorrow for the baby's future swept through me, and my decision was made.

I glanced at the clock. Three of the allotted seven or eight minutes had already gone. Every eye in the room was upon me, and I could feel the tension in their eagerness to do instantly what I asked, totally unaware of what I was feeling. I hoped they could not possibly detect the tension of my own struggle at that moment.

These nurses had seen me deliver dozens of breech babies successfully—yes, and they had seen me fail, too. Now they were going to see me fail again. For the first time in my medical life I was deliberately discarding what I had been taught was right for something that I felt sure was better.

I slipped my hand beneath the towel to feel the pulsations of the baby's cord, a certain index of its condition. Two or three minutes more would be enough. So that I might seem to be doing something, I drew the baby down a little lower to "split out" the arms, the usual next step, and as I did so the little pink foot on the good side bobbed out from its protecting towel and pressed firmly against my slowly moving hand, the hand into whose keeping the safety of the mother and the baby had been entrusted. There was a sudden convulsive movement of the baby's body, an actual feeling of strength and life and vigor.

It was too much. I couldn't do it. I delivered the baby with her pitiful little leg. I told the family, and the next day, with a catch in my voice, I told the mother.

Every foreboding came true. The mother was in a hospital for several months. I saw her once or twice, and she looked like a wraith of her former self. I heard of them indirectly from time to time. They had been to Rochester, Minnesota. They had been to Chicago and to Boston. Finally I lost track of them altogether.

As the years went on, I blamed myself bitterly for not having had the strength to yield to my temptation.

Through the many years that I have been here, there has developed in our hospital a pretty custom of staging an elaborate Christmas party each year for the employees, the nurses, and the doctors of the staff.

There is always a beautifully decorated tree on the stage of our little auditorium. The women spend weeks in preparation. We have so many difficult things to do during the year, so much discipline, and so many of the stern realities of life, that we have set aside this one day to touch upon the emotional and spiritual side. It is almost like going to an impressive church service, as each year we dedicate ourselves anew to the year ahead.

This past year the arrangement was somewhat changed. The tree, on one side of the stage, had been sprayed with silver paint and was hung with scores of gleaming silver and tinsel ornaments, without a trace of color anywhere and with no lights hung upon the tree itself. It shone but faintly in the dimly lighted auditorium.

Every doctor of the staff who could possibly be there was in his seat. The first rows were reserved for the nurses, and in a moment the procession entered, each woman in uniform, each one crowned by her nurse's cap, her badge of office. Around their shoulders were their blue Red Cross capes, one end tossed back to show the deep red lining.

We rose as one man to do them honor, and as the last one reached her seat and we settled in our places again, the organ began the opening notes of one of the oldest of our carols.

Slowly down the middle aisle, marching from the back of the auditorium, came twenty other women singing softly, our own nurses, in full uniform, each holding high a lighted candle, while through the auditorium floated the familiar strains of "Silent Night." We were on our feet again instantly. I could have killed anyone who spoke to me then, because I couldn't have answered, and by the time they reached their seats I couldn't see.

And then a great blue floodlight at the back was turned on very slowly, gradually covering the tree with increasing splendor: brighter and brighter, until every ornament was almost a flame. On the opposite side of the stage a curtain was slowly drawn, and we saw three lovely young musicians, all in shimmering white evening gowns. They played very softly in unison with the organ—a harp, a cello, and a violin. I am quite sure I was not the only old sissy there whose eyes were filled with tears.

I have always liked the harp, and I love to watch the grace of a skillful player. I was especially fascinated by this young harpist. She played extraordinarily well, as if she loved it. Her slender fingers flickered across the strings, and as the nurses sang, her face, made beautiful by a mass of auburn hair, was upturned as if the world that moment were a wonderful and holy place.

I waited, when the short program was over, to congratulate the chief nurse on the unusual effects she had arranged. And as I sat alone, there came running down the aisle a woman whom I did not know. She came to me with arms outstretched.

"Oh, you *saw* her," she cried. "You must have recognized your baby. That was my daughter who played the harp—and I saw you watching her. Don't you remember the little girl who was born with only one good leg seventeen years ago? We tried everything else first, but now she has a whole artificial leg on that side—but you would never know it, would you? She can walk, she can swim, and she can almost dance.

"But, best of all, through all those years when she couldn't do those things, she learned to use her hands so wonderfully. She is going to be one of the world's great harpists. She enters the university this year at seventeen. She is my whole life, and now she is so happy. . . . And here she is!"

As we spoke, this sweet young girl had quietly approached us, her eyes glowing, and now she stood beside me.

"This is your first doctor, my dear—our doctor," her mother said. Her voice trembled. I could see her literally swept back, as I was, through all the years of heartache to the day when I told her what she had to face. "He was the first one to tell me about you. He brought you to me."

Impulsively I took the child in my arms. Across her warm young shoulder I saw the creeping clock of the delivery room of seventeen years before. I lived again those awful moments when her life was in my hand, when I had decided on deliberate infanticide.

I held her away from me and looked at her.

"You never will know, my dear," I said, "you never will know, nor will anyone else in all the world, just what tonight has meant to me. Go back to your harp for a moment, please—and play `Silent Night' for me alone. I have a load on my shoulders that no one has ever seen, a load that only you can take away."

Her mother sat beside me and quietly took my hand as her daughter played. Perhaps she knew what was in my mind. And as the last strains of "Silent Night, Holy Night" faded again, I think I found the answer, and the comfort, I had waited for for so long.

"You are not your own; you were bought at a price.
Therefore honor God with your body."
1 CORINTHIANS 6:19-20, NIV

Yolanda Soo

THE COAL ORPHAN

Once upon a time in a big, big city there was a little five-and-dime. But this was a special five-and-dime because it was owned by a special man named Mr. Hesed. Most people in the city had never discovered the store, but those who had did not mind going out of their way to visit the special place, even though it was on the very edge of the city.

The best way to describe Mr. Hesed would be to say that he was like a Jewish Santa Claus. He was friendly, fair, and gentle. It was easy to be merry in his presence because his merriment was a contagious thing. Kindness exuded from him in a way that made the regular city folk wonder if it hadn't all been drained from the city and poured into this one man.

Yet Mr. H., as they called him, was no pushover. He was not old, but he was definitely not young. No one could tell his age, and he never told. Even more important than his age was his strength. When he saw some injustice, whether it be a shoplifter in his own store or some rough, mean people harassing the helpless, his softness took on a surprising sternness. His sudden, gruff authority always induced the offenders to stop, sending some scurrying away in shame. His strength was not physical but something beyond muscle—partly emotional, partly psychological. It seemed to sink into the depths of the soul.

The store itself also had a mythical air about it. No Muzak played in it, yet there was no more calming, soothing place in all of the city. That's why the city people who knew about it liked it so much. It was more relaxing than their expensive trips to the Bahamas and more restorative than a week on the ski slopes of Switzerland. People came more to visit the store—like they would a museum. Purchasing items almost seemed a superfluous act in Mr. H.'s store. And the children—there were *always* children in the store. Mr. H. could often be seen chatting with them and enjoying their company as much as he did any adult's. He loved the children and they loved him. They loved him not only because he was generous with his candy jars but because they felt in their bones how much he loved them. Mr. H. loved everybody.

There was one little girl, an orphan, who came to see Mr. H. every day. She would come running in and call for him, to say hello and to give him many hugs. He loved all the children the same, even the ones who tried to steal from him (and who always got caught). But he took special care of this little girl and called her "Daughter," for she had no mother or father to look after her. She lived on the streets and had to beg and do odd jobs for a living. But because she was still a child, when she ran into Mr. H.'s store, her eyes would be shining with hope, and the troubles of her world fell away in the joy of his presence.

One day, after she had run in for her daily hug, she disappeared into the aisles as he rang up some customers and chatted with them. When they had left, he called out for her, "Daughter, where are you?"

"Over here," she answered. "Come here and see!"

When he found her, she was the most comical sight. She was kneeling on the floor by the coal barrel and had picked up some lumps in her hands. She was caressing them, stroking them gently as she held them to her cheek, her eyes closed in enraptured bliss. She was covered from head to toe with streaks of coal.

"Aren't they glorious? They feel so soft, and I've seen what they do— they make fire. Fire that burns for a long, long time. Have you ever seen anything so black and beautiful? And the fire—it's such a *warm* fire. Absolutely perfect." For, living on the streets, she had seen homeless people who were lucky enough to have a few lumps of coal to burn during the cold, cold nights in the city. She knew those fires were brighter and hotter than all the others she had built with cardboard or wood.

"How much are they, Mr. H.?" she asked.

He replied sadly, "Twenty cents a lump." Times were hard, and the price of coal was high. He knew that she'd never be able to scrape the pennies together, let alone find people who could afford to give them up.

The little orphan girl's eyes brightened. "I'll get it! I'll get some money, I will!" And she clutched a lump of coal to her already-darkened dress and nuzzled it with her cheek.

"Yes, my daughter, I'm sure you will," he said comfortingly. He tousled her coal-streaked hair, gave her a hug, and said, "But first, you must have a piece of candy." He took her hand and led her to the front of the store, where he pulled out the brightest lollipop from his candy shelf and gave it to her.

"Thanks, Mr. H.," she said. "I'll be back in no time to get me my coal." She quickly kissed him on the cheek and skipped out the door with her lollipop.

Every day she came in to say hello to Mr. H. and then ran over to the coal barrel for a few minutes to look at it and stroke it longingly. Sometimes she would bring her friends in to show them her treasured coal. "Isn't it beautiful?" she would say. Some nodded in agreement; some just laughed at her. But all quickly lost interest and began to wander the store in search of more entertaining finds, leaving her to gaze and finger the much-desired coal.

Out on the street every day, she worked hard to stay alive and find the twenty extra pennies besides. She stood on street corners, asking for spare pennies. But almost everyone who saw her coal-streaked face and hands turned away, saying to themselves, "What a dirty little orphan! The city should really do *something* about keeping them out of sight. What an embarrassment!" She tried to get odd jobs, but the people who needed workers hired the older, stronger children. She was left with the smallest, most menial jobs that paid her only a couple of pennies.

Finally one day, after many, many weeks, the little orphan girl ran into the five-and-dime, crying out to Mr. H., "I got it! I got it! It took forever, and I never thought I'd get it, but I did. Can you see? Can you believe it? I got it! I finally got it!" Ecstatically, she reached down into an old sock she carried and plunked the twenty pennies down on the counter.

He smiled broadly. "And so you have, Daughter." He walked over to the coal barrel and picked out the biggest piece of coal she had ever seen, almost the size of his fist! Her eyes were round with excitement as he handed it to her.

"Now wait, my child. I have a special gift I want to give you."

"But this is all I ever wanted—my own piece of coal! And now I have it!" She was overjoyed at her new acquisition.

"I know, but I know you'll like this. It's even better than all the coal in the barrel."

Her eyes widened. "*All* the coal in the barrel?" she wondered. "What is it?"

"Do you want it?" She nodded eagerly. He said, "First, you must let me have the coal back." Her eyes darkened a little and her little smooth, coal-dusted brow crinkled. She looked puzzled first, then angry.

"The coal? But it's mine! I bought it with my own money! How could I ever give it back? It belongs to me!" she wailed.

"Yes, Daughter. It does belong to you. But I cannot give you the gift until you can give me what is yours."

"But how is that a gift?" she argued.

"You must see before you will understand," he gently replied.

As she hesitated and struggled in her heart, a tear ran down her face, washing a narrow trail of ivory skin clean from the thin layer of coal.

He assured her, "You know I'd never trick or rob you, don't you? You do believe that, don't you?" She nodded. He waited and said no more.

After what seemed an eternity, she gingerly placed the lump of coal on the counter between them. Mr. H. picked it up and began to squeeze it between his hands. She cried out in panic, "Wait! What are you doing to my coal?"

"Daughter," he said calmly, "do you want my gift? Do you trust me that it will be as I said—greater than all the coal in the barrel?" She hesitated, sighed, and then nodded.

He began squeezing again. He squeezed the coal harder and harder until it seemed as though his hands were burning red at times. It tore at the little orphan girl's heart to watch her beloved Mr. H. destroying her precious coal right there before her own eyes.

Finally, he stopped squeezing. His muscles relaxed, and he parted the front of his clasped hands to blow a little puff of air into them. Slowly, he held his hands in front of the little girl, who, by this time, was mournfully sniffling. She smelled a strange, burning smell. Then he unclenched his leathery hands. The orphan girl rubbed the tears from her eyes. There, in his hands, lay the most exquisite, brilliant, fiery clear creation she had ever seen in her life. She didn't know what it was. It looked like glass; but unlike glass, color and fire burned and leapt inside it. She reached out slowly to touch it but stopped her hand in midair, afraid that it might burn her.

"Go ahead, touch it. It's yours, child. It is called a *diamond.*" She took it, stunned silent, as Mr. H. watched her carefully. Cautiously, she touched it, then quickly pulled her hand away. When it did not burn her, she let her fingers run over the smooth facets. Mr. H. offered it to her and she took it, cradling the cool fire in her hands. She had to squint as she lifted it to the light and examined the daggers of colored fire dancing inside it. It burned more brightly than a thousand fires of coal.

She lowered the diamond and looked at Mr. H. "Th-th-thank you," she finally managed to stutter. "Thank you so much, Mr. H.!"

He said, "You are welcome. This diamond will buy you all the warm shelter, food, and clothes you need, and plenty besides. You will be able to have all the fires you want." He lovingly stroked her coal- and-tear-stained face.

All of a sudden, she noticed his hands. There in the middle of his palms were two small, red, round welts. It looked as if two red-hot irons had pierced the rough softness of his palms. She gasped. "Mr. H.! What are these? What happened to your poor hands?"

He answered, "These? These are the price I paid to buy you your gift."

She cried, "Thank you, thank you, thank you! I don't deserve this!" She flung her arms around his neck and covered his scarred hands with coal kisses. "I love you, Mr. H. How will I ever repay you?"

"No, my child," he said, "you do not have to repay me—because you never could. Remember, it is a gift." She nodded and understood.

"Love is patient, love is kind. . . . It always protects, always trusts,
always hopes, always perseveres. Love never fails."
1 CORINTHIANS 13:4, 7-8, NIV

Gilbert Morris

AN AARDVARK FOR CASSANDRA

"Ah—sir, may I help you?"

Caleb Roberts was bent over double, practically submerged in a huge circular box filled with stuffed toys. He surfaced, holding something that vaguely resembled a deformed buffalo. With a sigh he tossed the toy back, then turned to face the young woman who stood watching him curiously. "I'm looking for a purple aardvark," he muttered.

"A purple what?"

"An aardvark—small sort of an anteater. I don't suppose you've got one?"

The clerk answered, "We have some nice stuffed dogs and some darling bears."

"No, it has to be an aardvark, and it has to be purple."

"I don't think we have anything like that." The clerk stared at him with a slightly puzzled expression. "We've met, haven't we? You look so familiar."

Caleb Roberts was accustomed to this. He was tall and lanky and bore a remarkable resemblance to a youthful Jimmy Stewart. So many people had seen the actor in *It's a Wonderful Life* that they thought they recognized Caleb. He had the same awkward movements and boyish grin. "No, I don't think so," he said at once. "You see, my little girl's favorite toy is—well, was, a stuffed aardvark." He hesitated, and the clerk noted that his eyes filled with pain. "It was a gift from her mother—and after her mother died, somehow the aard-vark got lost. I've got to get her one for Christmas."

"Have you tried Wal-Mart?"

"Miss, I've tried *everyplace!*" A note of desperation ran through Caleb's voice. He nodded, saying, "Well, thanks anyway."

"I hope you find one," the clerk called after him. "You've got plenty of time until Christmas. It's only September."

Caleb found his car and drove away, feeling very tired. *I'm just not going to find one,* he thought wearily. *Cassandra will just have to settle for something else.* The thought depressed him, and he was unable to shake off the heaviness that clung to him. Since his wife, Cathy, had died, he'd tried to be father and mother to his five-year-old daughter. Being a freelance writer, he'd been able to be with her constantly, but he'd been worried about her. She had been very dependent on Cathy, and he had learned the bitter lesson that no man can replace a mother to a small girl.

By the time he reached his house, a small Cape Cod model, he had regretfully given up on the aardvark. *Maybe it wouldn't be good for her to have it, anyway,* he thought as he stepped inside. *It might remind her of her mother too much.* "Hello—I'm home," he called out.

"Daddy!" Cassandra rushed from the living room and threw herself at the tall man. When he grabbed her and lifted her for a hug, she clung to him. "I'm going to help you cook supper—you promised!"

"Why, I guess I did." He put her down and, as always, was slightly shocked by the resemblance she bore to her mother—same light blonde hair and dark blue eyes. Caleb felt a stab of loss but quickly put it away—a skill he'd had to learn over the past year and a half. The baby-sitter came into the hall, putting on her coat. "Was she a handful, Ginger?"

"Of course! Isn't she always?" Ginger took the bills that Caleb handed her and left, saying, "I'll see you tomorrow, Mr. Roberts. Bye, Cassandra."

Cassandra tugged impatiently at his hand, urging, "Come on, Daddy! Let's make the pancakes!" She loved to help him, and since pancakes were what he made best, she'd learned how to do some of the simpler things. For the next half hour she chattered as Caleb let her stir the mix and then pour the batter onto the griddle. "Look—this big one is for you—and this little one is for me," she said, nodding seriously.

After setting the table, they sat down. Caleb asked a brief blessing, then they ate the pancakes and turkey bacon. Afterward, as they washed the dishes, Caleb said, "Cassandra, I've got to go through my mail. Why don't you watch television until I get through with it?"

"And then will you read to me?"

"Sure I will!" As Cassandra plopped down in her blue beanbag to watch *Sesame Street*, Caleb sat down at his desk and sorted out his mail. He tossed the bills into one stack, the rejections from publishers into another, then dropped the junk mail into the wastebasket without opening it. The letters he took more time with. One he opened quickly—from the mission board. He was nervous as he tore it open, but when he read the first line, disappointment washed across his face. "We understand your desire to serve in Africa, but it is not our policy to send single men as missionaries. Your daughter is very young, and this presents an even greater problem."

Caleb slowly replaced the letter in the envelope and then slid it into a pigeonhole in the desk. He had tried every mission organization he knew of—but the answer was always the same. He mechanically opened and read the rest of his mail.

The last letter had a Savannah, Georgia, postmark and was addressed in a hand he'd never seen—a woman's hand, he thought. Opening it, he scanned the first line: "Your article in the June issue of *Christian Views* was very fine." The article had been entitled, "Can a Single Man Raise a Daughter?" and had traced the problems that had arisen in his struggle to be both father and mother to his five-year-old daughter. The response to the piece had been good, but Caleb had been shocked to discover how many men were having the same struggle. The letter was brief but encouraging. "I have never been married and have not had to face the problems you face. I have been soundly jilted by my fiancé, but my loss is not like yours. We do, however, have one thing in common—I also long to be a missionary to Africa, but God has not opened up a way for me. I will pray for you and your daughter."

The letter was signed Susan Blakely, and something about it intrigued Caleb. He finally decided it was the fact that the woman could admit to having been jilted with such a lack of bitterness. *Most women would be pretty angry, I'd think—too bitter to mention it to a stranger.* He turned his Mac on and answered the letter at once, giving a warm thanks and closing by saying, "Let's pray for one another. Cassandra and I certainly need help! And I will ask the Lord to open up a door for you to go to Africa."

Later that night he mentioned the letter to Cassandra. She demanded to see it, and when he read it to her, she said, "I want to write her a letter, Daddy." She ran to her room, and soon Caleb heard her voice, clear and precise, as she spoke into a microphone.

Cassandra's favorite toy was the tape recorder he'd given her for her birthday. She played with it constantly, singing and acting out little dramas she made up. She also recorded music from the radio and sent "letters" to people, some of them lasting over an hour. Caleb had encouraged her, buying tapes by the dozen and small mailing envelopes. He'd made stickers for those she wrote, mostly her cousins and her aunts, and the postman was kept busy with tapes. Finally she came back with the tape in the envelope, saying, "Will you mail this to Miss Susan for me, Daddy?"

"Sure, sweetheart. Now—time for bed."

When he tucked her in, he sat down and took her hand. "What will we ask Jesus for tonight?"

"For Miss Susan to go to Africa—and for Arkie." This was her name for the stuffed aardvark, and she held his hand waiting for him to pray.

"Honey," he said slowly, "maybe it'll be better if we don't ask for Arkie. How about another toy—like a nice teddy bear?"

"No, I want Arkie!"

I think it'll be easier to get Susan Blakely to Africa than to get that aardvark! Caleb thought, but surrendered and asked for both. As he left the room he muttered, "I wonder how much it would cost to get one of those stuffed toys *made?*"

The great aardvark search continued relentlessly, and tapes traveled back and forth between Cassandra and Susan. In the first week of October Caleb flew to Chicago to gather material for a story. He found himself spending more energy searching for Arkie the Second than in working—all to no avail. Later in the month he made a shorter journey, this time to Denver for a national meeting featuring missionaries from his denomination. The snowy mountain-tops that ringed the city gave him pleasure, but he got no encouragement from the director of missions.

"Caleb, you'd make a fine missionary," Dr. Kenneth Amis told him over coffee after one of the conferences. "I have no doubt of the call of God on your life, and we have need of a man with your qualifications in South Africa. But—"

"But I've got a five-year-old daughter and no wife," Caleb finished for the director. "I guess that's not going to change, Dr. Amis."

Caleb spent the rest of his stay visiting stores. He even found his way to small, dingy shops in the less affluent part of Denver in the hope of finding a used aardvark. He found nothing, and when he got back to Seattle, he found that Cassandra had received another tape from Susan.

"When are you going to let me hear some of your letters from Susan?" he asked. Cassandra never let him hear the messages she sent to Susan nor the replies she received regularly. Glancing at the neat row of tapes (copies of her letters to Susan and the replies) she kept in a wooden box with a picture of a black-and-white cat on the front, he felt a little peeved. "What in the world do you two say to each other? I'd like to hear them."

"No, Daddy. You have your letters from Susan, and I have mine." A dimple popped into her cheek as she smiled. "She's my secret friend. It wouldn't be right for you to listen."

Caleb shifted uneasily, for the correspondence between Susan Blakely and Cassandra had become tremendously important to his daughter. When a tape arrived, Cassandra retired at once to her room and played the tape over and over. When Caleb came home, he very often found her playing old tapes from Susan.

And Susan's name was frequently heard, for Cassandra had fallen into the habit of quoting her. "Susan says that game shows are silly and a waste of time," she announced one afternoon after receiving a new message. "So I'm not going to watch them anymore."

Caleb felt a stab of some emotion that was suspiciously like jealousy. He said shortly, "I've told you that before. You never paid any attention to *me*." At once he felt foolish and said quickly, "Susan's right. I'm glad she was able to help you." He smiled and gave her a kiss. "She gives me some good advice sometimes, too. Guess I'll see if she has any good stuff for me."

Susan always included a note for Caleb along with the tape for Cassandra. At first they had been brief, cheerful notes, sometimes with a Scripture verse done in beautiful calligraphy, sometimes with an amusing account of something that had happened to her. But somehow the notes had gotten longer. And not only Susan's letters, but his replies. They were both excellent letter writers, and once Susan had written, "A good, warm letter that reaches out from one person and touches the life and heart of another—well, it's almost an endangered species!"

Caleb opened her letter eagerly, murmuring, "I'm getting to be as greedy for Susan's letters as Cassandra is for her tapes." He paused abruptly, the idea causing his brow to knit in a puzzled fashion. He had always been somewhat shy, but since the death of his wife, he had become withdrawn. He'd justified it by the thought that it was natural for anyone who had lost such a companion to have that reaction. And besides, he had to spend most of his time with Cassandra, didn't he?

But as he slowly laid the letter flat on the desk, he thought, *I've gotten closer to this woman I've never seen than I have to anyone else since Cathy died.* Somehow the sudden realization came as a shock, and he sat there staring at the letter. *Well, I can say things on paper I can't say out loud, and I don't really have anyone to say them to anyway.* He thought back over the correspondence with Susan and again was a little disturbed to realize how he'd opened his heart to her, telling her some of the intimate things—such as how desperately he missed his wife and how inadequate he felt with Cassandra at times.

He glanced up at the telephone, the desire to call her rising in him. But he knew from her letters that she was at work, and he began to read the letter, which after a brief greeting, plunged ahead:

I've never told you, Caleb, how I got jilted. It's not a very dramatic story. (They'll never turn it into a made-for-TV movie!) I met a young man in college, and we both felt called to go to the mission field. When graduation came, I thought life was about to begin. We were going to get married, then go to mission school, and then off to the wilds of Africa.

But instead of a wedding, I got a letter. Charles had decided that he wasn't really called to missions. He told me he knew I'd never give up on going, so he was asking for release from our engagement. I gave it, of course. Oh, it was a very gentle sort of jilting, Caleb, but I must admit it left a big hole in my life. I haven't gotten my balance back yet, but God knows what tomorrow holds—and what I do now is wait until I get my marching orders. . . .

Caleb read the long letter twice, and all evening he was quiet and thoughtful. Finally after he put Cassandra to bed, he walked slowly to his desk. Picking up his address book, he opened to the *B* page and stared at the number at the bottom. For a full five minutes he sat there, then deliberately picked up the receiver and dialed the number. The tone sounded very loud, and when it rang three times he started to hang up.

"Hello? This is Susan." The voice was warm and rich—somehow just as he'd hoped.

Caleb licked his lips, then said, "Hello, Susan. This . . . is Caleb Roberts. . . ."

When Caleb opened his telephone bill for November, he stared at the total with blank astonishment. But then he glanced at the record of long-distance calls—almost all to Savannah, and nodded. "Never thought I'd be a telephone person," he said wryly. He'd always disliked telephones, keeping his conversations to the bare minimum. But for the past weeks he'd discovered a new joy in getting to know someone in that fashion.

Most of the calls took place after Cassandra had gone to bed. At first they had been brief, but soon an hour seemed all too short for all he wanted to say. He discovered that Susan had a delightful sense of humor, and at times he had to stuff his fist in his mouth to stifle his laughter. And he also discovered that he could tell Susan those things he could never speak of to anyone—except to Cathy.

As Christmas approached, he found himself talking over his plans for Cassandra, including his failure to find what his daughter really wanted—the stuffed purple aardvark.

Finally he told her, "Susan, I can talk to you about things. It's—it's made a big difference to me. And your tapes to Cassandra—why, she *lives* for those things! What in the world do you two talk about?"

"Oh, just girl stuff, Caleb," was all she would say.

Then in the middle of December everything stopped abruptly. No letters and no tapes from Susan! And when Caleb called to find out why she hadn't written, she said, "Caleb, I need a little time alone. Let me call you when I—when I feel more like talking."

Caleb heard the uncertain tone of Susan's voice, but he could only say, "I hope nothing's wrong. Please call me as soon as you feel you can."

Three days crawled by with no call from Susan. Caleb wanted desperately to call but felt he could not. They were the loneliest three days he could remember. Night after night he sat, rereading her letters and thinking of how this woman he'd never seen had come to bring such happiness to his life.

He lost his appetite and became so quiet that Cassandra asked, "Daddy, why don't you talk more?" He tried to be more lively, but it was hard work. He managed to keep up a front during his time with Cassandra, but at night he tossed and turned, thinking of Susan. He found himself praying for her fervently, convinced that she was in some sort of trouble. And as he did, he discovered that what he felt for her was more than he had known.

"God, what's wrong with me?" he agonized at two o'clock one morning. He'd wrestled with the problem until finally he'd gotten up and was pacing the floor. But God said not a word, and in despair Caleb went back to bed. Finally as the sun rose, he drifted off to sleep, but as he did, a startling thought rose from somewhere deep inside. He opened his eyes with a start and asked aloud, "I can't be in love with a woman I've never seen, can I, Lord?"

For the next two days Caleb sought God as he never had in his life. He hired Ginger to sit with Cassandra while he took long walks. Mount Rainier lifted its majestic head, dominating the city, but he paid no attention. Finally one gray, drizzly morning he was walking along the Sound, weary and spiritually numb. The sea whispered some sort of sad message, great gray waves looking over others coming in. The raucous cries of the gulls came to him, but he was too tired to pay attention to the sea or the gulls. He turned and made his way home, and after Ginger left, he sat down and stared at the carpet, as tired and confused as he'd ever been in his life.

"Daddy?" Cassandra came to sit beside him. She had a tape in her hand and a troubled expression in her blue eyes. "I did something bad, maybe." Tears appeared in her eyes, and he took her into his lap. "Daddy, listen to the tape—the last one I sent Susan. It made her mad, I think." The tears trickled down her smooth cheeks, and she began to sob. "I'm sorry, Daddy—but I wanted . . . "

Caleb was mystified. He held her close, saying, "I don't think you'd make Susan mad, no matter what you said."

"She never wrote after I sent it!"

A sense of apprehension came to Caleb. "All right, sweetheart, let's listen to it." He rose, and the two went into the bedroom. Cassandra put the tape into her tape recorder and pushed the play button. Cassandra's voice seemed to fill the room, and Caleb heard the grief in her tone as she said, "Susan, I miss my mother so much! I get so lonesome sometimes—and I cry when Daddy's not here." Caleb put his arm around Cassandra, the words cutting him like a razor inside. For a long time the voice went on, and then he heard her say, "Susan, why don't you be my mother? You and Daddy can get married, and I can be your little girl."

"You see, Daddy," Cassandra whispered. "That's why she won't write anymore."

Caleb tried to comfort the weeping child, but the words had come like a—well, like a *revelation* to him. He waited until Cassandra went to bed, then moved to the telephone. He dialed the number, and when Susan answered cautiously, he said, "Susan, Cassandra just played the last tape she sent."

Susan was very quiet, then said, "I've been very upset, Caleb. She's a very lonely little girl."

Caleb took a deep breath, then said, "Susan, I've got to talk to you. Will you listen?" He waited until she said, "Yes, Caleb," then he began to speak. The call was a long one—over an hour. Caleb felt awkward and uncertain. He spoke of his loneliness and his need for a companion. He spoke of Africa and their common dream to serve God in that place. For a long time he talked about Cassandra.

Finally Susan asked, "Do you love me, Caleb?"

Caleb paused for only one brief moment, then said, "Yes, I do, Susan. I've never seen you, but I love you. I want you to marry me."

The silence lasted so long that Caleb wondered if they'd been disconnected. Then Susan said, "I'll pray about it, Caleb. I've lost something once. I can't go through that again." There was a different tone then, and she said, "You'd marry a woman you've never seen?" When he assured her again that he would, she said, "I'll call you when I'm sure. Good-bye, Caleb."

The next few days were the hardest in Caleb's life. All the sounds and sights of Christmas meant nothing to him. He lived for the sound of the phone or for the letter that might come.

Finally on December twentieth the phone rang. Caleb leaped to pick up the phone, and when Susan's voice came to him, he gripped the phone so hard his fingers ached. She said, "Caleb, I'm coming to Seattle. I'll be on Delta Flight 1007 on Christmas Eve, if you want me to." She waited until Caleb assured her that he did, then said quietly, "I'm not making any promises. We have to be very sure about this, Caleb."

"Yes, we do." A thought came to him. "How will I know you?"

"I'll be wearing a red rose."

That night when Caleb tucked Cassandra into bed, he hesitated then asked, "Cassandra, how would you like a very unusual Christmas present?"

"You mean a new purple Arkie?"

"No, I don't think there are any more of those." He hesitated, then whispered, "How would you like a new mother?"

"Oh, Daddy, I've been asking Jesus to let Susan be my mother!" She threw her arms around his neck and held him tightly. "It's all I want for Christmas!"

"Come on, Daddy," Cassandra called out impatiently. She seized his hand and pulled him down the walk toward the car. Caleb unlocked the door, and after getting Cassandra installed in her seat belt, he got into the car and started the engine, saying, "Well, here we go."

"What time is it, Daddy? We won't be late for Susan's plane, will we?"

"Her plane comes in at eight-fifteen, Cassandra. It's only seven o'clock now." He glanced toward her, and as they made their way to the airport, he listened as she chattered excitedly.

I've never seen her so excited, he thought. *She hasn't slept much since I told her about Susan.* He swerved to avoid a Jeep all decked out with holly and bearing a huge papier-mâché reindeer head for a hood ornament. *She's bound to be disappointed—nobody could be as perfect as she expects Susan to be.*

"Cassandra, you know Susan is coming just for a visit. I mean, we'll all have to decide about—about—"

"About if you and Susan get married? Oh, Daddy, I've already decided. It's going to be so nice having a mother again!"

Caleb opened his mouth to warn Cassandra but then closed it. He'd been very excited when Susan had volunteered to come, but as the time had drawn closer, doubt had begun to eat at him.

The difficulty was that he'd had plenty of time to get to know his first wife. They'd been high school sweethearts and had attended the same college. He'd known all about Cathy's family, her hobbies, all her friends—everything! Now as they moved through the myriads of swirling flakes, he realized how little he knew about Susan. She'd told him about her family, of course, and they sounded very nice—but that wasn't the same as knowing them.

And he had been disappointed that she had never offered to send a picture of herself. More than once he'd hinted that it might be nice to exchange snapshots, but she'd said merely, "Oh, I don't take a good picture, Caleb."

Now as they drew near to the terminal, Caleb wondered—not for the first time—if physical appearance didn't make some difference. He was honest enough to admit that he was not handsome. He also had to admit that Cathy had been a very attractive woman and that had been part of the reason he'd been drawn to her. Stealing a glance at Cassandra, who was smiling as she talked about the Christmas lights, Caleb was reminded by the child's smooth features how pretty his wife had been.

Somehow they'd never talked about their appearance, and it struck Caleb now that there might be a reason for Susan's reticence. Even as he pulled into the parking area of the terminal, the thought came to him that Susan might be—well, somehow a little homely. As he got out of the car and walked around to let Cassandra out, this thought gnawed at him.

"Come on, Daddy!" Cassandra cried out. "Let's find the place where the airplane comes in!" She was wearing a red jacket with white fur around the hood. Her dark blue eyes sparkled as she smiled up at him.

The terminal was surprisingly crowded for a Christmas Eve. Caleb had thought that most travelers would have arrived at their destinations earlier, but people carrying luggage moved rapidly past them toward the landing gates. He paused to look up at the monitor that gave the data on flights and said aloud, "Flight 1007, arriving at eight-fifteen." He took a deep breath, then said, "The plane's on time—let's go to Gate 9."

As they made their way toward the gate, Cassandra asked, "Daddy, what if we don't know her? We've never seen her, and she won't know us." Cassandra paused and looked up at him, her blue eyes troubled. "We might never find her!"

Caleb squeezed her hand. "We'll find her, Cassandra. After all, there can't be too many fathers and daughters meeting this particular flight, can there?" He tried to shake off his own confused thoughts by smiling. "I told her to look for the prettiest little blue-eyed girl she ever saw. Now how could she miss *you*?"

"All right, Daddy," Cassandra said. "But there's such a crowd! I wish we knew what she looked like!"

Caleb blurted out, "So do I!" But then when Cassandra gave him a questioning look, he covered his statement by saying quickly, "Look, honey, the passengers get out of the plane one at a time. They walk down that long covered walkway—see right there? And they come out one at a time, or two at the most. Susan said she'd wear a red rose on her coat so we can't miss her."

"But, Daddy—it's winter! Roses don't grow in winter!"

"She'll get a rose, don't worry—" He broke off abruptly, for one of the women waiting for someone on the flight said, "Look, there's the plane!"

"Let's go watch it come up, Daddy."

"All right, Cassandra." He followed her to the window as the big plane taxied slowly across the tarmac. It came to a stop, and at once the warmly dressed ground crew jockeyed the plane into position. "Let's—let's just wait here, Cassandra. It's a little crowded up close to the door."

The crowd was pressing toward the area where the incoming passengers would emerge, but Caleb was feeling very nervous. *What if—what if it's all wrong?* he thought as panic flooded him. *What if I've gotten into this thing and it's not God's will at all? Maybe we moved too fast—Cassandra was so eager, but she's so anxious for a mother.* Despite the cold air, he began to perspire and heartily wished that he'd been more cautious. *Well, it's not too late to back out,* he thought, but somehow he knew that it was. He knew that Susan had suffered from being rejected once. *I can't do that to her,* he thought. Then as a cry went up from the crowd he thought, *Maybe she won't want to go through with it.*

"There they come, Daddy!" Cassandra cried out with excitement. "Hold me up so I can see! I don't want to miss the rose!"

Caleb picked Cassandra up in his arms and moved to stand in the broad aisle. "She'll have to pass right by us, Daddy!" Cassandra exclaimed. "Look! They're coming now!"

Caleb felt the child tremble with excitement, and he'd never been so nervous in his life. The first travelers to emerge were a middle-aged couple, and they were followed by two young women. They were grabbed at once by two young men, who kissed them soundly. The babble of voices rose as passenger after passenger came through the doors and was greeted by family and friends.

And then a young woman came through the door. She paused and looked around expectantly, but no one greeted her. She was not more than twenty-five, Caleb guessed, and wore a blue wool pantsuit and a small white tam on her head. She had a wealth of honey-colored hair that fell around her shoulders, and a pair of large gray-green eyes. She was very attractive and seemed to be looking for someone.

Caleb swallowed but did not move. *She's not wearing a rose,* he thought with disappointment, but then it occurred to him, *Maybe she couldn't find one. If it's her, she'll know us when she passes by.*

The young woman joined the crowd that swarmed toward the main terminal. She had, Caleb noted, a free stride, like a skier or a distance runner. He clutched Cassandra so hard in his excitement that she cried, "Daddy, don't squeeze so hard!"

And then the young woman came to where they stood. She had a clear, rosy complexion and a wide generous mouth that seemed to contain humor and compassion. *It's got to be her!* Caleb hoped.

But she gave the pair one brief impersonal glance—and then she was

186

gone, making her way down the corridor until Caleb lost sight of her.

"Look, Daddy—there she is!"

Caleb at once turned and saw the woman Cassandra was pointing at. He pulled her hand down at once, whispering, "Don't point, Cassandra. You know it's not polite."

The woman paused, as had the younger one, but no one came forward to meet her. She was, Caleb saw at once, in her middle forties. Her hair was going gray, and she was overweight. Caleb's heart sank, for she was a kindly looking woman with a broad, worn face—but definitely not pretty. He remembered suddenly that Susan had never said when she'd been engaged, but it came to him now that it must have been many years ago.

The woman looked down at the red rose she wore on her lapel, and when no one greeted her, she seemed disappointed. The weight of the worn suitcase she carried pulled her off balance, and she looked tired. She joined the rest of the travelers, and when she passed within five feet of the pair who watched, Cassandra whispered, "Daddy, it's her! See the rose?"

Time seemed to stand still as Caleb's mind reeled. He stood rooted to the floor, it seemed, unable to move.

And then he thought of the letters and the phone calls. All of the humor and the gentleness and the love he'd found in Susan seemed to sweep over him—and he knew what he had to do.

"Come on, Cassandra," he said. "Let's go meet Susan."

He half ran to catch up with her, and when he called out, "Susan! It's us!" she halted and turned. "I—I'm Caleb, and this is Cassandra." He could say not one more word, and he felt Cassandra clutching his hand very tightly.

"Ah, you come to meet someone?" The eyes of the woman grew warm, and she laughed. "Someone you have never met? That is good of you on Christmas." She had an accent, and there was something foreign about her.

This isn't Susan! Caleb realized instantly. "The rose—"

"Yes, it's beautiful, isn't it?" The heavyset woman touched the delicate flower, then smiled. "The young lady, she asked me to wear it—just before we landed."

"Which young lady—what was her name?" Caleb demanded.

"She never said her name, but she's a very pretty young woman wearing a blue suit and a white hat—like a tam, you know?"

Caleb twisted his head toward the main terminal. The woman reached out her hand and touched Cassandra's shoulder, then looked at Caleb. "She said if a man and a little girl come up to meet me, I'm to tell them that she'll be waiting for them at the entrance."

"Thanks a million!" Caleb cried, and shook the woman's hand so hard she blinked. "Come on, Cassandra!"

The two of them ran past the last of the travelers from the flight. They ran down the escalator—a thing Caleb had often warned Cassandra not to do—then turned when they reached the ground floor. Many watched with amusement as the two raced across the waiting area, but Caleb paid no heed. He was pulling Cassandra along so fast that her feet scarcely touched the floor.

When they rounded the turn that led to the main entrance, there she was—waiting for them with a smile on her lips. She stood very still, but when the pair came to stand in front of her, she whispered, "Merry Christmas, Caleb."

Caleb swallowed and took her hand. "It's—good to see you, Susan. Very good!"

Susan stood there, and the two looked into each other's eyes for a long moment. Then Susan pulled her hand back and took the small bag she carried over her shoulder. Opening it, she took out a brightly wrapped package and handed it to the girl, who was watching her with shining eyes.

"Merry Christmas, Cassandra. You can open this one now."

Cassandra tore the red-and-green paper into shreds, and when the gift was in her hands, she cried out, "Arkie!" She buried her face in the fur of a sad-looking purple aardvark for a moment and then leapt into Susan's arms.

Susan looked over the head of the ecstatic girl into Caleb's eyes. "God bless us every one," she whispered, her eyes clear and full of hope.

"I think he already has," Caleb answered. Then he said, "Come on. It's time to go home, Susan. We've got a lot to talk about." He put his hand gently on her cheek in an odd gesture, then smiled crookedly, looking a great deal like Jimmy Stewart at the end of *It's a Wonderful Life*. "But then, we've got a lot of time for talking, haven't we?"

Susan's eyes brimmed with tears, but she brushed them away. "Yes—a long time. Let's go home, Caleb! Come on, Cassandra—and you, too, you blessed little aardvark!"

I am indebted to S.I. Kishor, who wrote the delightful story "Appointment with Love." Any reader who is familiar with that earlier story will recognize its influence in the creation of "An Aardvark for Cassandra."

—Gilbert Morris

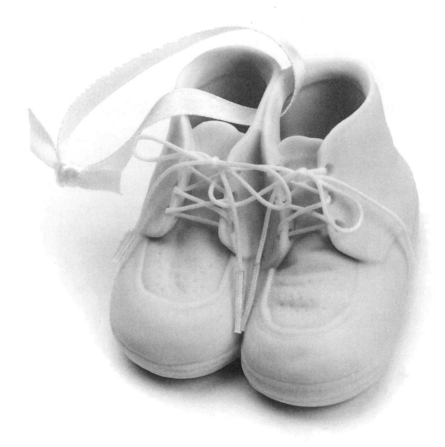

"In love he predestined us to be adopted as his sons through Jesus Christ,
in accordance with his pleasure and will."
EPHESIANS 1:4-5, NIV

Jim Kraus

THE GIFT

❖───────────────

But when the right time came, God sent his Son, born of a woman,

subject to the law. God sent him to buy freedom for us who were

slaves to the law, so that he could adopt us as his very own children.

GALATIANS 4:4-5, NLT

The moon had arched high into the night sky and hovered overhead, bathing the

world in a monochromatic light. A young Korean girl with black hair and liquid brown eyes stared out the small window of her room, struggling to prevent warm, salty tears from filling her eyes. She cried, keeping her tears silent, for her shame was great, and she would allow no one to share it with her. In the moonlight she picked up a white silk scarf, her tears splashing upon the soft fabric without a sound. She touched its smoothness and held it to her cheek. Then, from a small basket by the bed, she picked up a needle and thread and began to embroider a letter onto the long scarf.

After several hours she finished one character. During the hundred hueless nights preceding, she had stitched a hundred characters, each formed with a hundred stitches, each word formed by a thousand threads.

Now false dawn neared, and the city was coming awake. She lay the scarf at her side. She stood, and in her belly, in the warmth below her heart, she felt a twinge and a sudden twist—not of pain, but of completeness, of pleasure. Without thinking she lowered her hand to that spot, her fingers cupping that area, holding it tighter to her being. In her throat she formed a comforting small coo.

What her hand had protected now moved inside her, the marks of a new life. Her soul was filled with wonder—and anguish. She was awestruck by her capacity to nurture new life within her body, but to be an unmarried girl with child was a thing of immense shame, a dishonor that had crippled her proud father. For that she had left her village, left her family, left their cold stares, and had slept for more than a hundred nights in a simple, unadorned building on a cramped and twisting street no more than a mile from the airport in Seoul. It was here that she waited.

Her tears marked her sorrow for that life within her. Indeed, she would bring a child into the world, but she would never hold this child in her arms or stroke its tiny cheek.

At night, as the life inside her grew, her hand nestled just above it, she would listen as the planes roared overhead. As each plane passed she prayed that when her time came the plane carrying her gift, her child unseen, would pass overhead silently as it left. She did not think it possible to hear that roar, the roar of the plane taking her child to America, without her heart breaking and her life ending.

The first hint of fall sharpness filled the air, and thin wisps from cooking fires, heavy with the scents of fired meats and rice, curled through the crowded city. The young girl also felt a sharpness, but this came from inside her, a convincing nudge that ever increasingly spoke to her, whispering that her time was near.

An older woman tapped at her door the next evening as the moon slipped behind a cloud and the room turned dark. The streetlight from the warehouse across the road shone through the bare window. The young girl looked up at her visitor through her tears.

She was forty—maybe even fifty—and the deep lines in her face told her story, etched in her flesh. Wrinkles about her eyes spoke of her laughter, wrinkles on her forehead spoke of her tears, the sunken eyes spoke of her struggles.

"Your time is soon," the older woman said as she took the young girl's hand.

She could only nod, for the tears had muted her voice.

"Your child will be born in October," she said. "That is a good month for a child."

The young girl looked up, her eyes open wide in pain.

"It is a good month, for my child picked that month to be born as well," the older woman whispered. "He too left me. I had but a moment to hear his cry, and then he was gone."

Did the young girl see a tear on the old woman's face?

"You think your heart will burst when you say good-bye?"

The young girl nodded.

"I have come to tell you that it will not. Every year the pain will lessen. Every year October will arrive and then pass. And every year you will shed a few less tears that day. I have learned to live with that. God has allowed my heart to heal."

"But how?" the young girl whispered.

"Because I know that child was the most perfect gift I could ever offer. The family that took him in, they were American, too. They sent me a letter and a picture of my baby in their arms. I know he is loved. I know he has a better life than with a woman such as I was."

From a pocket in her coat she extracted a small, creased, black-and-white photo. A young man and woman held a small bundle by a Christmas tree. One could see the small dark eyes and the jet-black hair. The young couple was smiling, but it was more than just a smile. It was a reflection of their soul's immense happiness.

"I look at this every October," the woman said, "until my heart mends itself again."

And with that she reached out in the dark and touched the cheek of
the young girl, still wet with tears, then placed her hand ever so gently on
her swollen belly, over the baby about to be born.

It was a cold night, and snow had begun to fall, a fitting acknowledgment to
the season, for it was but a week before Christmas. An airplane roared across
the sky, streaking over the unlit prairie of the Midwest, miles above the
frozen stubble of barren fields.

This flight was near empty. Most businessmen had finished the year's
business, and most travelers would not venture forth till Christmas had come
a few days closer.

In the middle of the plane bound for Newark from San Francisco, with
a stop in Chicago, was an infant. The child was propped up in one seat,
alone and quiet. The child, no more than a few months old, was tightly
wrapped in a pink blanket in the manner of an Indian papoose. The seat
belt across the child looked like a giant's belt. The edge of the blanket had
been covering the child's head, and at that moment it fell away. It revealed
a beautiful sleeping Oriental baby with a thick shock of black hair falling
toward its closed eyes.

A single child on a large plane was no matter for concern, no subject of
curious stares. Yet there was more than a single child.

There was not just one Oriental child; there were near a dozen of them.
Spanning that first row of middle seats were three infants, all tightly bound in
their blankets, all secured nearly upright by a seat belt. The same grouping
was there for the next two or three rows. In the middle seat, or at the aisle, of

each row was one of a half-dozen women. They all looked exhausted, yet in each face one could see only calm, a palpable expression of love and purpose. Their glow nearly filled the plane's dim interior.

The children were mostly asleep, silent and still. The few that were awake were quiet. There were no tears, no cries, no struggles.

A businessman, making his last trip of the year, had boarded the plane in Chicago and had slept from takeoff to somewhere high above the rolling hill-sides of western Pennsylvania. He turned, seeing the single child, then viewing the dozen children in one surrealistic glance. His jaw dropped in surprise; he had been half-asleep when he boarded and hadn't paid any attention to the unusual travelers.

An elderly, gray-haired woman was seated by that first infant. She reached over to the child, now awake, and gently caressed its cheek with a gentle touch of her hand. She smiled. "It has been a long day," she said to her young companion with a hearty sigh. "And it is almost over."

The entire group had been traveling for close to thirty hours. They had begun their journey a day and a half earlier in Seoul, Korea.

She unbuckled the child's seat belt and transferred the small bundle into her arms. This child was wrapped in a white blanket, with a long scarf about its neck, the edges stitched with the dark, black characters of the Korean alphabet.

"I don't speak Korean," she explained to the businessman, who was watching, "but I was told that it meant `God's blessings upon my child.' The staff at the orphanage made sure that these handmade blankets and scarves went with the children. I believe their mothers have made them."

She placed the tiny baby back down on the seat. The infant looked about, puzzled perhaps, then yawned and closed its eyes.

"It will be good to get them with their new families."

The women were, she explained, members of an international adoption agency and were traveling back to the States with these children, each destined for adoption by an American family.

"This is the part that I both love and fear," she said. "I love the joy, but it hurts me to let go of these babies, even though it has been such a short time that we've been together."

She paused as she stroked the cheek of the small child beside her. "I look at these tiny faces, and every moment I am near to being overwhelmed that these women have given such a gift. To bring a life into the world only to let it go so soon."

She reached up and wiped at her eye. It could have been a tear.

"I am always reminded of Mary and Jesus when I take these trips. To bear a son only to lose him. It is so hard." She paused again. "But the faces on the families at the airport will erase that pain in a moment."

She smiled at the businessman, whose business was all but forgotten for the moment.

"You'll see. Just wait. You'll see."

The landing announcements began, signaling the end of the flight and its arrival at Newark. Each of the women began to fuss over the babies that were within arm's reach, smoothing blankets, smoothing down wispy black hair, smoothing their own anxious feelings.

The plane landed, taxied, and parked. The first passengers departed from

the chilly jet way, the businessman among them, and opened the door at the
end. They were greeted with an explosion of signs, balloons, streamers,
posters, and cameras. Each face inside the gate was wide with excitement and
anticipation. Their eyes darted to those first passengers and then immediately
focused past them, looking farther down the long jet way.

Near to an empty ticket counter was a young couple in their twenties.
On the man's shoulder was a huge video camera—perhaps he had been
unwilling to merely experience the moment without documenting it, produc-
ing some form of permanent record. His wife, small and blonde, clutched a
poster board to her chest. On it, neatly lettered in blue marker, were the
words "Welcome home, Danny! We love you!"

There were near a dozen family groupings, each presenting identical
tableaus. Off to the left stood two sets of grandparents holding flowers and
balloons imprinted with teddy bears. Grandmothers whispered animatedly to
each other, arms interlocking. Grandfathers stood, hands in pockets, feet
apart, rocking slightly in their nervousness.

Another group included children, their faces alive with excitement. One
hid for a moment behind a parent's leg, then darted out closer to the door,
only to scoot back to the safety of the family. There were lights from a dozen
video cameras flooding the scene in brilliant sharpness.

Tenderly carried by one of the women volunteers, the first child made its
way to the gate. The escort scanned the crowd, looked over to the young
couple beside the ticket counter, and walked toward them.

The elderly woman held the child, tightly wrapped in the white blanket and the scarf edged with a Korean blessing, and smiled. She murmured

a few words to the couple and then without hesitation presented the baby to the outstretched arms of the small blonde woman. She had dropped her sign, being far more concerned with the infant than making a statement with her poster. Her husband was so intent on watching that first moment as his wife carried their new child that the camcorder was all but forgotten at his side.

She leaned over and peered at the baby's face, cooing to him, tugging at the blanket to ensure warmth in the chilly terminal. A hurricane of kisses and hugs stormed through the terminal as each family greeted its new child.

The young husband and wife were now father and mother. Because of that immense and overwhelming joy, they were oblivious to the activity and emotions running in torrents all about them. That young husband, now a father of several minutes, gently draped one arm over his wife's shoulder. The camcorder was at his feet as his other hand touched the cheek of his new son, tenderly, gingerly, and then with a growing sense of assurance. A tough finger carefully touched the smooth cheek of a baby born thousands of miles—and a culture—away. The small baby boy, intent on focusing his eyes, looked up, lifted his tiny head, and peered at the faces before his eyes. Three sets of eyes locked together in that instant, forming a bond that time couldn't break. It had been a life shared by two, and now, a mere heartbeat later, it was shared by three. That split, that three-part division, meant that their lives now became bigger, more expansive.

The mother's eyes never left the face of her baby, tears rolling down her cheeks, her joyous smile filling and warming the space around her.

The young blonde woman, now a mother of but a dozen heartbeats duration, gently smoothed the white silk scarf about the baby's shoulder. She lifted an edge close to her face to look at the stitching, and without thinking, without knowing why, she gently stroked it to her cheek. She must have felt the uneven surface, the uneven bumps of the stitches along the elegant silk, and she closed her eyes for a breath. In that moment she felt the hand of the baby's mother and felt the love that she had sewn into the small piece of silk. She smiled and opened her eyes and touched the silk to her baby's cheek. He seemed to know what had touched his cheek and smiled up at her. A tear from his new mother fell, splashing on that scarf, mixing in with a tear that had been shed many months ago in a foreign land by a scared, lonely girl.

A family was born in front of that empty ticket booth, a miracle echoing through that drafty airport. It was a gift that brought that family into being. It was the most precious gift that poor girl in Korea might ever offer. And she would never truly understand how much joy and happiness her gift had brought.

The businessman had started to walk to claim his bags, but he stalled there, observing the scene. A lump rose in his throat as he thought about his children at home, how he missed them, how he was thankful to be part of a family. He thought also about his adoption into a family—God's family of believers. He was once like that Korean infant, alone and helpless. But unlike this child, the businessman had made the decision to be adopted by God. God had stood before him, waiting for him to surrender himself.

Before he headed home, the businessman bowed his head in a silent prayer, thanking God for the miracle he had witnessed. Before opening his eyes, he said, "Little Danny, I pray you also will be adopted a second time—into God's family. Amen."

"And by the light of that same star, three Wise-Men came from country far; to seek
for a king was their intent, and to follow the star wherever it went."
"The First Noel"

Daniel Taylor

THREE CHRISTMAS MEMORIES

❖

A first memory of Christmas . . .

In a small, white boarded house in a California lemon orchard, long before

California was a symbol of anything. A small child who had not yet learned to talk—

or knew how but didn't bother.

No memory of presents, or Santa Claus, or food. One memory only: a dark living

room. No one else around. Me on the sofa. Darkness everywhere. Darkness

Except in the corner. Except in the wondrous corner. There—mysterious, painfully beautiful, almost frightening, almost holy—was the light . . . the uncontainable Christmas light.

Could this trucked-in California tree have been anything but sparse and scrawny? Must it not have looked a little silly in the bright glare of day to busy people with places to go and things to do?

No matter. For at this moment the world was dark, and I was innocent, and the tree was the central mystery of life. The reds burned fiercely, and the blues bespoke calm and peace, and the greens whispered forever and forever. And I was enchanted. And I was worshipful. And I wanted it never to end.

But this was not the best part. This only pointed to the best. From its wide lower branches the tree tapered upward, higher and higher, toward the ceiling, a ceiling as faraway for a not-yet-speaking child as heaven itself. And there at the top, faraway and yet so near, was a star—a bright and morning star.

The reds and blues and greens came together in this whiteness. The star reigned over the tree like a king over a kingdom. It shone in the darkness, and the darkness could not overcome it.

A star. A light in the darkness. This is a first memory of Christmas.

A memory of a childhood Christmas . . .

If I lived there now, I would think I was poor. Ugly, low, red-brick apartments, stuck together on a barren Texas plain. A tiny living room, a hallway, one bedroom for Mom and Dad, one for the three boys. For a backyard, acres of dirty white Texas sand, waiting patiently for the next wind.

I was too ignorant to be anything but happy. I had my family. I had a dry gully out back in which to dig for treasure. I had dozens of anthills to choose from—little mountains swarming with big red ants, begging for the attention of a young boy.

Yes, life was good. And never better than our one Christmas there.

As always, we opened our presents on Christmas Eve, a testament to my parents' understanding of young boys, and perhaps to my father's aversion to early rising. The presents were fewer than usual. I do not remember being disappointed, but I did notice. This was OK. We were together, and this was Christmas. It would be all right.

I unwrapped one of the two packages with my name on it. *My name*—meant for *me*—a gift ordained since the beginning of time for one little boy in Texas. . . .

Ahh . . . socks. Nice fuzzy new socks. Neat. . . . Wonderful. . . . The best. Socks. Just what I needed. Really—a fine gift. They would go perfectly with . . . something or other.

And then the *big* package! The one that, shaken a hundred times, had made no noise. The package that had sparked the imagination.

Mmm . . . pajamas. Great. New pajamas. Swell. Roy Rogers. My favorite. I smiled bravely. I glanced under the tree on the off chance that something might have been overlooked.

And then . . . something magical. A crashing sound against the front door! A loud and frightening crash. We boys looked instantly to my father. His eyes were opened wide in mock alarm.

"What was that?" he shouted.

"What was that?" we shouted back.

"Go see!" he shouted.

"Let's go see!" we shouted back.

We raced to the door and cautiously ripped it open.

A bicycle! A first bicycle. A *red* first bicycle. A bicycle to be shared by three unbelieving yet believing boys.

And my first thought was Santa Claus. I raced into the front yard. I looked up into the sky for his sleigh, spinning around quickly, neck craning. I absolutely refused to place any significance in the sound of a pickup truck racing away up the street. It was Santa Claus for sure. He had dropped a bicycle from his sleigh for me and my brothers. It was, to be sure, a good and magical world in which we lived.

Of course, I saw nothing but stars in that cold Texas sky. High, bright, uncountable stars. But no matter that I did not find Santa. What mattered was that I lived in a world where unexpected blessings drop thickly from above; that I lived in a world where richness need not be measured in dollars—such a world as was proclaimed by one bright, shining star . . . two thousand years ago.

A memory of a young man's Christmas . . .

This was the Christmas of dying. His name was Jon. He was the hoped-for lifetime friend, given this time for less than half a life. Tall, gentle, mischievous. We had suffered together through countless Sunday school teachers and the agonies of adolescence. We had survived high school hazings and army lottery numbers. He had gone to study medicine and I to study words, but somewhere . . . somewhere along the way his cells had begun a quiet and deadly revolt.

And now it was Christmastime, and it was near the end. And I was in my second winter in Minnesota, a California boy explaining to my family in letters why the Norwegians tell Swedish jokes, and the meaning of terms like *windchill*. And they were telling me that Jon was weaker and that he was skinny again, like he had been when we first met in Mrs. Pinkerton's class at Calvary Baptist.

And so, as my father had taught me, I ignored the financial facts and pretended I could afford a plane ticket home, trading the Christmas-card December of Minnesota for the tepid California sun.

It was the Christmas of sad laughter. Conquer-the-world board games, once played with ruthless, Napoleonic zeal, were played now only "for old time's sake." We could not make ourselves forget that the pieces were only bits of plastic and that Jon's body was perhaps even less.

One evening, however, Jon looked at me with the shy look of friendship that had always been ours, touched now with the seriousness of someone who has seen his end.

"You know that letter you sent a while back. It meant a lot. It was a turning point. It's all right now."

That was all. "It meant a lot. It's all right now." That was all he said and all he needed to say.

The letter had been written when he still looked healthy but the statistics looked very bad. It had been a reminder of what he and I had once both believed but which he had put on hold in recent years. It had been a letter about God and death and the meaning of life, the kind of letter you don't know how to start and that never ends.

So we spent Jon's last Christmas playing games and laughing quietly and knowing that all was well.

Christmas marks a birth that looks forward to a death, a death and resurrection that make it possible for us to look forward to our own deaths—and at our lives—without fear, knowing that all is well.

A first Christmas memory—light in the darkness.

A childhood Christmas memory—unexpected blessings from above.

A young man's Christmas memory—all is well.

This is what the star announced.

This is the gospel.

This is the good news that is Christmas.

"Break forth, O beauteous heavenly light, and usher in the morning. . . .
This Child, now weak in infancy, our confidence and joy shall be."
"Break Forth, O Beauteous Heavenly Light" JOHANN RIST

Hans Christian Andersen

THE LITTLE MATCH-GIRL

❖

It was terribly cold; it snowed and was already almost dark, and evening came on,

the last evening of the year. In the cold and gloom a poor little girl, bare headed and

barefoot, was walking through the streets. When she left her own house she certainly

had had slippers on, but of what use were they? They were very big slippers, and

her mother had used them till then, so big were they. The little maid lost them as she

slipped across the road, where two carriages were rattling by terribly fast. One slip-

per was not to be found again, and a boy had seized the other and run away with it

He thought he could use it very well as a cradle someday when he had children of his own. So now the little girl went with her little naked feet, which were quite red and blue with the cold. In an old apron she carried a number of matches, and a bundle of them in her hand. No one had bought anything from her all day, and no one had given her a farthing.

Shivering with cold and hunger, she crept along, a picture of misery, poor little girl! The snowflakes covered her long fair hair, which fell in pretty curls over her neck; but she did not think of that now. In all the windows lights were shining, and there was a glorious smell of roast goose, for it was New Year's Eve. Yes, she thought of that!

In a corner formed by two houses, one of which projected beyond the other, she sat down, cowering. She had drawn up her little feet, but she was still colder, and she did not dare to go home, for she had sold no matches and did not bring a farthing of money. From her father she would certainly receive a beating; and besides, it was cold at home, for they had nothing over them but a roof through which the wind whistled, though the largest rents had been stopped with straw and rags.

Her little hands were almost benumbed with the cold. Ah, a match might do her good, if she could only draw one from the bundle and rub it against the wall and warm her hands at it. She drew one out. R-r-atch! how it sputtered and burned! It was a warm, bright flame, like a little candle, when she held her hands over it; it was a wonderful little light! It really seemed to the little girl as if she sat before a great polished stove with bright brass feet and a brass cover. How the fire burned! How comfortable it was! But the little flame went out, the stove vanished, and she had only the remains of the burnt match in her hand.

A second was rubbed against the wall. It burned up, and when the light fell upon the wall it became transparent like a thin veil, and she could see through it into the room. On the table a snow-white cloth was spread; upon it stood a shining dinner service; the roast goose smoked gloriously, stuffed with apples and dried plums. And, what was still more splendid to behold, the goose hopped down from the dish and waddled along the floor, with a knife and fork in its breast, to the little girl. Then the match went out and only the thick, damp, cold wall was before her. She lighted another match. Then she was sitting under a beautiful Christmas tree; it was greater and more ornamented than the one she had seen through the glass door at the rich merchant's. Thousands of candles burned upon the green branches, and colored pictures like those in the print shops looked down upon them. The little girl stretched forth her hand toward them; then the match went out. The Christmas lights mounted higher. She saw them now as stars in the sky; one of them fell down, forming a long line of fire.

"Now someone is dying," thought the little girl, for her old grandmother, the only person who had loved her, and who was now dead, had told her that when a star fell down a soul mounted up to God.

She rubbed another match against the wall; it became bright again, and in the brightness the old grandmother stood clear and shining, mild and lovely.

"Grandmother!" cried the child. "Oh, take me with you! I know you will go when the match is burned out. You will vanish like the warm fire, the warm food, and the great, glorious Christmas tree!"

And she hastily rubbed the whole bundle of matches, for she wished to hold her grandmother fast. And the matches burned with such a glow that it became brighter than in the middle of the day; grandmother had never been so large or so beautiful. She took the little girl in her arms, and both flew in brightness and joy above the earth, very, very high, and up there was neither cold, nor hunger, nor care—they were with God.

But in the corner, leaning against the wall, sat the poor girl with red cheeks and smiling mouth, frozen to death on the last evening of the old year. The New Year's sun rose upon a little corpse! The child sat there, stiff and cold, with the matches, of which one bundle was burned. "She wanted to warm herself," the people said. No one imagined what a beautiful thing she had seen and in what glory she had gone in with her grandmother to the New Year's Day.

"Rich and poor have this in common: The Lord is the Maker of them all."
PROVERBS 22:2, NIV

Lissa Halls Johnson

KASHARA'S GIFT

◆

I couldn't believe it. The Christmas decorations were up even before the Halloween

candy had been sold out. And I knew this was going to be the worst Christmas yet.

Who did my parents think they were kidding? Their "Christmas trees all over the

house" were, in reality, paper bags cut out in the shapes of Christmas trees and painted

green. They decided "the best Christmas presents ever" would be stuff we made from

whatever we could find. Oh joy. I'm excited. Can you tell?

At school it was just as bad. The minute Thanksgiving ended, kids were bringing Christmas goodies for their friends. Secret pals were going to be big this year. During the last week of school we would be required to bring something special every day for our secret pal. On the last day, we were supposed to do something rather fantastic for them. I suppose it was the rich kids who thought up this lovely idea.

The geographical placement of our school has become the designating line in town between the have-lots and the have-nots. In the old books I've read it seems that the railroad tracks decided what kind of person you were, depending which side you lived on. In our town we don't have railroad tracks. We have a high school.

If you enter or leave school through the massive oak front doors of the school, you're cool, have money, drive your own car, and won't need a job until after you leave that nice university your parents paid to put you through.

If you enter or leave school through the back doors with peeling green paint, your clothes probably are on the worn side. If you want money, you have to work at some minimum-wage job. Good luck on getting one, though, because they go first to the unskilled guys with families. Out the back doors of our school the walls are decorated with the voice of graffiti, the streets decorated with mute rundown cars, and the Saturdays decorated with yard sales no one will go to because they know the stuff is already so used up, stained, and broken that there's no use left in it.

I guess what makes it worse for me is that a long time ago I used those front doors of the high school. I was in kindergarten then. Our family owned shiny bikes and great clothes and ate dinner at home only on the nights when Mom felt like cooking. Then my dad got hurt in an auto accident. His job didn't want him back because he couldn't work like he used to. My mom couldn't get a job because she never learned a single trade. We sold everything and moved to the back side of the high school.

My old friends pretended they didn't know me. And I could hardly make any new friends because no back-door kid trusts a former front-door kid. Especially a *black* front-door kid. It's like you were a traitor from the start.

In English, they passed out names for secret pals. I don't know who did this stuff because it was always rigged that front-door kids got front-door kids and back-door kids got back-door kids. It must have been an unspoken code of law that the back-door kids didn't play the secret-pal game. They never exchanged so much as a piece of peppermint candy. They snickered to cover their envy and made cruel jokes about what the front-door kids exchanged.

"Kashara Sanders." I kept my head down on the desk. Maybe if I ignored the teacher, he would think I'd gone home for the day.

"Kashara," he repeated. He sighed and walked around his desk and between rows five and six until he reached my desk. He stuck a piece of folded paper underneath my arm. He touched my arm, and I jerked it away. I didn't need any sympathy from a teacher.

As he read through the rest of the list, I heard various shoe sounds, shrieks of excitement, whispers, and silence, depending on who had picked up their pal's name.

I suppose I would have thrown mine out without even reading it, but my biggest flaw has always been curiosity. I waited until I was out the back door and almost home before I dug the name from my jeans pocket. *Heather Claremont.* I turned the paper over, looking for another name. This had to be a joke. A total joke. Heather Claremont? Heather's family is the richest family in town. No kidding. Her dad not only owns half the land the mall is built on but he's also the town's foremost judge. He's on his way to being a superior-court judge. Fairness is supposed to be how he lives. But judging by his daughter, he's got a long way to go.

I sat on the low cement wall surrounding some person's house and stared at the name on my paper. I couldn't get over it.

"Kashara. Who'd you get?" Tifron sat next to me. He reached into his sock for a piece of paper like mine.

"Heather Claremont." I could tell my voice reflected my shock.

Tifron tipped his head back and laughed. "No way, girl. I think someone's pulled a major trick on you."

Tifron was one of the few people who talked to me. He talked to everyone. He could even get along with a brick wall. No one was his enemy.

"Here." I shoved the paper at him. "Let me see yours."

I opened his piece of paper and wasn't surprised at the name. A back door.

"You going to do anything?" Tifron asked, stuffing his paper back into his sock.

220

"I don't know," I said, still shocked. "I wasn't going to." Then a small, evil smile took over. "But maybe this is a way I can really make a statement."

Touching my arm with his finger, Tifron made a sizzling sound, then yanked his hand away as if burned. "Whoa, girl! I'd hate to be on the receiving end of your gifts."

"What's wrong with it, Tifron? I don't have the money like she does. She'll expect something I can't give her. Besides, she has everything. There's nothing I can give her that she can't get better quality or more of."

"Then give her something she can't get."

"Funny. As if we have the money to even buy her a candy bar."

"I didn't say *buy* her anything," Tifron said, his face moving into a rare serious look. "Think about it, babe." He pushed himself off the wall and sauntered off down the street.

I opened the paper and stared at it once more. I didn't like what Tifron said. I used to believe in being good to people and stuff. You know, like the Bible tells you to. It was easy when life was easy. It's easy to be nice to people when you can buy them stuff they like. It makes them smile. It's easy to be nice to people when they're nice back. And people are always nice to you when you're dressed nice and have cool clothes and perfect hair and all that. They aren't so nice when your clothes are kinda old looking because you have to buy them used and out-of-date from Goodwill.

Give her something she can't get. I snorted at the thought. What could I give her that she couldn't get?

I slid off the wall and headed home. Once there, I took a handful of pretzels for a snack, said hey to the folks, and dumped my stuff on my bed. I looked around my room, hoping for some sort of inspiration. Do I play this secret-pal game or not?

I decided not to make a decision. It could wait another day.

But several days passed, and I still hadn't made a decision. Then, I looked at Heather's face. What a dumb thing to do. I'm a total softy, even though I pretend to be hard. The first two days when she had reached the end of the day and got nothing from her secret pal, I could see something in her face. It was a strange emptiness. Come on! A girl like Heather couldn't possibly think of secret-pal time as important. Could she?

I dragged myself home, talking to myself the whole way.

"You fliphead! You can't play this game by the normal rules."

"And why not?" I asked me.

"Because it's not a normal thing. If you had gotten a back door, you could skip it. But you didn't. You got a front door, so you have to play by those rules."

I sighed, hating my own logic. I could get out of it if I really wanted. But I could not get Heather's sad face out of my mind.

The first thing I had to do was make a card. I dragged out our stack of secondhand magazines and cut out letters and phrases and pictures until I had what I wanted. I cut one panel off a paper sack and glued the message onto it. I then folded up the sack and gave it to Tifron to give to Heather.

He passed it to her at lunch, when there were so many bodies around that no one could have told who actually slipped the bag onto her plate. At first she gingerly picked it up by one corner, her face scrunched into a "eeewww!" kind of look. Fortunately, the corner she chose allowed the bag panel to fall open.

"It's a threat!" shrieked Lindy, known for her exaggerations. "Someone wants to kill you."

At that, Heather gripped the paper with both hands and opened it. Her face broke into a smile. "Wishing you all the gifts you could never buy for yourself this Christmas . . . ," the cutout words and letters said. "Hoping with you, Your Secret Pal."

"*Yes!*" Heather exclaimed, her manicured nail pointing at the photo of a gorgeous male model with too many perfect muscles to be believed. Kids started gathering around to look at the magazine cutouts of a tropical island, a bride, the moon, some stars, a picture of a sunset clustered with clouds, and the latest James Bond standing next to his latest car.

"Great idea," Tifron said, slapping me on the back. "What's next?"

I slumped against the balcony railing. "I haven't a clue."

The next day, Heather didn't cringe when a large paper bag appeared on top of her lunch tray. She eagerly looked inside. This time her face crumpled into one of disgust. She took out a loaf of bread tinged with mold. Next came a bag of crumpled, dry doughnuts (thanks to the Dumpster behind Ed's Doughnuts). If Heather were a cat, she'd be spitting and getting her claws ready. Then she took out another paper-bag panel. "Enjoy the simple things in life. Take your best friend to feed the ducks. Think about all you have been blessed with."

I held my breath, expecting her to get really mad. Instead, I watched her body go from rigid to soft and relaxed. She held the bag of bread next to her and smiled.

Tifron walked up to me. "Moldy bread? Never would have thought of it myself."

I looked down at the ground, ashamed. "It started out because I was angry about all she has. And then I thought about how when you can buy everything you need, you forget about the simple pleasures in life." I shrugged. "I guess it was really a lesson for me to be nice."

"One more day," Tifron cruelly reminded me. "Tomorrow's the big finale. It's supposed to be a grand gift. You ain't got much that's grand."

"I know."

"Maybe you're just lookin' at the wrong end of the picture."

That got me to thinking. I kept thinking of what I *couldn't* give Heather. Or maybe I was thinking about what I couldn't get myself. If I looked at the picture honestly, I'd see the selfish person I had become. *I* wanted all the things money could buy. *I* wanted to be respected and liked because of how I dressed, what I drove, and where I lived.

"What can *I* give Heather?" I muttered over and over all the way home. I tried doing some kind of mental inventory. But I couldn't find much there. I was really good in math. But she could afford any tutor she needed. I didn't have some great ability to style hair or do nails or cook or bake or do any of that kind of stuff for her.

Going through my stuff at home didn't help much either: a few favorite

224

books . . . a sporadically used diary . . . a couple of dead batteries . . . my stuffed dog and bunny from when I was little.

I went to bed with useless ideas rolling around in my head. I woke early, still with no answer. I took out the scissors, the glue, and some paper. I began to cut and paste, ideas popping into my head quicker than I could use them. The whole time my heart told me, "She's going to hate this. She is *really* going to hate this."

I got to school late and breathless. I stuffed the bag tied with string into Tifron's locker. I was afraid to go to lunch.

The cafeteria was *the* place for revealing secret pals. That way everyone could *ooh* and *ahh* over all the gifts. The back-door kids either stayed outside where they could ignore the action or went upstairs and stood around the balcony railing to watch.

I debated all the way to school and through every single class about where I would be. I hadn't had the guts to sign my name to the gift, so I could stand on the balcony and watch Heather's face without her knowing it was from me. Outside, I could be oblivious to the whole thing altogether. By the time my curiosity had won me over, the cafeteria had already seen many secret-pal revelations. I made my way upstairs, trying to see what was going on around one table. A crowd had gathered. Kids tried to see over shoulders. All went silent, then a roar of laughter followed. Silence. Then a roar.

"What's going on?" I asked Tiana.

"I'm not sure. I think Heather got something that everyone is interested in."

I gulped. My homemade book depicted life at the school, caricatures of teachers, students, front-door and back-door life. Heather was the main character. I bit my bottom lip.

The laughter ceased. Heather stood up in the middle of the parting crowd. From above, it could have been a flower unfolding around her. "Who did this?" she demanded, looking at her friends.

The cafeteria noise fluttered to a silent stop.

"Who did this?" She stamped her foot, tears pouring down her face. She began to search the whole cafeteria.

From another part of the balcony Tifron must have pointed. Not wanting to be the culprit, everyone moved away from where his finger aimed. I was frozen in place, unable to blend in with the crowd that was inching away.

Heather parted the kids before her and marched up the stairs to the balcony. By the time she reached the top step, I was alone. "No one . . . " she said, her voice strong yet full of tears. "No one has *ever* had the guts to give me gifts like you have this week."

"I'm sorry," I said, unable to look her in the eyes. "It's just that I knew you were expecting *something*. But I didn't have the money to get you anything."

Heather went on as though I hadn't said a thing. "This book—" she held out the page with magazine cutouts and phrases pasted all over—"is the funniest thing I've ever read. You have caught all my friends perfectly in this story. More important, you taught me that the best gifts don't have to cost a lot of money."

Heather took my chin in her hand and pulled it up so she could look at me. She opened her mouth to say something, then hugged me. A real hug that a friend would give. Startled, I couldn't hug her back.

To this day I don't understand what happened that week. But now the doors at the high school open for everyone. There are no more front-door kids or back-door kids. We are all just friends.

"Delight thyself also in the Lord; and he shall give thee the desires of thine heart."
PSALM 37:4, KJV

Lawana Blackwell

A Husband for Miss Dearborn

❖

I had no idea that the Christmas of 1878 would be my most memorable ever. How could I even guess, when the season practically began with my getting into trouble at school?

The first day of December started as any other in Kirklea, my village in the county of Shropshire, England. The only sounds in our redbrick, one-room school-house were an occasional rustle of pages and Miss Dearborn's soft voice as she led the youngest students through the primary numerals. It seemed a safe time for Claire

Pendly, my best friend, to twist around in her desk and whisper, "Have you asked your father about Shrewsbury?"

I sent a casual glance to the far corner of the room. Miss Dearborn was still guiding little fingers over rows of "nines" on their slates, so I leaned over my open *History of the British Empire* text to whisper back, "He sat up the night with old Mr. Tanner, so I didn't have the chance."

Claire's brown eyes narrowed suspiciously. "You've been saying that since last week. I don't believe you really want to go."

"Of course I do," I whispered back, then felt guilty for the half-truth, which Father says is the same as a lie. But there was *some* honesty in my answer, for I could think of no greater fun than accompanying Claire and her family to visit relatives in Shrewsbury, the big city to the south of Kirklea. She had six brothers and sisters, and even though they squabbled quite a bit, they were just as quick to laugh and josh. Not having siblings of my own, I found it exhilarating, if sometimes exhausting, to be in their company.

It was the idea of leaving home for five days of the winter holidays that dampened my enthusiasm for the outing. I chewed on my lip and thought, *What if Father needs me?*

"Your father will be just fine without you," Claire whispered, as if reading my mind. "He's got Mr. and Mrs. Tripp."

She was right, of course. Mr. and Mrs. Tripp had been servants in our household since before I was born, and they practically doted upon my father and me. It was silly of me to think that a thirty-seven-year-old man couldn't manage for less than a week without his thirteen-year-old daughter!

Ignoring the lump in my throat, I was just about to assure Claire that I would indeed ask Father, when Miss Dearborn's voice floated over the other industrious students' heads. "Emmeline and Claire."

Claire paled and wheeled back around. The whole class looked to where Miss Dearborn stood, her mouth set in a firm line. "This is the second time today I've had to reprimand you for talking during lessons," she said. "I will speak with both of you after school."

After school again! I thought, feeling every eye in the room now upon me. What would Father say? My teacher was still waiting, so I had no choice but to answer, "Yes, Miss Dearborn," and Claire mumbled the same. Two hours later we were waiting at her desk while she stood at the door and waved farewell to twenty-seven fortunate students spilling out into the crisp winter air.

Finally the clatter of shoes against the front steps fell silent, and Miss Dearborn limped back across the room. Even in my present state of disgrace, I winced inside with every thump of her cane against the floorboards. Miss Dearborn didn't deserve her handicap, for she was undoubtedly the nicest schoolmistress in all of England. Far more pleasant than our former schoolmaster, Mr. Hearst, who left Kirklea this past summer to take a position with Her Majesty's Inspectors.

It suddenly struck me to wonder if Miss Dearborn's cane was the reason she never married. What a shame if it were so, for it certainly wasn't her fault that a horse stepped on her foot when she was a tot. Even the limp couldn't detract from her lovely green eyes and kind smile. The younger children were constantly clinging to her at recess, and even we older students found ourselves competing with each other for the best marks so we could earn her praise.

But the thing I appreciated most about Miss Dearborn was that she never brought up the fact that I was the vicar's daughter. One of the most frustrating things about having a minister for a father is that people expect you to be *perfect* every minute of the day. I wish I had a shilling for every time someone has wagged a finger above my nose, saying such things as, "Shame on you, disgracing your father like that!" Well, I would imagine that the children of dairy farmers, greengrocers, and wheelwrights should be just as concerned about disgracing their fathers.

Miss Dearborn was at her desk now. She leaned her cane against the side and sat down easily in her chair. "Now, whatever am I going to do with the both of you?" she began, staring up at us. "If you weren't the only two on the seventh level, I'd put you on opposite sides of the room."

"I'm so sorry, Miss Dearborn," I told her, lowering my eyes. I meant it, too, for I hadn't set out this morning to be disobedient. How much easier life would be, especially for children, if talking weren't so enjoyable.

"We have in this classroom twenty-nine students on eight different levels," Miss Dearborn went on. "Do you understand how necessary it is to have order during lesson time?"

Claire, who colored easily because of her auburn hair, now had two splotches of crimson across both cheeks. Still, she managed to sniff, "We do, Miss Dearborn."

Miss Dearborn became thoughtfully silent for what seemed like hours, though it couldn't have been more than a few seconds. Meanwhile, I shifted on my feet and wondered what punishment would be meted out. I eyed the wooden cane propped at an angle in front of me. *Is she going to . . . ?*

"Tomorrow morning, I want you both here a half hour before the other children," she finally said. "And every day until the winter holidays."

"A half hour?" I asked, not quite sure of my hearing. What sort of punishment was this? Then I realized we would likely be put to work for the next two weeks; sweeping the floor, scrubbing the chalkboard, and such. Well, I honestly didn't mind, for I felt we should pay some sort of penance for causing Miss Dearborn so much grief.

"Thirty minutes," Miss Dearborn said, in answer to my question. "I would be tempted to have you come even earlier, but the classroom isn't warm enough until then."

An audible swallow came from Claire, and then she said, "What do you want us to do when we get here?"

"Talk."

"Ma'am?" we both said at once.

Our teacher nodded. "I would like you to sit in your desks and visit with each other until time for school to begin. Surely with the morning and recess to talk, you'll find it easier to restrain yourselves during lessons."

After another moment of silence, I cleared my throat. "Miss Dearborn, . . . that's all?"

"For now," was her answer. "But if this doesn't work, I shall be forced to ask your parents to meet with me."

"Oh, it'll work!" I assured her with haste. Gratitude welled up inside of me, and I gushed, "Thank you for not punishing us."

Miss Dearborn's expression softened into a smile. "I do believe in using punishment, but only as a last resort. And I remember how nice it was to have a friend with whom to share my thoughts."

A hint of sadness was in her voice at that last part, and I thought, *Why, she's lonely!* In all of my thirteen years, it had never occurred to me that adults needed close friendships as much as young people did. I suppose I thought that if you put *any* two adults in the same room, each would be quite happy with the other's company, just as any three-year-olds would be. Miss Dearborn boarded with the elderly Holt sisters, who were lace spinners and lived in a stone cottage on Market Road. They were both pleasant, but they spent most of their time sitting in the sun with their pillows and pins. It seemed unlikely that Miss Dearborn, being new to Kirklea and quite a bit younger than the Holts, enjoyed any close companionship at all.

"Emmeline?"

I blinked at my teacher's voice and realized I had drifted off into what Father calls a fog. "Yes, Miss Dearborn?"

She gave me a bemused little smile. "You may go now."

Claire and I lived at opposite ends of Kirklea, but we walked together a little way down the lane past the school yard. Our shoes made little crunching noises upon the snow, and a bracing December wind caused me to pull up the hood of my wool cloak.

"Are you going to tell your father about this?" Claire asked me with envy in her voice. She and I both knew that the option of telling her parents had already been taken out of her hands, for her younger siblings, Mary, Amos, and Margaret, would have raced home to see who could be the first to tattle.

"I have to," I replied.

Since Kirklea School was sponsored by the church, one of Father's duties as vicar was to meet with Miss Dearborn every Saturday in the Holt sisters' parlor to assist in planning the lessons for the coming week and charting the students' progress. Miss Dearborn had ample opportunity to inform him of my actions, as Mr. Hearst had always been quick to do. . . . She hadn't yet, though. Somehow I knew that she trusted me to tell Father myself, and not wanting to betray that trust, I always confessed my misdeeds as soon as possible.

We walked together in snow-numbed stillness for several steps, and then Claire looked sideways at me and smiled. "You know, other than the trouble we're going to be in at home, it's going to be fun."

I hadn't thought of that. Who wouldn't enjoy an extra half hour every day with her best friend? Taking Claire's mittened hand in my own, I said, "You know, we should do something nice for Miss Dearborn."

"Such as . . ."

"Find her a friend."

"A friend?" Raising an eyebrow, Claire said, "Every child in town loves her."

"But she hasn't got a close friend," I pressed. "Doesn't she seem lonely to you?"

"I never thought about it. I suppose she should have someone her own age."

235

"Absolutely." We weren't sure of her exact age, but I'd once asked Mrs. Tripp how old she thought Miss Dearborn was, and she had cocked her head and answered, "Oh, not more than twenty-five, I would guess."

My feet slowed their steps, for the end of the lane was nearing, and I knew we would soon have to go our separate ways. "The only problem is, I can't think of any woman her age who isn't married."

"Why can't she have a married friend, then?" Claire asked, then shook her head. "They're just so busy with their husbands and children, like my mother is."

Finally reaching Market Road, we stopped walking to say good-bye. I hated leaving without agreeing upon a proper plan because we couldn't very well discuss this in Miss Dearborn's presence in the morning. That was when the answer came to me.

"There are some men in town who aren't married."

"*Men?* Are you serious?"

"And some look to be about her age . . . like Mr. Casper at the mill."

"Men can't be friends," Claire declared stoutly.

"Of course they can," I told her. "Why, my parents were best friends when Mother was alive." I hadn't been around to witness their friendship because my mother went to heaven soon after I was born, but Father had told me about it once when we visited her grave. It was then that I realized how much my father needed me to fill—as much as possible—the void Mother had left.

Claire was staring at me with her arms folded. "Then you're saying we should find Miss Dearborn a *husband?*"

That hadn't been my original plan, but I found myself smiling. *Why not?*

236

My punishment from Father was to be sent upstairs immediately after supper. From Mrs. Tripp I received a frowning "tsk, tsk" at the same time she was serving me an extra-large portion of bread-and-butter pudding. Usually I *loathe* going to bed early, but it turned out that the extra time to think was most profitable. I whispered my idea to Claire at our desks the next morning.

"I've written down the names of the unmarried men in Kirklea who look to be Miss Dearborn's age," I said, pulling a folded sheet of notepaper from my pocket. "There are four."

Claire raised an eyebrow. "And . . ."

"Why don't we get one of them to ask her to the Christmas Eve service?"

It was the highlight of the village year. The evening began at the church with a live manger scene, the reading by my father from Saint Luke, and caroling. Refreshments and games came afterward at the town hall. I couldn't imagine a more romantic evening on which to begin a courtship.

"How can we get someone to do that?" asked Claire with her usual skepticism. "And who?"

First looking up to make certain that Miss Dearborn was still at her desk and out of whispering range, I suggested we begin with Mr. Moberly, who owned a large dairy farm across the River Lyn. "He can provide her with a nice big house," was my practical reason.

"But how?"

I knew Claire wasn't going to like my answer, but I plowed on ahead anyway. "We've got to ask him to ask her."

As I expected, Claire protested that a grown man wasn't going to listen to two young girls about such a matter. I listened to her arguments, but then silenced her by leaning closer, my eyes narrowed accusingly. "I suppose if *you* don't care if Miss Dearborn is alone for the rest of her life, I'll just have to take care of it myself."

She looked at me as if trying to decide if I was bluffing and then nodded. "All right," came out with a sigh. "I'll help. When should we do this?"

"Saturday morning," I replied, giving her an appreciative smile.

Three days later I sat at the breakfast table and explained to Mrs. Tripp why I didn't want a second helping of poached egg and sausage. "I've got to go somewhere," I said, smiling to show that I appreciated her usual concern that I would starve before my next meal. There was a quiet click from across the table as Father set his teacup back upon its saucer. "You have a big day scheduled, Emmeline?"

I answered that Claire and I planned to take a long walk. That was true, too, because Mr. Moberly's farm was a good distance away. Somehow I had the feeling that Father wouldn't approve of our plan to become involved in Miss Dearborn's personal life. When he listened to my prayers at night, I would even add my request about finding Miss Dearborn a husband *after* Father left my bedside. "May I be excused now?" I asked.

As he nodded, I thought about how handsome he was, even though his hair was becoming flecked with gray. "It's nippy out there," he warned. "Bundle up tight."

We both chuckled then, because that is what *I* usually said to Father. It's not that he hadn't sense enough to keep warm, but he could be terribly forgetful at times. I would feel terrible if I didn't remind him and he became sick from paying calls around the village without his hat or comforter.

It took Claire and me, once we met at the greengrocery, a good part of an hour to reach Mr. Moberly's farm. A tired-looking housemaid shrugged and told us that Mr. Moberly could likely be anywhere now that the milk wagon was loaded and on its way. We found him outside of a paddock, repairing an old feeding trough. He looked surprised to see us, and after he got over the shock of our request, he shook his head. "Can't be takin' that teacher nowhere," he said, his face assuming its usual pinched expression.

"She's very pretty," Claire offered timidly.

"Crippled." Mr. Moberly positioned a nail on the end of the trough and held his hammer poised over it, obviously a signal of our dismissal. "Need a woman who can help with farmin'," we heard him mumble to himself as we walked away.

Mr. Casper at the grain mill was next. He stopped loading sacks of flour long enough to grin and answer, "I'm gettin' married come spring." It turned out that he had been courting a lady from nearby Albrighton. I wondered as we left how that information had escaped the Kirklea gossip mill.

Our next attempt was Mr. Kemp, the smithy. We watched with fascination as the sparks flew from his hammer and anvil, but we left defeated after he politely suggested that schoolgirls should be minding their own business.

There was only one candidate left: Mr. Wichell, whose family owned the Elderdown Inn. No one in Kirklea was quite sure of Mr. Wichell's occupation other than running occasional errands for his father, but Claire and I reasoned that he would one day inherit the inn and be able to provide adequately for Miss Dearborn. Besides, he was rather nice-looking, with an aristocratic face and thick eyelashes.

It was going on eleven o'clock when we found him in the mews behind the inn, feeding an apple to a roan mare. I was relieved when he listened to our request with an interested expression.

"But how do you know Miss Dearborn will go with me?" Mr. Wichell asked. "She won't hardly look at me in town." My nose suddenly picked up a whiff of rum, but then I reminded myself that he sometimes helped his father in the dining room of the inn. Surely an occasional glass sloshed or spilled on him.

Claire, having grown bolder, said, "She's probably shy around men."

"You think so?" Mr. Wichell rubbed the end of his nose, which was red from the cold, and then laughed out loud. "All right, then. I'll do it!"

239

"You won't tell her that it was *our* suggestion, will you?" I asked.

He laughed again and then replied, "I won't if you won't!"

Claire and I parted for our homes, our spirits lightened. While Mr. Wichell hadn't been our first or even second choice, it had been gratifying to see how quick he had been to accept our suggestions. *Maybe they'll fall in love right away*, I thought. I hugged myself and noticed how beautiful the village had suddenly become under its icing of snow. Romance was so much fun!

When I got back to the vicarage, Mrs. Tripp helped me remove my outer clothing and then asked me to fetch Father for dinner. "He's in the parlor, I believe," she directed.

I found him in his favorite chair, a faded old thing with cushions that lapped around him like water. It was his usual place to read the *Shrewsbury Chronicle*, so I was surprised to find him without a newspaper in his lap. He was just sitting there, staring into space with a sadness in his expression that disturbed me, and I walked over to touch his arm. "Father?"

He blinked and then smiled at me. "So, my wandering daughter is back."

I leaned over to kiss his cheek. It was clean-shaven, as usual, and smelled of soap. "What are you doing in here?"

"Just thinking."

"About what?"

Getting to his feet, he tousled my hair and answered, "About different things."

The sadness on his face was gone now, and I chided myself for being away for so long. *He's used to my being here on Saturday mornings*, I thought.

Once the winter holidays were upon us, it was easy to stay home, for there

240

was plenty to do. Mrs. Tripp and I had hundreds of cookies to bake—some to save for the tree we would have later, and still more to put aside for the Christmas Eve service. Even though she covered my hair and clothes with a cap and apron, I managed to get flour and bits of drying dough on other parts of my body, including one ear. Still, it was great fun pressing cookie cutters shaped like holly leaves, ginger men, and bells into the sweet-smelling dough.

I was glad to have so many things to do, for without them the days would have crawled by. My dilemma about going to Shrewsbury was solved when Claire's brother, Amos, broke his leg and her parents canceled the trip. My sorrow about Amos's leg was genuine, mind you, and I had even asked Father for sixpence to purchase him a bag of boiled sweets.

Often I found myself wondering if Miss Dearborn was as impatient as I was about the coming Christmas Eve service. Perhaps she would be so happy to have a beau that she would wear something special for the occasion. *An emerald-colored gown would be perfect,* I thought. *To match her eyes.* And Mr. Wichell would declare her the most beautiful woman in Kirklea—no, the whole world!

But when I delivered the sweets to Amos Pendly three days before the Christmas Eve service, Claire drew me aside. "I was going to come to see you later," she said. "I saw Mr. Wichell in town this morning, and he said that Miss Dearborn turned him down!"

"No!" I gasped.

"She told him that she already had an invitation."

My shoulders fell. "The Holt sisters must have asked her first. And she wouldn't hurt their feelings by backing out."

"That's what I thought as well," Claire said.

With a sigh, I told her that perhaps Mr. Wichell and Miss Dearborn would have an opportunity to spend at least a little time together during the party at the town hall. "We have to keep praying."

Two days later, after Father had listened to my prayers at my bedside, he took my hand and said, "I've something to tell you, Emmeline."

"Tell me?" I echoed, wondering at the somber tone of his voice.

He nodded. "I've asked Miss Dearborn to accompany us to the Christmas service and to celebrate Christmas Day with us here."

I opened my mouth, but no sound came out. *So, it wasn't the Holt sisters after all!*

"I should have told you long before now," Father went on, "but I didn't know quite how. It's been a while since I've courted anyone."

This time I had no trouble speaking. "Courted!" I gasped.

A look of pain came across Father's face. "I loved your mother deeply and still cherish her memory. But I've been lonesome for so long now, and I care deeply about Miss Dearborn. I believe she feels the same about me."

How could he be lonesome, I asked myself, *when I have always been so conscientious about staying home as much as possible?* My thoughts must have shown on my face, for he then said with a gentle voice, "You're the most important person in my life, Emmeline, and I know you love me with all your heart. But I believe we have enough love here to share with Miss Dearborn."

The full impact of his words hit me then. "You're going to . . . *propose?*"

He nodded. "Soon."

"But aren't you too old for her?" I squeaked.

"That's for Miss Dearborn to decide," he replied, and then his eyes crinkled at the corners. "I'm thirty-seven, and you think I've already got one foot in the grave?"

I frowned, resisting his effort to tease me out of my reservations.

His expression grew serious again. "Don't you *like* her?" he asked.

I didn't like her at all at the moment, but then reason took over, and I realized that it wasn't Miss Dearborn's fault that my father had fallen in love with her. She was still the same wonderful teacher she had always been. *She may even turn him down.* My thoughts became so confused that I let out a sigh. Father moved to sit on the side of my bed and put his arm around me.

"I don't want anything to change," I sniffed.

"Of course you don't," he said. "Change can be frightening. But you'll enjoy having a mother, you'll see."

I didn't answer, and we sat there for a long time, his chin resting upon the top of my head. As angry as I was with Father, I was grateful for his allowing me some silence in which to mull over everything he had just said. The many prayers I had said for Miss Dearborn to find a husband came back to haunt me.

"Father?" I said after a while.

"Yes?"

"Does God ever answer a prayer differently from the way you wanted him to?"

"Well, it's happened to me before," Father answered in a dreamy voice. "He knows the desires of our hearts before we're even aware of them."

"Could I *want* a mother and not even know it yet?" I asked him, for I knew with some mysterious certainty that Miss Dearborn would accept.

Father squeezed my shoulder. "Why don't you ask God?"

"Will he tell me?"

"If you listen."

"I'll try," I promised.

On Christmas Eve, Dan, our sorrel horse, pulled the sleigh bearing Father and me to the Holt sisters' cottage. I sat with a blanket wrapped around my knees and held the reins while Father went to the door. Minutes later he and Miss Dearborn both came down the walkway. I had only seen my teacher at church since the start of the winter holidays, and a lump came to my throat when I noticed how natural she and Father seemed together as my father held Miss Dearborn's arm to steady her against the icy cobblestones.

244

He helped her up beside me into the carriage and spread my blanket over both our laps. "You look so lovely tonight, Emmeline," Miss Dearborn said in her soft voice. Even though the sunlight was beginning to fade, I noticed the flush across her cheeks. Was it because of the cold, I wondered, or the vicinity of my father, now seated at her other side?

"Thank you," I replied somewhat stiffly, but opened the collar of my cloak a bit so she could admire the royal-blue velvet of my dress. "Mrs. Tripp had so much to do that she didn't finish it until yesterday."

She gave an understanding nod as the sleigh started out with a slight lurch. "If it hadn't been for the dear Holt sisters pitching in this morning, mine wouldn't have been ready either."

"You're wearing a new dress?"

Miss Dearborn allowed an arm to escape her cloak, revealing a sleeve of emerald sateen, the same color as her eyes.

"It's very nice," I told her, finding myself strangely meaning it. I then settled back in quiet for the rest of the ride. The runner of the sleigh moved through the snow with a swishing sound, and Father's voice was as comforting as usual as he pointed out the sun setting behind Kester Hill.

Presently we approached Saint Luke's. The church's doors and windows were trimmed with fir branches and red ribbons, the loving labor of the Missionary Ladies' Society. Other sleighs were arriving, depositing bundled villagers as near to the door as possible, and Father waited his turn to do the same. I watched the light from the stained-glass windows throw colorful patterns on the snow and pleasantly thought, *It's the same as it was last year.*

Even with Miss Dearborn with us. And it would be the same next year. Not completely, of course, but almost. Just as my life would be. The only thing different was that I would have a mother to listen to my prayers with Father. And to help me remind him to bundle up tight. I would even feel free to go to Shrewsbury with the Pendlys next winter, if Amos didn't break another limb.

The desires of our hearts, I thought, inhaling deeply of the clear, fir-scented air. God had indeed given my answer.

"Doesn't the church look beautiful, Emmeline?" Father asked after pulling up the reins. He was leaning forward slightly to study me with a concerned expression. Miss Dearborn's face was turned to me with the same worry, and I wondered if they had misunderstood my contented silence for sulking.

I smiled at both of them. "Beautiful."

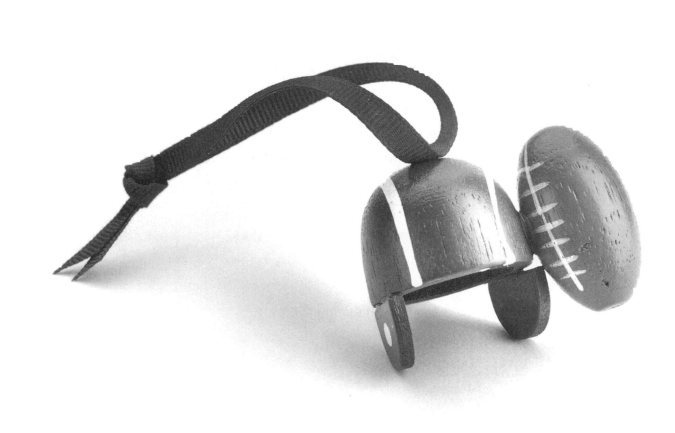

"And, lo, the angel of the Lord came upon them, and the glory of the Lord
shone round about them."
LUKE 2:9, KJV

Walter Wangerin Jr.

LO, THE ANGEL OF THE LORD

◆

We all considered Aunt Moravia to be slightly insane. Harmless, really, but a bit vexing

for people who had proper schedules and reasonable goals and normal views of existence.

As long as I knew her, Aunt Moravia was convinced that she had swallowed a glass

piano. It caused, she said, a delicate and irritating music in her pancreas.

Near the end of dinner she would suddenly stand up, place one bony hand on her

abdomen, the other on the small of her back, and whisper, "Do you hear it? Oh, honey, can't

you hear it?"—then silently begin to weep and retire to her bedroom.

Honey was my father, her nephew. Moravia was my great aunt, actually. She was as old as stone.

When company came she would stay secluded in her bedroom. But suddenly this thin, shuffling, bent old woman would throw open her door and begin to sing "Pomp and Circumstance" in a tremendous, yowling vibrato. The piece has no words, so far as I know. But Aunt Moravia sang the brass and the drums with an angry sort of gusto. Then she would slam the door and sink again into a grave silence.

I said, "Aunt Moravia, when people come to visit us, why do you sing?"

She opened her eyes wider and wider. She had no eyebrows or eyelashes anymore, but she wore black mascara on her upper and lower lids, making me think of death or of God. And she had yellow teeth as long as pickets for fences. "It is a shame upon your mother's meat!" she hissed.

248

I think Aunt Moravia liked me. She never pointed at me the way she pointed at my mother. Sometimes she would stand in the kitchen and raise her whole arm and point at my mother for fifteen minutes altogether, aiming her long finger wherever Mom happened to go.

And she answered my questions.

"What's the matter with my mother's meat?" I asked.

She glared down her long nose at me, though I was already a good head taller than she. "Dressed to kill!" she declared. It was the passing of judgment. "No humbleness in her roasts and gewgaws. Phaw! Phaw! And an haughty spirit before a fall!"

Mostly Aunt Moravia wore black.

Sometimes she emerged from her room in her underwear, carrying a candle, peering in every dark corner of the house, weeping. She did this only deep in the night when everyone else was sleeping. Except me. After Mom and Dad and Sarah were sleeping I often got up to draw in a large, linen sketchbook.

Actually, I used to think she was looking for her jewelry, because she also had the habit of hiding the most expensive pieces in odd places throughout the house—a single earring, for example, in a knothole in a basement joist. But she wasn't. I didn't know what she was looking for. Because during my senior year in high school Aunt Moravia began to conclude her midnight searches by holding the candle behind me and staring at my sketches as if *they* were the shadow in which something precious was hidden.

The first time she did this, she dripped tears on my neck, and I thought it was hot wax from the candle. I jumped up and stifled a scream. The poor old woman gasped and burst into genuine tears, so I put my arms around her and held her until she stopped sobbing.

Once, I pointed at the words I had written in my book, and I whispered, "Aunt Moravia, when you look at this, what do you see?"

"Nothing, Vladimir," she said with such sadness that it made me sad.

"Well, but then what are you looking for?" I asked.

She shook her old head. Without mascara, without eyebrows, with only white wisps of hair left, and her thin, gaunt and chewing cheeks, there was no severity in her aspect. Age and a stunned sort of sadness only.

She raised her candle high and said, "Vladimir, I am looking for the Son of God."

I sketched athletes. I myself was no jock, but I had a great admiration for the unconscious gesture of strength, the languid motion of dexterous torsos, the stunning beauty of extreme stress in perfect bodies. I liked to catch contestants at the moment of peak accomplishment, outdoing themselves and *knowing* it. I used pencil or charcoal or pen-and-ink. I paid attention to my own frame in order to understand the figure I was drawing— so that figure lent me a sort of aptitude. Walter the artist, the vicarious champion!

I planned to make a career of my art. Maybe cartooning. Or graphic design. Maybe illustrating books. I didn't know.

There was no one, really, with whom I could discuss my dreams. I've already told you about my Aunt Moravia. She didn't have conversations; she uttered oblique decrees. My sister, Sarah, was always willing to sit and talk with me, but the girl was only ten years old and altogether too agreeable. I mean, she didn't know how to ask questions or how to disagree with me. She smiled too much. She wanted hugs too much.

My parents were kind. They loved me. There is no doubt about that. My mother especially would stop cooking when I came home and ask after my day and listen for a while. She would bend her head toward me, and a long lock of hair would fall over her left eye. She wouldn't sweep it back again. Lately she seemed oblivious of herself and her appearance. A bit of a shambles, my mother was in those days. And that hanging lock of hair would so consume my attention that soon I couldn't continue telling what little news there was in my day, and I left—hearing her say behind me, "That's nice, dear."

She *was* a patient and forgiving woman. Never once did she blame Aunt Moravia—her husband's aunt, you understand—for the criticism Moravia cast on her.

Finger-pointing can be most unnerving. I know it would cause me to blow up. Or else to walk away. But my mother just went about her business, allowing herself only the comment, "Aunty, you don't mean it, you don't mean it"—whatever *it* was. Aunt Moravia never explained why she held the accusing finger against my mother.

But, in fact, neither my mother nor my father could bring themselves to be interested in any career of mine. Not that year.

In December of my high school junior year, my older brother, George, who was then a senior at the university and a wide receiver for his football team, ran downfield with tremendous speed, executed a quick buttonhook, leaped to catch a high pass, and was at that same instant struck from behind at the knees.

We were watching the game on television. All of us. *This* was the career my parents dearly cared about. George's record was outstanding, both in high school and in college. He had been identified by sports reporters as an early pick for the NFL draft. And *he* had maintained humility even to Aunt Moravia's satisfaction—a truly unbelievable star. His was not false modesty. He looked people directly in their eyes. He understood his talent very well. But (here's the thing the reporters couldn't understand) he loved God and gave God the glory for any accomplishment of his own. It made him impervious to the grand temptations and the praise of the world.

I would have talked with George about my art. In fact, we planned a month together after his graduation. It would have been the first time in nearly four years that we went off alone as brothers. Yes, George would have had advice for me. And God would have been a part of it. Yes.

But we all saw that hit from behind. A flying, brutal, human body put George's body into a slow, backward turn. He held on to the ball. Even as his feet swept up above his face, he tucked the ball in the crook of his right arm and crossed it with his left hand. There were no hands free, then, to catch the ground. He came down on the back of his head.

Mother groaned.

That was the only sound in our living room.

We sat very still. George lay on the field a long time. The managers and the doctors huddled close and hid him. When finally with dexterity they slipped a stretcher underneath him and drove him slowly away, Dad said, "Broke his neck." He went into the kitchen and made a telephone call. He came back in silence. Fifteen minutes later the phone rang and he answered it, and then he came and told us: "The coach confirms it. George's neck is broken."

He lived two weeks after that.

We flew to the city where they kept him.

When I went into the hospital room with Sarah and Aunt Moravia, George didn't know us. Not us. He talked to Mom and Dad continually.

He seemed to be whining. Like a spoiled child. It scared me to hear that one in his voice. He kept asking why he wasn't being sent in. "Sent in." He was upset because he thought the coach was benching him for no good reason, and he was begging Mom and Dad to go talk with the coach.

One of the few times I ever saw my mother angry with George was late one night when she and I alone were in his room.

George wasn't coughing. The doctor had said that he *must* cough to clear his lungs. The fluid could cause pneumonia.

But George said it hurt to cough. He acted as if he didn't deserve to hurt so much. He seemed to be blaming people. He was blaming Mom.

But he could scarcely breathe.

And Mom was crying. "Cough," she said.

She held a plastic tube to his lips. "Blow into this," she said.

He wouldn't.

The tube was attached to a device in which were four blue balls; they would rise up if one blew hard enough.

"Blow," she said.

He wouldn't. He twisted his head left and right, whining and making baby curse words.

So she grabbed his jaw, stopped his head from turning, opened his mouth, and put the plastic tube between his teeth.

He clamped down with his teeth and crushed the plastic.

Mom slapped him.

"Cough!" she cried. "George, if you don't cough, you're going to die. Cough, George! Cough! Cough!"

He refused. Mom knelt down beside the bed and put her arms around him and cried. "I'm sorry, I'm sorry, I'm sorry," she said. "Oh, George, I am so sorry."

My father said nothing so long as I was there. Maybe he talked to George in private.

Aunt Moravia once burst out singing at the top of her lungs.

"O Trinity, most blessed Light
O Unity of sovereign might,
As now the fiery sun departs,
Shed thou thy beams within our hearts!"

She had remarkable lungs that day. Wide, white eyes, black and shadowy lids, yellow teeth, she was an apparition in the room. My sister whispered to the nurse who peered in. "It's OK. Aunt Moravia's crazy."

Sarah and Moravia and I went home for the last week of school before the Christmas holidays.

George died on Christmas Eve.

His funeral was two days later.

We did not celebrate Christmas that year.

And our house thereafter fell into a silence.

And then in December of my senior year, it occurred to me that *all* of us were like Moravia—slightly insane. All except Sarah, who was in the fourth grade. Dad and Mom each kept their own sort of silences—Mom, generally disheveled, mildly sloppy; Dad, furiously neat and precise and forever busy about something.

And me, too.

Because Sarah had to come into my bedroom and take me by the hand and lead me downstairs and outside.

"Snow," my sister said. She puffed steam from her mouth. I wanted to tell her to go get a coat. Neither of us was dressed for this. "Look," she said, "it's snowing."

"Yes," I said. "And—?"

"Look," she said. She pointed at the fir trees in our yard, their arms laden with cold white loads. "Wally, it's beautiful," she said.

I looked at the fir trees. I looked down at Sarah. Her mouth was pulled down at the corners. She was not delighting in beauty.

She took my hand again and pulled me around to the back, where our property bordered on a small lake. "Look!" she demanded. I did. People were ice-skating in mittens and gloves. There was one particular girl who skated backward at an astonishing speed. Yes, yes, I did look at her. Suddenly she jammed the teeth at the toe of her blade into the ice, flew upward, and executed a breathless spin in the air, landing in a grand sweep backward. I thought of drawing her face at the instant of landing: triumphant.

Sarah grabbed my arm and yanked down with such power that I knelt before her.

My sister has a dark, pinched face. Her eyes can be intense with looking. They remind me more of mine than of George's because George was social, open to everyone, no need of a private moment, a happy man. Sarah, who loves me, is as private as I am.

"Wally," she spoke with some anger into my face, "are we going to have a Christmas this year? *They* are," she said, pointing at the lake. *"They* are," she said, pointing at the trees. "How come we're not?"

"Sure we are," I said.

"Liar," she said. "There's no Christmas here. You never talk to me anymore. You're mad at me," Sarah said. The tears began to glitter in her eyes. "You're mad at me, and I don't know why."

"No, I'm not," I whispered.

"Liar!" she said. The tears spilled over.

I said, "You should go get a coat on."

"Wally, don't send me away!" she screamed. "Please, please tell me what I did. Why are you mad at me?"

"I'll go get us coats," I said.

But she took my sweater in her two hands. "I don't know what I did," she wept. "Wally, what did I do?"

Now she was crying very hard. My sister, Sarah—she was lonely. She was lonely for me. For me, too.

I put my arms around her, and I started to cry, too.

"I'm not mad at you," I whispered into her ear. I put my cheek against her cheek, and I said what I had never said before, nor even had thought before. "I'm mad at God. George was good, Sarah. I don't just mean good at football. George loved God. I don't understand why God would take him away. That's what I don't understand."

Now I noticed that Sarah with her small hand was patting my back.

She whispered in my neck, "I prayed that God would let me die instead." Oh, now the sobs shook her poor thin body, and she couldn't talk for a long time. "But God didn't let me die. Georgie died. So Mom and Dad are sad. But I'm not mad at God, Wally. I wish you weren't mad at God."

I didn't answer.

Soon I felt that Sarah was shivering. I was cold, too.

I said, "Let's go in."

She pushed me back in order to look into my eyes. Ah, there was that Moravian glister in her stare. Yes, yes, a certain fierce madness in her glance, too. She said, "Wally, are we going to have Christmas this year?"

"Yes," I said. "I promise."

So Sarah and I became a small conspiracy.

The closer it came to Christmas, the quieter our parents grew. We were aware of that. We shared the evidence with one another. But we *could* discuss it precisely because we believed we were about to break their gloom with gladness. What a surprise our Christmas Eve would be!

No, it didn't occur to Dad to get a tree. Sarah and I went forth on our own, selected a blazing blue spruce, and hid it behind the garage.

Sarah made ornaments by putting papier-mâché in gluey strips over various-shaped light bulbs, then, when they had dried, breaking the glass within. I used primary colors to paint the ornaments. It looked like a dazzle of Mexican craft to me.

We bought presents. We made presents. Sarah spent time in my room weaving three scarves for Mom and Dad and Aunt Moravia. I began a painting.

At first I simply intended to paint the best figure I knew how, an athlete of symmetry and splendid strength. But the sketches began to talk back to me. Of their own they took upon themselves the features and the habitual stance of my brother, George. It *was* George. I was trying to sketch George.

When I realized what was happening, I experienced a strange agony. I didn't *want* to paint George. This was somehow an intrusion from last year. He had already consumed one Christmas and one whole year; he didn't deserve this one, too.

But Sarah happened to notice the sketch. Immediately she saw the resemblance and complimented me. "Good idea, Wally," she said offhandedly. "What a good present for Mom and Dad."

"Really?"

"Sure. A memory. A sort of memorial, huh?"

"Yeah. A memorial."

So I went at the task with intensity and passion. I surprised myself by how constantly I kept thinking about the painting—and by how easily George appeared beneath the color and the strokes of my brushes. I didn't think to look at a photograph, and then it became a matter of propriety that I did *not* look at pictures of George. It had to come out of my own memory only.

In fact, I managed to gather all the pictures of George from the living room and hide them.

I discussed the pose with Sarah. We decided that he should have outstretched arms. Ambiguous. It was the moment this athlete turned and sought the bullet pass. It was our brother's native openness, his pure love of people and life—and God. Sarah wanted to see his teeth again. She had always thought his teeth were beautiful, white and sturdy and even and strong. I never knew she had observed him so closely. In this detail I discovered how deeply my little sister could love. Sarah knew how to love.

It was our plan, once the painting was done, to frame it in a subdued, wooden frame, and on Christmas morning to surprise our parents—with a Christmas tree, with gifts, with carols and cookies and prayer and good memory and love.

And love.

On the morning of Christmas Eve day, I woke to a roaring. I truly did not recognize the noise for a full thirty seconds—but then I knew that it was Dad.

Dad was shouting downstairs. He was angry. The language spilled from him, uncontrolled. "Where are they? Where are they?" he yelled. "Who took them? I swear, I'll break the hand that touched them!"

My stomach immediately went tight.

There was a short interlude.

And then thunder. My father uttered cursings as I had never heard him curse before. "You tell him," he bellowed, "that they will be back where they belong when I come home at lunch, or I'll break *his* neck!"

The front door slammed.

He raced the engine. He drove away, skidding sideways on the ice.

Quickly there was a knock at my door, and Sarah came in, dead white. "Dad says you have to put George's pictures back. You have to, Wally. I told him we were cleaning them. I don't think he believed me."

I dressed. I tried to sneak the pictures back. There were three of them, a high school graduation picture, a prom picture, and an official photograph of George in his football uniform, taken the last year of his life.

While I put the last one in its place on the piano, I noticed my mother staring at me from the kitchen. Her gaze was gaunt, her eyes were stricken, as if I had hit her. She took the hem of her apron and covered her face.

I went to her. "Mom," I said, "Mom, it's OK. We didn't mean any harm—"

She turned her shoulders against me and sobbed with a huge, gulping effort.

Aunt Moravia appeared. Black sockets, white eyeballs, she raised her arm and pointed her forefinger at me. It was the most horrible thing she could do. She did not lower the arm. I walked away and she followed, pointing the accusing finger, pointing at my heart, pointing guilt into me—but I did not deserve the guilt. I did not!

Sarah and I decided that more than ever we needed a Christmas here. So we began to trim the tree out in the lawn shed, still hidden from view but ready to move indoors on the instant.

Dad came home at noon. He went straightway into the living room. I followed. He looked for each of George's pictures. He saw them. He left without eating lunch. He left in three minutes, saying nothing at all to me.

Mom had vanished. The kitchen was empty. Together, then, we baked cookies, Sarah and I, saying very little to each other, fearing that the result of all our effort was in mortal doubt. It could crash. We could fail miserably.

But this was Christmas Eve. And next year I would be gone from home, leaving Sarah behind, the only child. We sensed the endings yet to come. Therefore, though we spoke little, we felt much together. I hated it that my eyes seemed so close to tears the whole day through.

This was the plan:

Always the family went to church on Christmas Eve. All of us. It was the children's pageant, the story of the birth of our Lord. George had been Joseph, once. I had been Joseph, and Sarah had been Mary, and we had all been Gabriel: "Behold," we had, each one of us, roared: "I bring you good tidings of great joy, which shall be to all people."

George had smiled in wondrous confidence as he announced the strategies of God for the salvation of the world. I—well, I mumbled, filled with shyness and uncertainty. I always wished that I were born as free as my brother. Sarah spoke with simple sincerity. That was last year. That was the day George died. Mom and Dad were not with us when Sarah spoke her piece—and not till midnight did they call to tell us the news, and to cancel Christmas.

Sarah said it was as if she had walked into church from the starry heavens of God: "For unto you is born this day in the city of David a Savior, which is Christ the Lord."

In the past Dad would always drive the long way home through the city so that we could view the Christmas adornment of richly lit houses. Cold drive home. Warm drive home. Mother would laugh in those days. Aunt

Moravia—well, she would suddenly roar Lenten hymns: "O sacred Head, now wounded, with grief and shame weighed down. . . ."

There would be warm kitchen-talk, hot cider, and Mom's Danish pastry after we got home. Then swiftly to bed. And in the hours that followed, Mom and Dad would prepare the living room for the morning, for our bright arising.

Well, Sarah and I had no doubt of several things: Yes, we would as always celebrate the evening at church. But no, they would not be arranging the living room for joy tonight.

Therefore, after all had fallen still within the house, *we* would. Tonight we would be bearers of good tidings and great joy. That was the plan.

It failed.

Stony was the silence during dinner. Mom wept. Dad spoke no word. Indeed, his mouth was so severely shut that he seemed incapable of eating food, let alone speaking to us.

Aunt Moravia stood up and grabbed herself fore and aft. "Do you hear it?" she whispered. "Oh, honey, can't you *hear* it?" Dad did not respond. She glared at him with such a baleful, black-and-white, death's-head, smoking accusation that I felt the sweats of guilt in my own armpits. He still didn't respond. Aunt Moravia picked a piece of fish from her plate and threw it at my father. Sarah let out a yip. Dad did not move. He did not speak. He did not raise his eyes. His aunt retired to her bedroom.

Yes, we went to church. It was an agony. Sarah and I felt compelled to smile and say "Merry Christmas" to all the people our elders resolutely would not answer. I hated the pasty smile on my face. And I began to suffer an earnest resentment against my father. He could at least acknowledge these people. They were his friends, not mine. He was offending them. He was offending *me*.

In fact, it occurred to me during the bright children's pageant that my father had been offending me this whole year through. I was not responsible for George's death! Nor was I George. I was Walter, their second son, who deserved some time, some word, some conversation, some love, something.

I grew angrier and angrier throughout the service.

At the end of it Sarah whispered to me, "Stop it, Wally. You look like Dad." Instantly I was furious with her, and then I, too, chose not to return the season's greetings to those who greeted me.

"Merry Christmas, Walter!"

Your Christmas may be merry. You have no idea about mine.

No, we did not drive through town to enjoy the Christmas decorations of our neighbors. We went straight home. We went straight into the house. Clearly, Mom and Dad were about to go to their bedroom without a word to us. No cider, no Danish, no talk—not a word at all.

So I said, "If my pictures were missing this morning, would you have gotten so angry then?"

Dad froze with his foot on the first step, facing away from me. He took the second step.

So I shouted: "What's the matter with this house? Why can't you care about us now?"

Mom began to beg, "Please, Wally, please don't talk now. Not now. Later, maybe—"

"Now is the *right* time!" I yelled. "Now is the *only* time—"

And my father whirled on the step, his eyes inflamed. He raised his arm and pointed exactly as his aunt would point. Low and slow he began to speak in a diction almost thrilling for clarity.

"George died," he said, "not you, Walter. George, my firstborn, is dead. This is the day he died. This day, this hour, this minute, *now*. And all my dreams and my own childhood and fatherhood and all my days died with him. A father has the right to grieve. No one, Walter—do you hear me?—no one knows the pain of the grief of a father who has outlived his son. No one!" He began to walk toward me. I was rooted to the spot. There was not the slightest doubt in my mind: he was approaching me to hit me. "A private and unbearable pain," he whispered. "Are you so selfish that you can't give me this day? This day? Steal his pictures! Blame my sorrow! Walter—"

Suddenly Aunt Moravia was standing between us, facing my father. She lifted an old bony hand and slapped his face. He stood still a moment, then turned on his heel and took the stairs two at a time.

Mom was crying hard now. She followed him.

Aunt Moravia began to point at me again. As a sepulchral ghost she intoned, "But a prating fool shall fall." That was more than I could take. I rushed upstairs to my own room.

And then came the knock.

Sarah said, "Can I come in?"

I didn't answer. She came in anyway.

And she had the crass stupidity to say, "Are you ready, Wally? Let's go get the tree now."

I turned my back to her. "George has stolen this one, too." I said. "Go away and leave me alone. Just go away."

When I looked over my shoulder, I saw that she was gone. The door was open, but my sister had left so silently that I had not heard her go.

So now the guilt was a drowning within me. I was a wicked human being. And the only one to whom I could have gone for conversation and comfort I had just wounded horribly.

Oh, Sarah, I'm sorry. George is dead. Mom and Dad are beyond us now. Aunt Moravia was ever too far gone to be of help. But you, my sister, you were my darling and my friend. I've broken us and sent us each into solitary. Sarah, I am so sorry.

I couldn't sleep.

Late, late in the night I switched the light on over my worktable. I took out George's portrait and lay it in the light. I gazed long and long at it. Yes, the features were his. Yes, but I must have imagined for them an expression I myself had never seen in George before he died. He gazed directly back at me. At me, Wally. His teeth were strong and white, his arms cast open before me, but these eyes were older than my brother had ever been. Ageless, watchful, blameless, and knowing. *Brother, give me thine heart—*

Suddenly there was a light immediately above my head. Candlelight.

And then drops of hot wax fell on my neck, and I almost cried out in pain. But these drops were not hot; they were warm. Nor were they painful. I jumped up and whirled around and found Aunt Moravia standing in her slip immediately behind me, weeping, weeping a full flood of tears all down her pale checks. No eye shadow, no eyelashes, few hairs—she was a weak and bent and shaking woman.

She was pointing at the painting of George.

"There he is," she whispered. Now she turned and looked up into my eyes. "Vladimir, Vladimir, thanks be to God, who used your poor hand to do it."

Never before had Aunt Moravia held me, neither my hand or my self. But now she set her candlestick down and put her ancient arms around my stomach and buried her head in my shirt, whispering, "You have drawn him, Vladimir. You have given him room in our house. There in the face of young George—there is the Son of God."

Sarah was not in her room. She was bundled in the shed by the Christmas tree. Ah, my sister was so sad and so cold. I said nothing at first. I opened my coat and wrapped it around us both and tucked her as tightly as I could against my stomach.

I cried for what I had done. I was the weaker one. She was the stronger. For soon she put her hand against my cheek.

"I'm so sorry, Sarah," I whispered.

She didn't speak. She stroked my throat a while.

I said, "George didn't steal this Christmas. No one can take Christmas from us. Where the signs are, there it is. Where the signs are, there is the baby, wrapped in swaddling clothes, lying in a manger."

"I know," said Sarah. "I never thought Georgie would take it away. I just thought that Christmas would bring Georgie to us again. And Mom. And Dad. And you, Wally. You, too. I was so lonely for you."

For where that babe, the Christ child, is, there are we all gathered in a single place and peace together.

"We three kings of Orient are, bearing gifts we traverse afar, field and fountain,
moor and mountain, following yonder star."
"We Three Kings of Orient Are," JOHN H. HOPKINS JR.

O. Henry

THE GIFT OF THE MAGI

◆

One dollar and eighty-seven cents. That was all. And sixty cents of it was in pennies.

Pennies saved one and two at a time by bulldozing the grocer and the vegetable man and the butcher until one's cheeks burned with the silent imputation of parsimony that such close dealing implied. Three times Della counted it. One dollar and eighty-seven cents. And the next day would be Christmas.

There was clearly nothing to do but flop down on the shabby little couch and howl.

So Della did it. Which instigates the moral reflection that life is made up of sobs, sniffles, and smiles, with sniffles predominating.

While the mistress of the home is gradually subsiding from the first stage to the second, take a look at the home. A furnished flat at eight dollars per week. It did not exactly beggar description, but it certainly had that word on the lookout for the mendicancy squad.

In the vestibule below was a letter-box into which no letter would go, and an electric button from which no mortal finger could coax a ring. Also appertaining there unto was a card bearing the name "Mr. James Dillingham Young."

The "Dillingham" had been flung to the breeze during a former period of prosperity when its possessor was being paid thirty dollars per week. Now, when the income was shrunk to twenty dollars, the letters of "Dillingham" looked blurred, as though they were thinking seriously of contracting to a modest and unassuming D. But whenever Mr. James Dillingham Young came home and reached his flat above he was called "Jim" and greatly hugged by Mrs. James Dillingham Young, already introduced to you as Della. Which is all very good.

Della finished her cry and attended to her cheeks with the powder rag. She stood by the window and looked out dully at a gray cat walking a gray fence in a gray backyard. Tomorrow would be Christmas Day, and she had only a dollar and eighty-seven cents with which to buy Jim a present. She had been saving every penny she could for months, with this result. Twenty dollars a week doesn't go far. Expenses had been greater than she had calculated. They always are. Only a dollar and eighty-seven cents to buy a present for Jim. Her Jim. Many a happy hour she had spent planning for something nice for him. Something fine and rare and sterling—something just a little bit near to being worthy of the honor of being owned by Jim.

There was a pier-glass between the windows of the room. Perhaps you have seen a pier-glass in an eight-dollar flat. A very thin and very agile person may, by observing his reflection in a rapid sequence of longitudinal strips, obtain a fairly accurate conception of his looks. Della, being slender, had mastered the art.

Suddenly she whirled from the window and stood before the glass. Her eyes were shining brilliantly, but her face had lost its color within twenty seconds. Rapidly she pulled down her hair and let it fall to its full length.

Now, there were two possessions of the James Dillingham Youngs in which they both took a mighty pride. One was Jim's gold watch that had been his father's and grandfather's. The other was Della's hair. Had the Queen of Sheba lived in the flat across the air shaft, Della would have let her hair hang out the window some day to dry just to depreciate Her Majesty's jewels and gifts. Had King Solomon been the janitor, with all his treasures piled up in the basement, Jim would have pulled out his watch every time he passed, just to see him pluck at his beard from envy.

So now Della's beautiful hair fell about her, rippling and shining like a cascade of brown waters. It reached below her knee and made itself almost a garment for her. And then she did it up again nervously and quickly. Once she faltered for a minute and stood still while a tear or two splashed on the worn red carpet.

On went her old brown jacket; on went her old brown hat. With a whirl of skirts and with the brilliant sparkle still in her eyes, she fluttered out the door and down the stairs to the street.

Where she stopped the sign read: "Mme. Sofronie. Hair Goods of All Kinds." One flight up Della ran, and collected herself, panting. Madame, large, too white, chilly, hardly looked the "Sofronie."

"Will you buy my hair?" asked Della.

"I buy hair," said Madame. "Take yer hat off and let's have a sight at the looks of it."

Down rippled the brown cascade.

"Twenty dollars," said Madame, lifting the mass with a practiced hand.

"Give it to me quick," said Della.

Oh, and the next two hours tripped by on rosy wings. Forget the hashed metaphor. She was ransacking the stores for Jim's present.

She found it at last. It surely had been made for Jim and no one else. There was no other like it in any of the stores, and she had turned all of them inside out. It was a platinum fob chain simple and chaste in design, properly proclaiming its value by substance alone and not by meretricious ornamentation—as all good things should do. It was even worthy of The Watch. As soon as she saw it she knew that it must be Jim's. It was like him. Quietness and value—the description applied to both. Twenty-one dollars they took from her for it, and she hurried home with the eighty-seven cents. With that chain on his watch Jim might be properly anxious about the time in any company. Grand as the watch was, he sometimes looked at it on the sly on account of the old leather strap that he used in place of a chain.

When Della reached home her intoxication gave way a little to prudence and reason. She got out her curling irons and lighted the gas and went to work repairing the ravages made by generosity added to love. Which is always a tremendous task, dear friends—a mammoth task.

Within forty minutes her head was covered with tiny, close-lying curls that made her look wonderfully like a truant schoolboy. She looked at her reflection in the mirror long, carefully, and critically.

"If Jim doesn't kill me," she said to herself, "before he takes a second look at me, he'll say I look like a Coney Island chorus girl. But what could I do— oh! what could I do with a dollar and eighty-seven cents?"

At seven o'clock the coffee was made and the frying-pan was on the back of the stove hot and ready to cook the chops.

Jim was never late. Della doubled the fob chain in her hand and sat on the corner of the table near the door that he always entered. Then she heard his step on the stair away down on the first flight, and she turned white for just a moment. She had a habit of saying little silent prayers about the simplest everyday things, and now she whispered: "Please, God, make him think I am still pretty."

The door opened and Jim stepped in and closed it. He looked thin and very serious. Poor fellow, he was only twenty-two—and to be burdened with a family! He needed a new overcoat and he was without gloves.

Jim stopped inside the door, as immovable as a setter at the scent of quail. His eyes were fixed upon Della, and there was an expression in them that she could not read, and it terrified her. It was not anger, nor surprise, nor disapproval, nor horror, nor any of the sentiments that she had been prepared for. He simply stared at her fixedly with that peculiar expression on his face.

Della wriggled off the table and went for him.

"Jim, darling," she cried, "don't look at me that way. I had my hair cut off and sold it because I couldn't have lived through Christmas without giving you a present. It'll grow out again—you won't mind, will you? I just had to do it. My hair grows awfully fast. Say `Merry Christmas!' Jim, and let's be happy. You don't know what a nice—what a beautiful, nice gift I've got for you."

"You've cut off your hair?" asked Jim, laboriously, as if he had not arrived at that patent fact yet even after the hardest mental labor.

"Cut it off and sold it," said Della. "Don't you like me just as well, anyhow? I'm me without my hair, ain't I?"

Jim looked about the room curiously.

"You say your hair is gone?" he said, with an air almost of idiocy.

"You needn't look for it," said Della. "It's sold, I tell you—sold and gone, too. It's Christmas Eve, boy. Be good to me, for it went for you. Maybe the hairs of my head were numbered," she went on with a sudden serious sweetness, "but nobody could ever count my love for you. Shall I put the chops on, Jim?"

Out of his trance Jim seemed quickly to wake. He enfolded his Della. For ten seconds let us regard with discreet scrutiny some inconsequential object in the other direction. Eight dollars a week or a million a year—what is the difference? A mathematician or a wit would give you the wrong answer. The magi brought valuable gifts, but that was not among them. This dark assertion will be illuminated later on.

Jim drew a package from his overcoat pocket and threw it upon the table.

"Don't make any mistake, Dell," he said, "about me. I don't think there's anything in the way of a haircut or a shave or a shampoo that could make me like my girl any less. But if you'll unwrap that package you may see why you had me going a while at first."

White fingers and nimble tore at the string and paper. And then an ecstatic scream of joy; and then, alas! a quick feminine change to hysterical tears and wails, necessitating the immediate employment of all the comforting powers of the lord of the flat.

For there lay The Combs—the set of combs, side and back, that Della had worshiped for long in a Broadway window. Beautiful combs, pure tortoise shell, with jeweled rims—just the shade to wear in the beautiful vanished hair. They were expensive combs, she knew, and her heart had simply craved and yearned over them without the least hope of possession. And now, they were hers, but the tresses that should have adorned the coveted adornments were gone.

But she hugged them to her bosom, and at length she was able to look up with dim eyes and a smile and say: "My hair grows so fast, Jim!"

And then Della leaped up like a little singed cat and cried, "Oh, oh!"

Jim had not yet seen his beautiful present. She held it out to him eagerly upon her open palm. The dull precious metal seemed to flash with a reflection of her bright and ardent spirit.

"Isn't it a dandy, Jim? I hunted all over town to find it. You'll have to look at the time a hundred times a day now. Give me your watch. I want to see how it looks on it."

Instead of obeying, Jim tumbled down on the couch and put his hands under the back of his head and smiled.

"Dell," said he, "let's put our Christmas presents away and keep 'em a while. They're too nice to use just at present. I sold the watch to get the money to buy your combs. And now suppose you put the chops on."

The magi, as you know, were wise men—wonderfully wise men who brought gifts to the Babe in the manger. They invented the art of giving Christmas presents. Being wise, their gifts were no doubt wise ones, possibly bearing the privilege of exchange in case of duplication. And here I have lamely related to you the uneventful chronicle of two foolish children in a flat who most unwisely sacrificed for each other the greatest treasures of their house. But in a last word to the wise of these days let it be said that of all who give gifts, these two were the wisest. Of all who give and receive gifts, such as they are wisest. Everywhere they are wisest. They are the magi.

"While mortals sleep, the angels keep their watch of wond'ring love."
"O Little Town of Bethlehem," PHILLIPS BROOKS

Angela Elwell Hunt

AVNER AND THE MORNING STAR

———————————◆———————————

And we have the word of the prophets made more certain, and you

will do well to pay attention to it, as to a light shining in a dark place,

until the day dawns and the morning star rises in your hearts.

2 PETER 1:19, NIV

When God created the earth and space, he flung billions of stars through the velvet heavens.

Upon each star he placed an angel. "Now I will create man," God told the angels "Each time a baby is born, one of you will leave your star to guard the child. You will keep him safe from harm for as long as he wants my help."

Avner sighed. He waited on a shy little star, a nearly-nothing nova far from earth. *I may be on a tiny star,* he thought, *but I will train to be the mightiest guardian angel in God's service.*

Avner practiced zipping through space until he could fly to the sun and back a billion times in a second. He sat in the very center of his blazing star until he was sure he could withstand the heat of Satan's fiery darts. He built up his angelic muscles by hurling asteroids through space.

While Avner readied himself, boys and girls were born on earth, and people filled the planet. Thousands of guardian angels were already busy.

"Whew," Rigel whispered to Avner as he flew by. "I've just spent weeks guiding Abraham's servant toward Rebekah, God's chosen bride for Isaac."

I am faster than Rigel, thought Avner. *I could have brought Abraham's servant to Rebekah in the single beat of a human heart.*

Another night Altair whizzed by. "What an adventure!" he called. "I've just saved Shadrach, Meshach, and Abednego from a blazing furnace!"

I could have saved them from a hundred furnaces, thought Avner. *The feeble fires of earth are nothing like the terrible heat of my star.*

"Greetings!" Sirius called to Avner one morning. "I've just saved the prophet Daniel. I grappled with hungry lions and held their mouths closed all night!"

I could have shut their mouths with my little finger, Avner thought, flexing his muscles. *So why doesn't God send me to serve a child of earth?*

Finally an angel captain summoned Avner to the throne room of heaven, where the archangels Michael and Gabriel knelt before God. "It is time for Gabriel to visit the girl called Mary," God said. "The birth of her child will bring great joy and great trouble."

"I can guard her child," Avner volunteered, stepping boldly into the light of God's holiness. "I can protect a child of earth from anything."

Michael smiled. "You will be called when it is time," he told Avner. "Go to your star and wait."

As he waited, Avner zipped impatiently around his star. His powerful speed made the star spin faster and burn hotter. Just when he thought it would shine brighter than the earth's sky, he heard God's voice: "Go. The child will be born in Bethlehem."

As Avner's star blazed overhead in the Bethlehem night, Mary's child was born. In the first instant Avner gazed upon the boy's face, he knew this was no ordinary baby. The love and wisdom in the child's eyes had existed long before earth. Avner began to tremble. God had asked him to safeguard the only Son of God.

While Avner hovered invisibly above the newborn Jesus, he heard other angel voices shout the wonderful news. Now all creation must have heard that God existed in a tiny, helpless baby. Avner spread his protective wings wider over the man and woman who watched the babe in the manger.

Avner's bright star brought the first serious trouble. Men from the East followed it in search of the newborn King, and they stopped to ask jealous King Herod for news. Avner appeared to Joseph in a dream and sped the young family out of Bethlehem just before Herod's soldiers killed every baby boy in the city.

Great joy and great trouble, Avner thought, remembering what God had said. *'Tis a good thing that Jesus has a fast guardian angel.*

Jesus' family settled in Nazareth, and Avner blinked in amazement when the one who had filled the universe with his presence, first took three wobbly steps in a fragile human body. He marveled that one who had commanded billions of powerful angels obeyed a poor man and woman. He was astonished when the one who had spoken the world into existence skinned his knee and ran to his mother for comfort.

Avner watched over Jesus for many years. When Jesus was ready to begin his work, he went into the wilderness to pray. For forty days he did not eat, and he grew hungry, lonely, and tired.

When Jesus was at his weakest, Satan and his army approached. Avner unsheathed his blade of light.

"Put your sword away," Jesus said.

Avner slowly lowered his weapon while Satan's army giggled. They parted to make way for their wicked master, who furiously attacked Jesus. Pleasure, money, and power would be his, the devil promised, if Jesus would obey Satan instead of God.

Jesus lifted his weary eyes and refused the devil's temptation. Satan howled in fury and fled, and Avner moved in to shelter Jesus from the rain of fiery darts from Satan's retreating army.

Great joy and great trouble, Avner thought, as his wings withstood the flaming arrows. *'Tis a good thing Jesus has a fireproof guardian angel.*

One night Jesus went to a garden with three of his closest friends. Jesus knelt in prayer, but his friends went to sleep. "Father, if you are willing, take this choice from me," Jesus prayed, as great drops of sweat rolled down his forehead. "But I want whatever you want."

"Why are you so sad?" Avner asked, appearing next to Jesus. "I am strong enough to protect you."

"You don't understand," Jesus answered. "You are an angel and will live forever. I must find strength enough to die."

"No!" Avner cried, slashing the clouds with his sword of light. The heavens rumbled in protest.

"Put down your sword," Jesus whispered. "Tonight I need a strong friend."

While the disciples slept, Avner sat with Jesus. *Great joy and great trouble,* he thought, a protective feeling rising inside him. *'Tis a good thing Jesus has a strong guardian angel.*

The sound of approaching footsteps halted Jesus' prayer. "Go," Jesus said, and Avner vanished. As the angel watched from the night sky, Jesus put out his hands. Soldiers bound him and led him away.

Avner watched in horror as Jesus stood alone before cruel men who had long forgotten God. Angels on distant stars covered their faces in shame and fear as the Son of God walked down a dusty street to be crucified.

Avner flew to the throne room of heaven. "Surely it is time to act!" he cried to God. "Let me annihilate those who would do this to your Son! With one stroke of my sword I could destroy them all, for I am the mightiest guardian angel!"

"No," God answered. "I did not send my Son into the world to destroy mankind."

Gabriel lifted his anguished face. "The Son of God carries the sin of the world," he said. "Return to your star and wait."

From far away Avner heard all creation groan as Jesus died. The angels covered the sun and stars with their wings; the heavens wore black in mourning. But on earth, most men and women went on as if nothing had happened.

Avner drifted back to his star, now gleaming bloodred in the sky. *Great trouble and great sorrow,* he thought miserably. *And I am a great failure.*

After three sad days, Michael appeared before Avner. "Go to the tomb where they laid Jesus," the archangel commanded. "Roll away the stone you will find there."

Avner zipped to the tomb in a second, and one tap of his finger pushed the huge stone aside. The tomb was empty.

Suddenly Jesus stood beside him, and Avner fell to his knees. "Tell those who will come here that sin and death are defeated," Jesus said. "Not by might, but by love, mankind has been redeemed."

In a flash of understanding, Avner realized that Jesus did not want him to be creation's mightiest guardian angel. He wanted Avner to love man as much as he did.

"Yes," Jesus said, knowing Avner's thoughts. "Through great joy and great trouble, I love the people of earth. In the days to come, many will choose to follow me."

"How can I help them?" Avner whispered.

Jesus smiled. "The angel army needs a captain," he said. "A mighty and loving guardian angel."

When God created the earth and space, he flung billions of stars through the velvet heavens. Upon each star he placed an angel, and the single shining star that lingers until morning is Avner's. He's so busy taking care of God's people, you see, that he sometimes forgets to put the light out.

"Inasmuch as ye have done it unto one of the least of these my brethren,
ye have done it unto me."
MATTHEW 25:40, KJV

Grace Johnson

THE COBBLER

❖

Once upon a time in a little German village, there lived a cobbler named Gunther. In the windows of his little shop, shoes and boots of varying sizes waited for their owners to claim them or in some cases for people to buy them. Inside was the lovely smell of shoe wax and of the leather that lay upon the cobbler's bench and was strewn beside it in bits and pieces. And on any given day, except Sundays, Gunther could be seen hard at work with his tools—cutting, pounding, and stitching. For in all the countryside it was known that there was not a finer cobbler.

On this particular day snow had begun to fall, and the wind blew hard about the corners. It was very early in the afternoon of December 24, and Gunther bent over his bench, as usual. One might think that on such a day the cobbler would have left his work to prepare himself for Christmas. But there he was, hard at work.

Suddenly the door opened, and in swept a very tall man in a flowing black cape lined in scarlet. He carried a pair of elegant black boots in his gloved hands.

Looking up, Gunther recognized the high city official from the next town, a town much larger than Gunther's little village. Gunther stood up out of deference and bowed just a bit. "Lord von Schlimmel," he said politely.

Lord von Schlimmel thrust the pair of shiny boots into Gunther's hands. "I need these for a Christmas Eve ball."

Gunther opened his eyes wide. "But Christmas Eve is *tonight!*"

"Exactly!" Lord von Schlimmel smoothed his gloves and pointed a finger at the shoes. "Which is why I shall need them by five o'clock. You see what's wrong with them—where they're coming apart."

Gunther turned the shoes over, his eyes taking in each detail and knowing quickly what must be done. "But, Lord von Schlimmel, with all due respect, it's already one o'clock, and I've been working since daylight. And I see that there's a considerable amount—"

"I shall expect them to be done by *five* o'clock!" Lord von Schlimmel reiterated imperiously. "In the meanwhile—good day." He swept grandly out the door in the same fashion in which he had entered.

Gunther glared after him. He sighed and shook his head gloomily.

"Ah! My favorite cousin in the doldrums! And on Christmas Eve?" said a new voice. It was Griselda, bright and warm in a red cape, blonde curls peeking from under her bonnet. She came in the door almost as soon as Lord von Schlimmel had left. She carried something large and awkward, draped with a large brown cloth so that one could not make it out. This she proceeded to lay carefully beside the door.

Immediately from the other direction, which led to the kitchen, appeared a little lady—just the right amount of plump with wide brown eyes and graying hair done up in a bun. She held a feather duster and cleared her throat pointedly. "Excuse me—"

Gunther was staring at Lord von Schlimmel's boots. "Ja, Frau Dibble?"

"What would you like me to clean today?"

"It doesn't matter. Do whatever."

The housekeeper nodded. "And about supper—will there be anything special, it being Christmas Eve?"

Gunther moved toward the cobbler's bench. "I don't care. Do up some fish soup. There are some crackers to go with it, I think."

"Not a bit of *Stollen?*" remonstrated Mrs. Dibble. "Or some *sacher torte?* Maybe a few gingerbread cookies—"

"Nein, nein!" Gunther sat down hard at his bench to punctuate his words. "Soup is enough."

"If that's your wish then. But just let me turn up the lamp; it's clouded up so." She moved to a little table on which stood an oil lantern and turned up the wick. Immediately there issued forth a great cloud of smoke. "Oh, my!" she gasped. Her duster flailed back and forth to no avail.

"Frau Dibble, *please!* You may go now!" cried Gunther, coming to the rescue.

Mrs. Dibble retreated as fast as her short legs would carry her, waving the duster in the air. "Merry Christmas to you, Griselda," she called, disappearing toward the kitchen.

"And to you, Frau Dibble," Griselda responded warmly. She surveyed Gunther, who had gotten the lantern under control. "Gunther!" she said reprovingly but with kindness in her voice. "It's Christmas Eve!"

"Ja, Griselda, it's Christmas Eve, and I tell myself that it, too, will pass. Ah, but I forget my manners. You will sit?" He waved his hand toward a chair.

Griselda loosened the strings on her bonnet and hung her cape over the chair back and sat down, all the while regarding him solemnly.

"It's not the same anymore," he said.

Griselda's eyes clouded sympathetically. "You miss your Hilda and your little Karl. And it's worse at Christmastime?"

Gunther sighed. "Ja. Other days are not so bad. I have friends. I have my work. But on Christmas Eve *families* are together. Everybody has someplace to go." His shoulders slumped. "So—ja, I'm lonely. But soon the holidays will be over."

"Gunther!" remonstrated Griselda. "You have *us!* You're my *cousin!* You're always welcome at our house!"

"Ja, I know. And I thank you. But you have six children to see to—"

"Who all love you!"

"And your Hugo—"

Griselda shook her head sadly. "Oh, dear! You and Hugo. I know he's grouchy and sometimes things don't go so good—"

Gunther was definite. "So don't worry about me." He searched for a new subject. "Are you singing with the *Glaubensbrüder** today?"

"But, of course," she said firmly. "And then later we'll sing together, Gunther, you and I."

Gunther shook his head. "It's too much effort if the heart isn't in it." He tapped the boots that lay before him. "Besides, I have these to repair for Lord von Hoity-Toity by five o'clock. I shall have to put aside everything else and work as if the Furies were after me!"

Griselda was firm. "Nevertheless, I will come. It's part of `keeping Christmas' for me—to remember when we were children and the family gathered together and we sang and sang—"

Gunther stared reflectively past the shoes in his window, past the falling snow, seeing another time and place. "Ja, when Christmas was magical and we thought it would always be like that. Not knowing that one day it could mean more loneliness and pain than any other day."

"Oh, dear Gunther!" Griselda rose and came toward him. "It's still the day we celebrate that Jesus *came*, the Bright and Morning Star, to *lighten* our darkness, to be *with* us in the loneliness." She put her hand on his arm. "Do you believe it?"

"That he came? Ja, ja. I read in the Scripture. Every day I read."

"And he is still here," she persisted.

Gunther wrinkled his brow thoughtfully. "I suppose."

*A singing group comprised of German men.

"Ach du lieber! I almost forgot!" With a cry Griselda ran to pick up the object she had set on the floor and then whisked off its brown cover. Underneath was a gingerbread house. "Made by the children. They wanted you to have it." She glanced about the shop. "We *knew* you'd not have a single thing to remind you of Christmas. Here!" She thrust it toward him. "Now I must go, but I'll be back." She gathered up her coat and bonnet. "The fun is already beginning in the village square. Open your door—*and your heart!* Maybe you can hear it!"

And with that she was gone.

Gunther stood in the middle of his shop holding his gift and thinking that Griselda's good cheer only made his own sadness seem the greater. He looked down at the gift from the children. "Now what would I want with a gingerbread house?" he muttered.

Gunther was hard at work on Lord von Schlimmel's boots when Mrs. Dibble entered. "Herr Gunther, you still want no lunch?"

"Nein," he said without looking up.

"But it's three o'clock!"

"Ja, and my work isn't going well. These must be done by five, and some of my stitching isn't right, and there's more to do than I thought."

"Maybe some tea or coffee then? And a little marzipan?"

He shook his head. "Nein."

"One would think we could have a little more cheer around here, especially on Christmas Eve!" grumbled Mrs. Dibble as she left the room.

Gunther sighed deeply and rested his chin upon his hand. He was very tired—tired inside himself mostly. Perhaps if he rested a few moments. . . . He put his head down on his arms.

It could not have been more than two minutes before his shop door jingled as someone entered. Gunther fought to drag himself from a sleepy stupor.

"Oh my!" said a woman's voice. "He surely needs us!"

"He doesn't have a Christmas tree!" exclaimed a child.

"And there's nothing pretty in the window!" said another.

Gunther rubbed his hand across his eyes. "Good day."

"Merry Christmas!" responded the woman warmly, holding tightly to the hands of two children.

"You've brought shoes?" he asked in polite friendliness, rising from his bench.

"No shoes."

Gunther was puzzled. "Then you've come for something else?"

"Oh, yes, definitely for something else," she said, removing her cloak. Gunther could not have told whether the woman was young or old. But for some reason he noted tiny spring flowers embroidered across her dark dress, and a long scarlet apron that gave her a bit of a dashing air. And her eyes sparkled.

She took the children's coats and laid all the wraps across a wooden chair with a sense of getting straight to the heart of the matter—though what the "matter" was totally escaped Gunther. "This is Greta," she said, and a little girl with smooth blond hair curtsied. "And Franz!" The woman pointed as Franz bowed solemnly. "And I'm Carrie," she smiled, extending her hand.

"I'm Gunther—and—" But Carrie was already walking around inspecting things. "I've not seen you before," he said. "Where do you live?" He was slightly embarrassed to realize he was following her about.

"Oh, somewhere on the edge of things, you might say." Carrie picked up a boot and peered out the window. "Yes, definitely at the edge of things!"

"I see," said Gunther, although he definitely did *not* see. He glanced at the children, who seemed to be everywhere at once. He had a vague feeling that he might be losing control of his shop.

"Oh, look, Greta!" shrieked Franz, pointing to the gingerbread house that lay on the floor in a corner.

"A gingerbread house!" cried Greta, running and kneeling before it. "See the little door and windows, Franz! And all the candy!"

"It's very pretty," said Carrie, crossing in front of Gunther.

"But he just has it on the floor in the corner," said Franz.

"That's not a very good place," agreed Carrie.

"I beg your pardon," said Gunther pointedly, wondering if the three had forgotten he was there.

Carrie was unperturbed. "Let's see—" She spied a stool. "Ah, children, pick it up—very carefully. Let's put it right up on this stool. There!" She stood back to observe.

Greta clapped her hands. "That makes it more special, doesn't it, Carrie?"

"It does!" She cocked her head thoughtfully. "Of course, pretty as it is, it hasn't anything to do with the *real* meaning of Christmas." She turned to Gunther. "Gunther, don't you have a crèche—a manger scene?"

"Ja, but if you don't mind my saying so—"

"Then where is it?"

"It's . . . it's up in the attic."

"Why's it up there?" piped up Greta.

Franz glowered. "Oh, Greta, you ask so many questions!"

"Why, Herr Gunther?" persisted the child.

Gunther blinked. Must he reveal his innermost self to these people? And yet he could not lie. "I—I put the crèche up there—when Christmastime didn't seem happy anymore."

"Oh," said Greta.

Meanwhile, Carrie was again walking about the shop. She seemed to be eyeing the windows from various angles.

"Excuse me!" said Gunther in a tone that implied it was time for an explanation.

"Yes, of course," replied Carrie. "Don't worry; you're *not* in our way!" She didn't see Gunther roll his eyes. "Children," she announced grandly, "bring the candle in!" As the children ran outside, she said matter-of-factly, "We left it just outside the door so we could look things over first."

"Of course!" Gunther let as much sarcasm creep into his voice as he dared. He sat down; things were clearly out of his control.

Carrie smiled at him charmingly. "You'll like it very much. I know you will."

The children entered, carrying a very large, beautiful candle and a box.

"Right over here," directed Carrie. She eyed the selected window. "It must be just right." She moved several shoes to the side, put two pairs of boots on the floor, and took the candle, placing it carefully in the window.

Suddenly Greta was beside Gunther. "Could I sit on your lap?"

"Well, ja, I suppose you may," he responded, surprised, but feeling he ought to be willing.

Greta settled herself. "Herr Gunther, did you ever have a little girl like me?"

"Nein. But I had a little boy. About the size of Franz."

"What was his name?"

"Karl," answered Gunther, not sure he wished to continue the conversation.

Greta nodded. "And did Karl have a mama?"

Franz snorted in disgust. "She asks so many questions!"

"It's all right, Franz," said Carrie, kneeling before the window, arranging greens from the box around the candle. "It's good to talk about those things." She looked meaningfully at Gunther. "It is good to talk about them, Gunther."

Gunther returned her look thoughtfully. "Her name was Hilda."

"And did you love her very much?" asked Greta.

"Karl and I both did."

Franz came to stand beside Gunther. "I suppose they died and that's what made Christmas not seem happy anymore."

"Ja," Gunther replied softly.

Carrie gave the greens a last pat and struck a match. The candle glowed with a wondrous light. "There now!"

Greta slid off Gunther's lap, and both children ran to the window, shrieking, "It's beautiful! It's beautiful!"

Gunther stood up. It was time to get to the heart of things. "Excuse me! But would you mind telling me why you came here?"

"Because you needed us," Carrie replied simply.

"I see," he said, thinking again that no, he did *not* see. "Then may I ask why you've put a candle in my window?" He felt himself growing in both frustration and sarcasm. "My shop was perfectly fine without it!"

Carrie stepped back and surveyed the candle's glow for a long moment. "Well, it's like this. There's a beautiful old legend that the Christ child walks about on Christmas Eve seeking to enter the hearts of men. And it's a candle in the window that invites him across the threshold."

The children on either side of Gunther tugged at his arms. "Did you hear that story before, Herr Gunther? Then you know why we brought the candle and why Carrie put it in the window."

Gunther frowned. "But I still—"

"Oh my!" cried Carrie. "It's time we were going. Come, children." She scooped up their wraps and started toward the door.

Franz stood his ground. "But, Carrie, you didn't tell him yet!"

Carrie stopped in her tracks. "Oh, mercy! You're so right. And it's the most important thing, too!" She walked back to Gunther. "It's *so* special, Gunther! So very special!" She sat down and waited for him to sit beside her. Then she put her hand on his arm and leaned toward him. "And this is what it is . . . !"

Soon an entirely different atmosphere had descended upon the cobbler shop. Gunther swooshed about in a frenzy of physical activity and jolly goodwill. In one arm he held a pile of evergreen boughs, and with the other he busily laid them everywhere. Gunther was not known for his decorating abilities, and things may have been placed a bit haphazardly, but the entire shop was beginning to smell like a wonderful pine forest.

"Frau Dibble!" he boomed. "We need more evergreen boughs!"

His housekeeper appeared with an armload of greenery and a puzzled expression. "At this rate there won't be a bush or tree left outside!"

"No problem!" Gunther took her load and continued about the shop.

Mrs. Dibble folded her hands. "What's gotten into you this past hour? Ah! I have heard that some people use greens to banish demons lurking in the darkness. Have you gotten superstitious?"

Gunther zoomed past her. "Nein, nein! I have no problem with demons."

"He has no problem with demons," Mrs. Dibble said to no one in particular.

Gunther abruptly stopped in his tracks. *"Ach du lieber! Stollen!* We need *Stollen* and *Hutzelbrot!"* He was in motion again. "Some cookies, too? Maybe tart jam."

Mrs. Dibble rolled her eyes. "Suddenly he has no problem with food either!"

"But you must hurry! Or they may not be done in time."

She wiped her hands on her apron. "Stubborn as I am—*Stollen* and cookies are *already* baking. I did them just in case. Soon the shop will be filled with wonderful baking smells!" She started for the kitchen but stopped. "In time? In time for *what?*

Gunther stood very still as a sense of awe and reverence came over him. "In time for my Visitor."

"What visitor? You have people running in and out of here all the time."

Gunther smiled. "When my Visitor comes, you shall know it. I promise!"

"You've never seen this person?"

"Nein. But surely—surely I will!"

Mrs. Dibble's eyebrows went up and then down. "I think you may be a bit daft."

Gunther, undeterred, was again in motion. "Indeed! And what do you term `daft'?"

"Please forgive me, but a bit out of step with the rest of us."

Gunther beamed at her. "That's it! That's it! Frau Dibble, such an astute lady you are! Out of step! Out of step with the old *me!* Isn't it wonderful?"

Suddenly Mrs. Dibble was staring at the candle in the window. "The candle? I've never seen it before. How did it get there?"

"Franz, Greta, and Carrie brought it to me."

"Franz, Greta, and Carrie? Who are they?"

"I don't really know."

"Then where are they from?"

Gunther deposited the last evergreen bough on the table beside the lantern. "They live somewhere on the edge of things. That's what Carrie said."

"Ja? Well, I'd better go to the kitchen." She shook her head, muttering to herself, "I wonder if he's all right."

"Go up to the attic first and fetch the crèche," Gunther called after her.

"I already did. It's just here in the hall," she said, bringing it to him.

Eagerly Gunther pulled back the flaps of the old dusty box. "What could be more appropriate for *him* to see!" And as Mrs. Dibble started again for the kitchen, "And milk! We should have fresh milk."

"Helmut has already brought over fresh. It's by the back door," she called.

"Well, put it in a nice pitcher. We don't want to serve it just out of a jar."

Suddenly the housekeeper cocked her head, listening intently. "Do you hear something outside? I'll go and look."

She soon reappeared with her arm about a frail woman, slightly stooped, wrapped in a tattered blanket. "I found her huddled on the walk, moaning and shaking with the cold."

In one bound, Gunther was next to the poor woman. "Let us help you. Here, sit, please."

The woman sank down in the chair gratefully and let out a little moaning breath. "I saw the candle in the window, and it had such a beautiful glow I had to stop and look—." She stared past them, and her old eyes became dreamy—"and remember," she added softly. "Then I felt faint and then—I don't know."

"You fell against the shop." Mrs. Dibble patted her shoulder comfortingly. "Just sit here and rest. Would you like to take your blanket off?"

"Oh, no!" The woman pulled the blanket closer. "I'm still a little cold."

"Are you hungry?" Gunther asked solicitously.

She shook her head. "Nein."

"Ah, but I think some good, hot fish soup would do you good—and some bread. Frau Dibble, will—"

"Nein! Truly, I cannot eat anything. I know I can't."

Mrs. Dibble looked at her more closely. "Do you feel sick?"

"A little," she murmured.

"Your eyes don't look well." She felt the woman's forehead. "You have a fever!"

"Perhaps. But I'm better already. I can take the blanket off now. In here it is warm."

Mrs. Dibble folded the blanket and set it beside the chair. "You just stay right here, and I'm going to get you something for your fever." And she hurried out.

The woman stared about the shop with wide-eyed interest. Meanwhile, Gunther, being a somewhat shy man, felt it easier to busy himself with his task. So he went back to his box, took out an object, and began to unwrap its brown paper.

The old woman continued to gaze about her. "It's so beautiful in here," she said, "with all the branches, the gingerbread house, and the candle. Most of all, the candle. I never saw such a pretty one." Her eyes continued around the room. "It's almost as if you're getting ready for someone. Oh, but of course, it's Christmas you prepare for."

"Well, that too, I suppose." Gunther carefully set a wooden figure of the Virgin Mary on the table. "But I'm also expecting a very *special* Visitor."

The old woman spied the figure and let out a cry of delight. "Oh—oh!"

Gunther smiled. "You like this?" He observed her for a moment. "Would you like to hold it?"

She reached both hands toward the carving. "Oh, could I?" Gently she touched the figure.

Gunther went back to his task, unwrapping and setting the crèche figures on the table, all the while observing his guest.

The old woman stroked the wood lovingly. "When I was a little girl we lived next to a church, and at Christmastide there were figures like this—a little larger, maybe. Papa would take me there, and while he and the pastor would talk, the pastor would let me touch them and move them around a little." Her eyes became dreamy. "I thought it was the most wonderful thing. . . ." Her voice trailed off, and she seemed to be in another world.

Mrs. Dibble bustled in. "I couldn't find the medicine. So I had to go next door. Now, just let me give you two spoonfuls, and you'll soon feel better. Actually, you look better already! A visit to the cobbler's shop must agree with you!"

Suddenly the woman lifted her head. "Singing. I hear singing."

"Ah, it's the *Glaubensbrüder!* Every Christmas they come, and Gunther's cousin sings with them." Mrs. Dibble pulled a stool close and sat down beside her. She patted her hand. "Listen. You will like this."

"Silent night! Holy night! All is calm, all is bright," sang the men, and Griselda's pure, sweet voice rose above them like a lovely bird in flight.

Afternoon had cast soft shadows into the corners of the shop. The lantern and the candle sent shafts of light dancing over the rough floor and playing among the evergreen boughs. Gunther watched as its glow lit the face of his kindly housekeeper and saw it turn the features of the old woman into beauty as she sat entranced, listening.

"Son of God, love's pure light . . . the dawn of redeeming grace." Yes, yes, it was so! Gunther felt himself caught and lifted beyond his shop, beyond the core of his loneliness, beyond pressures and cares.

As the song died away and the footsteps and voices of the singers retreated down the street, the woman sighed. "Like heaven! I will never forget it!" She stirred herself. "But I must go now. I'm much better. Truly I am."

Gunther's brow was wrinkled in deep thought. "Would you like to take the crèche home with you?"

Her eyes flew wide in surprise. "What do you mean?"

"Would you like to take this crèche with you?" Gunther repeated.

"Oh, I couldn't!"

"But you could if I *gave* it to you."

The woman's lined face crinkled in wonderment. "A gift! For *me*? But why would you do it?"

"Because I want you to have it."

"But it's part of getting ready for someone you're expecting."

Gunther was silent for a long moment. Then he said softly. "I feel that the One for whom I wait would want you to have it."

The old woman clasped the wooden figure to her, and tears coursed down her face. "No one has ever—" There was a sob in her voice. "It's the most wonderful gift I've ever had!"

Mrs. Dibble and Gunther smiled with happiness.

"I must go," she said again.

"Is there someone who could come for you?" asked Gunther.

"Nein. There is no one."

"Then I'll go along," said Mrs. Dibble, "and see you safely home."

"And I'll put the figures in the box for you." Gunther paused and frowned. "Now what else was it that I should be doing?"

Mrs. Dibble wrapped the blanket about the woman. "Lord von Schlimmel's shoes, maybe?"

"*Ach du lieber!*" cried Gunther in horror. "In all the excitement, I forgot!"

"It's already half past four," she offered.

"I'll never be able to do them by five o'clock!" Gunther tucked the last figure in and closed the box. "Wait! What am I thinking of? I should nearly kill myself for a pair of boots for Lord von Hoity-Toity? Ridiculous!"

"But what will you tell Lord von Schlimmel?"

Gunther's eyes twinkled with sudden merriment. "That he can dance in his stocking feet if need be!" He placed the box in the woman's arms with a courtly bow. "These are yours! God bless you."

She held the box close. "It's been one of the loveliest afternoons of my life." Her eyes brimmed with tears. "You have given me so much. I will treasure these, and I'll never forget you."

304

When the woman and Mrs. Dibble had gone, Gunther strode about his shop, wagging his head haughtily from side to side. "Lord von Schlimmel! *Ach Himmel* to Lord von Schlimmel! On Christmas Eve I'll *not* spend my time on Lord von Schlimmel's boots!"

Suddenly he stood still, and his face broke into a great smile at a new thought. "Of course! Why didn't I think of it before? I shall make a pair of shoes for the One for whom I wait!" He rustled eagerly through his cobbler's bench, eyeing his materials. Then he stopped. "But how can there be enough time?" He knit his brow, searching for an answer.

Abruptly he clapped his hands. "The shoes! The shoes for Prince Frederick!" he shouted. The count had come all the way to Gunther's village to ask him personally. Such an honor! And they were the very finest pair he had ever made. He only need do a few more stitches and finish off the lacings. The count would come for them next week. Surely by then he could make another pair for the little prince.

From a high shelf in the back of the shop he took down a carved box and drew out the shoes of a child. Lovingly he touched the leather and turned them over in his big hands. "Ja! *These* will be for the Christ—the *very finest for him!*"

At the cobbler's bench he went to work, breaking out in a joyful "Good Christian men rejoice, with heart and soul and voice. . . ."

So caught up was he in his work and his song that he did not hear the jingle of his door nor the footsteps of the man who entered—until a voice said, "You have a fine shop here."

"*Ach Himmel!*" cried Gunther. "I didn't hear you come in."

"I am liking your song," offered the man.

"And I am thanking you!" returned Gunther heartily, surveying his visitor. The man had dark eyes, sandy-colored brows, and hair that seemed to go every which way and met with a beard thick and long. His coat was torn and threadbare, and his shoes were coming apart at the seams. (Always Gunther noted a man's shoes.) And he carried a large, lumpy black bag.

The man nodded toward the shoes on Gunther's bench. "You're doing fine work there."

"It must be my *very best* work! It's for Someone special."

The man nodded. "I see."

"Ja. Now what may I do for *you?* And wouldn't you like to lay down your bundle?"

"I would." He swung it off his back. "Groceries for the family." He shifted uneasily on his feet. "Could I see some of your boots, perhaps?"

"Ja, ja." Gunther put down his tools and took off his glasses. He picked up a pair of boots. "Now these are of the finest leather. And the lacings will never wear out." Gunther stopped and wondered what he could be thinking. How could anyone in such tattered clothing afford *new* boots? "Actually, I think the size is too big." He picked up another pair. "Now these are second-hand, so they don't cost so much. But I've put fresh uppers on them."

"They're—very nice," said the man hesitantly.

Gunther moved to the other side of the shop. "But then—a pair that would cost even less is over here. They may be patched and stitched up, but they are a fine pair of boots."

The man again shifted uncomfortably. "Well—I—let me think. . . ."

"Actually, as I think of it, they've sat around here for so long, you would do me a great favor if you would take them for *nothing*." He held them out. "Please, take them!"

The man shook his head. "I'm sorry. I think I have a little confession to make. I have no money. I saw the candle in your window, and it looked so friendly that I came inside to get warm."

Gunther clapped him on the back. "Never mind. This is good. You are welcome."

At that moment Mrs. Dibble entered. "Here I am, finally."

"Did you see her safely home?"

Mrs. Dibble frowned in puzzlement. "Not exactly. We walked a ways. Then I saw someone I knew, and I turned to greet her—only momentarily—and the woman was gone! I couldn't find her anywhere. I hope she's all right."

Gunther looked concerned. "Ja, I hope so." Then he remembered the business at hand. "Frau Dibble, please get some milk and *Stollen* for my guest."

Mrs. Dibble's eyes flew open wide, and she gaped in astonishment at the "guest." "You mean to tell me. . . ?" She pulled herself together and started toward the kitchen. "Ja, I will do it."

Gunther reached for the man's coat. "Let me take your coat. And come—sit here at the table. You're hungry, I think?"

"Ja, I am." He glanced at his bag. "Those are not groceries."

"I thought as much."

He sat down gratefully and leaned his elbows on the table. "Those are scraps of wood I picked up where they are building—for a fire in the stove. I shovel snow for marks, when I can. Lately there has been cold but not so much snow." He grimaced. "So then, in the meanwhile I must be a beggar."

Mrs. Dibble appeared with a tray. She placed cups, a pitcher of milk, and a plate of fruitcake and cookies on the table.

"Eat," encouraged Gunther warmly. "Eat as much as you can!"

Mrs. Dibble peered at the guest in amazement until a look from Gunther caught her attention. She straightened herself. "Well, now, will there be anything else?"

"I think not."

"Then I'll be going. It's getting late, and Herr Dibble will be waiting."

"Ja, ja, you go home. Thank you. And Merry Christmas!"

After another long look, Mrs. Dibble shrugged her shoulders and left, shaking her head.

There was a commotion at the opposite side of the shop. "Oh my!" said Gunther. "I'm afraid I know who it is."

The door flew open, and in swept Lord von Schlimmel. He drew himself up pompously. "I've come, of course, for my boots."

"And here they are." Gunther held his breath as he took them and turned them over.

"But, my dear fellow, you've scarcely done a thing to them!"

"Something more important came up."

Incensed, Lord von Schlimmel glared at him. "But *what* do you expect me to do?"

In a burst of daring, Gunther put his arm about Lord von Schlimmel's shoulders, moving him jovially but firmly toward the door. "I expect you to dance in your stocking feet! Or barefooted, even! Perhaps you will start a new style! And now—" Gunther opened the door—"good night and Merry Christmas!" He closed the door on the confused nobleman.

He returned to the table and seated himself across from the beggar as muttered imprecations outside faded in the distance. "I wasn't very nice, was I?"

"I thought you were wonderful!" The beggar paused in his eating. "You're making a pair of shoes for someone more important than Lord von Whoever?"

Gunther leaned across the table. "I'm waiting for the dear Lord."

"Who?"

"For the Christ child. Do you think that I've taken leave of my senses?"

The beggar peered from under his shaggy brows and over his cup of milk. "I couldn't say. You look quite sensible to me."

Eagerly Gunther rose, took a worn Bible from the shelf, and brought it to the table. "You know how the dear Lord came to earth long ago?"

"Ja," said the man slowly. "When I was a child I heard it."

Gunther tapped the Bible lovingly. "In here, in these pages, I find the dear Lord. And it comforts me here—in my heart."

"Ja? Even when things seem pretty bad?"

Gunther was thoughtful. "Sometimes I still feel very sad. But maybe not so much as if I didn't read. When my Hilda and my Karl first died, every night I lay on my bed and cursed and cried. Now I say, `O Lord, Thy will be done.' And it helps."

The beggar munched more slowly on his *Stollen.* "And now you—you wait for him? To come here?"

Gunther opened the Bible. "Last evening I was reading where a rich man named Simon invited the Lord to his house and how a woman, a sinner, showed her devotion to the Lord, and Jesus said to Simon—" Gunther pointed—"right here he says, `Simon, . . . I entered into thine house, thou gavest me no water for my feet. . . . Thou gavest me no kiss. . . . My head with oil thou didst not anoint.' But he tells how the poor woman did so much!"

The beggar reached for a cookie. "Ja?"

"And I said to myself, `Gunther, that Simon must have been just like you! Always thinking of himself!' So you see, when the dear Lord comes, I want to be ready. When he comes to me, should I behave like that Simon? Nein, nein! God forbid!"

His visitor was visibly moved. "That's very beautiful. But if you'll pardon my asking, why do you think he's coming here to you?"

"Someone came to tell me *this very day* that he would come. Could I have imagined it?" He glanced at the candle. "No, I think not."

The beggar wiped his mouth with the back of his hand. "I've eaten too much of your food. But I'm warmed and filled. And I must go."

"Ah, then here are your boots. Please! You must take them! And I shall help you with your coat." Gunther looked down at the coat he held. How could he let anyone go out into the cold in such a coat? "This isn't warm enough. Wait." He returned with a warm coat of his own. "Here, put this on."

"Oh, nein! How can I take your own coat?"

"Take it! Take it! I have two coats. Now what would I want with two coats? One is plenty!"

The beggar buttoned it up in wonderment and picked up his bag. "You've given so much—the shoes, a coat. You've given me food for my stomach and food for my soul. I'll not forget."

Gunther followed the man to the door. When he had gone, Gunther stepped outside. He looked searchingly up and down the street. The wind had ceased to blow, and large flakes fell silently. He could see no one. "Surely, he'll come soon," Gunther murmured as he returned to his bench. "In the meanwhile, I *must* finish the shoes."

It was not long before a little girl entered. Gunther saw her out of the corner of his eye as he kept working. "How are you?" he asked.

"Fine," said a small voice.

"You brought something for repair?"

"Nein."

"Then why are you here?"

"I thought I could help you, maybe—"

Gunther poked a lacing through the leather. "I'm afraid not. I could use a strong boy, not a little girl. Sorry."

Still the child stood there.

"What's your name?" he asked.

"Maria."

"Well then, Maria, don't you think you should be going home?"

"Nein."

"Why not?"

She moved a step closer. "Because I don't have a home."

Gunther tightened the last of his stitching. "Everybody has a home. Where did you stay last night?"

"I don't know the name of it."

He laid the shoe down and turned toward her. Great dark eyes stared back at him from a pale, thin face. She clutched a tattered black shawl over a faded cotton dress. And she had no shoes, only thick rags tied over her feet.

"Are you hungry?" he asked.

Maria nodded solemnly. "Ja."

Gunther picked up a soft polishing cloth. "Then go over to the table. Do you see the bread and the cookies? And the milk in the pitcher?"

The child peered into the pitcher. "Ja, I see it."

Gunther moved the cloth over the shoe carefully, lovingly. "While I work, you sit right down there and eat until you aren't hungry anymore." Out of the corner of his eye he watched as Maria ate and drank hungrily, almost voraciously.

The front door flew open, and in came Griselda. "Gunther, I'm back! Did you think I was never—" She stopped short and stared about the shop in amazement. "Gunther! The greenery and—what on earth has happened?"

"Maybe not on earth but in heaven," returned Gunther cheerily. "Come, and I shall tell you of it."

Griselda's eyes were caught by the child. "And I see you have a visitor!"

"That's Maria, who seems to have no home and who is very hungry."

Flinging off her cape and bonnet, Griselda sat down on the other side of the table. "Hello, Maria."

"Hello." The child scarcely looked up, so busy was she with her eating.

"Merry Christmas!" said Griselda. There was no response, and Griselda noted the unkempt, matted hair that clung about the pale face. "Did you know it's Christmas, Maria?"

"Nein," said Maria between great gulps of milk.

"Where did you come from?" pursued Griselda.

With one hand Maria took a cookie. With the other she pointed. "A place—far, that way."

"Why did you come in here?"

"Because I saw the pretty candle in the window," she said, munching contentedly.

"The candle! Gunther, it's lovely! Where did it come from? And what caused you to put all these boughs about?" She studied him carefully. "And most of all, what turned you into a completely different person from the one I left earlier?"

Gunther continued to polish, but more slowly. "It's a strange story, one that I'm not completely sure I believe myself anymore. But it changed me—you see that?"

"I do see it!" she said with a smile.

He leaned forward. "I—am anticipating—and anticipating is part of hope, isn't it?"

"It is."

"I'm anticipating a visit from the dear Lord himself! I was given the candle and a message that he would come." Gunther tapped his head. "You think I'm crazy?"

Griselda surveyed him earnestly. *"Never!"* she said firmly. "And I know that he is here for those who reach out to him."

"Oh!" With a cry of wonder, Maria had run to the gingerbread house.

Griselda smiled at the child. "It's a pretty little house, isn't it?"

Maria gazed in wide-eyed wonder. "I like the little windows and the pretty candles. But real houses aren't like that."

Griselda knelt beside her. "What kind of house did you live in, Maria?"

"I lived in lots of houses."

"With your mama and papa?"

"Nein. I never saw them."

"With whom, then?"

"Different people." The little girl gently fingered the house. "The last lady said it cost too much to feed me, so I got up this morning before it was even light and went away."

A glance passed between Griselda and Gunther. Gunther laid the shoes down carefully. His eyes caressed them proudly. "They are all done!"

Griselda stood up. "Then it's time for us to sing, Gunther, you and I, before I must get home to the family. Come! It will be like old times! And," she said with a gesture toward Maria, "we even have an audience! Would you like that, Maria?"

The child nodded solemnly.

And sing they did! Beautiful Christmas melodies echoed throughout the cobbler's shop.

When the last note died away, Maria said softly, "I liked your song."

"I must go now," said Griselda, tying on her bonnet. Suddenly she moved to the little girl. "Maria, would you like to go home with me?"

For the first time Maria smiled. "Ja, I would like that."

"Then come." Griselda wrapped the tattered shawl around her. Then to Gunther she whispered, "I'll find out about her, Gunther, and who knows? Once one has six children, what's one more?" Griselda's face crinkled into a smile.

Gunther was staring at Maria's feet. "Maria, I think . . ." Slowly he walked to his cobbler's bench and picked up the shoes. The shop seemed very still as he turned them over in his hands. At last he turned back to Griselda and the child. "I think you need these, Maria. Let's put them on you. Perhaps *you* are the one I was supposed to make them for."

Maria sat down in wide-eyed astonishment as her rags were removed and the new shoes substituted. "I never had new shoes before! They're so beautiful!" She walked about, filled with happiness.

Griselda glanced at Gunther. "They were to be for the Christ child?"

"I know he'll understand," Gunther replied a little sadly. Now Maria was gazing at the gingerbread house. "Maria," he said, "would you like to take the gingerbread house with you? It could be your very own." He looked at Griselda. "Couldn't it, Griselda?"

"Oh, ja, your very own! What a lovely idea!"

"I never had anything like that! My very own?"

Gunther placed it in her arms. "Your very own."

When they had gone, Gunther walked slowly about in the stillness of his shop. He looked at the stool. "The gingerbread house might have amused him," he said aloud. "And surely he would have thought the crèche so special." He looked into the milk pitcher. "The milk is all gone. And the bread and the cookies. Or nearly so."

At his bench he picked up the carved shoe box and opened it. "And the shoes! The best pair I ever made!" Tears rolled down the cheeks of the cobbler. "But he'll understand. I know he will!" He shut the empty box with a final snap and sat down.

Shadows were dark in the corners now. The candle glowed steadily, but the oil lamp sent fitful fingers of light over planks and beams. "Ja, Gunther," he said at last, "you keep a stiff upper lip. But you don't fool yourself!" He leaned his chin on his hand. "Christmas Eve will soon be over. And still he has not come."

Gunther had fallen asleep with his head on his arms. He had not heard the town clock chime ten—nor eleven. Then something caused him to awaken. He glanced toward the door, but all was quiet. He moved to the window and peered out. A blanket of snow lay tranquil and undisturbed around the shop.

He took out his pocket watch. "Just a few more minutes," he said sadly, "and I shall blow out the candle and go to bed."

He heard a sound behind him and whirled about, his heart leaping in hope.

Before him stood Carrie, Franz, and Greta. "Merry Christmas!" said Carrie.

He peered at them with a mixture of disbelief and puzzlement. Carrie and the children had been the means of changing his life on this day. Whenever he thought of them throughout the afternoon, it was with affection and gratitude—and joy at the special rapport they had shared. Now the old bitterness and loneliness had returned, and the three before him could not dispel it. "You've come back," he finally said in a flat tone.

Carrie unbuttoned her cape. "Of course!"

"You're out rather late, aren't you?" The moment he said it, Gunther knew it had sounded harsh.

"Oh, that's our best time," said Franz cheerfully.

"Everything's so soft and beautiful," added Greta. "The starlight makes it look like angel dust on the rooftops."

Carrie nodded. "We saw the torches of worshipers on their way up to the midnight service. It makes a lovely, shining necklace against the dark hillside."

Gunther moved toward his cobbler's bench. "That's very—nice," he said, trying to keep an edge out of his voice. He motioned toward a chair. "Please, do sit, if you like."

Carrie sat down, and the children sat on the floor beside her. They seemed rather subdued; the shop was very still.

"Why have you returned?" Gunther asked at last.

"To hear of your Christmas Eve, Gunther," Carrie responded warmly.

"There's nothing to tell. No one came."

"That can't be!"

"Well, my cousin, and the housekeeper, and the *Glaubensbrüder,* to sing."

Carrie leaned forward. "No one else?"

"Not the Christ child!" Gunther's frustration welled up within him. He felt he would have cried if he were not a grown man. "I was *ready* for him!"

"But was there no one else?" persisted Carrie.

"Only a sick woman. A street beggar. A homeless child."

Carrie leaned back in her chair thoughtfully. "I see. Did you turn them away?"

Gunther stood up. "Nein! Nein! They had needs! I couldn't turn them away! The beggar needed a coat, and I gave away the crèche and the shoes and—" He broke off and stared at Carrie in consternation. "Is—is that why he did not come? Because I gave away all the things that were to be his?"

Carrie jumped to her feet. "No! No! Oh, you mustn't think it!" She almost ran to the big Bible, which still lay on the table. Quickly she opened it. "Here. Look, Gunther. You must see this!"

Gunther sat down before it slowly, greatly puzzled.

She pointed. "Here it is. Read it, Gunther. Please!"

Gunther looked at the passage in Matthew's Gospel and read aloud. "Then shall the King—" He looked questioningly at Carrie.

She nodded. "The dear Lord Jesus."

Gunther's finger followed as he read. "Then shall the King say unto them on his right hand, `Come, ye blessed of my Father, inherit the kingdom prepared for you from the foundation of the world: For I was an hungred, and ye gave me meat: I was thirsty, and ye gave me drink: I was a stranger, and ye took me in: Naked, and ye clothed me.'"

Gunther looked up, and his eyes brimmed with tears. "Those things are what I would have wanted to do for the Lord! If he had come, I would have done them!"

Carrie laid her hand on his shoulder. "I know you would have! But there's more. Franz and Greta know it by heart. Franz—"

Franz got up solemnly. "`Then shall the righteous answer him, saying, Lord, when saw we thee an hungred, and fed thee? or thirsty, and gave thee drink? When saw we thee a stranger, and took thee in? or naked, and clothed thee?'"

"And, Greta, how did the Lord answer?" prodded Carrie.

Greta moved until she was close and could look up into Gunther's face. "And the King shall answer and say unto them, `Verily I say unto you, Inasmuch as ye have done it unto one of the least of these my brethren, ye have done it unto me.'"

Gunther stared from one to the other incredulously. "It—says—*that?*" he said slowly.

Carrie pointed to the page. "It does! See here."

Gunther tried desperately to adjust his mind to it all. "When I gave the shoes to Maria, it was indeed for *him?*"

Carrie nodded.

"And the coat—the crèche for the woman—" A new understanding was growing within him. "The Christ child came to me in these people," he said in wonder. Gunther sat in hushed contemplation. "It makes one think of things—differently, doesn't it?" he offered finally.

"It does!" Carrie smiled at him as she moved toward the candle. "May I say an ancient candle prayer? To the One who has visited us, to give light to those who sit in darkness."

"I would like this." Gunther closed his eyes and with folded hands listened enrapt to the sweet voice that called into the room the presence of the Christ.

"Lord Jesus, thou whose birth we celebrate, we have lit our candle in the presence of each other—and the holy angels. Kindle in our hearts thy flame of love, that day shall break and shadows flee away. Amen."

When he opened his eyes, Carrie and the children were gone. He stared about him. "In the presence of the holy angels?" he said aloud. Could it possibly be? Carrie and Franz and Greta?

Gunther stood up and walked to the candle and stared hard into the flame. Slowly he shook his head in wonder. *"We have lit our candle, Lord Jesus, and you came!"*

He knelt beside the window. *"Kindle in my heart thy flame of love, that day shall break and shadows flee away,"* he murmured softly.

And Gunther looked into his heart and knew that it was so.

349

Look! The virgin will conceive a child! She will giv